The award to Nadine Gordimer of the Nobel Prize for Literature in 1991 was an affirmation of her distinctive contribution to twentieth-century fiction and to the creation of a literature that challenges apartheid. In this study, which may be used as an introduction as well as by those already familiar with Gordimer's work, Dominic Head discusses each of her novels in detail, paying close attention to the texts both as a reflection of events and situations in the real world, and as evidence of her constant rethinking of her craft. Head shows how Gordimer's concerns, apparent in her earliest novels, are developed through increasing stress on the politics of textuality; and he pursues the implications of this development to consider how Gordimer's late work contributes to postmodernist fiction, and to a recentring of political engagement in an era of uncertainty.

CAMBRIDGE STUDIES IN AFRICAN AND
CARIBBEAN LITERATURE

NADINE GORDIMER

CAMBRIDGE STUDIES IN AFRICAN AND
CARIBBEAN LITERATURE

Series Editor: Professor Abiola Irele, Ohio State University

Each volume in this unique new series of critical studies will offer a comprehensive and in-depth account of the whole *oeuvre* of one individual writer from Africa or the Caribbean, in such a way that the book may be considered a complete coverage of the writer's expression up to the time the study is undertaken. Attention will be devoted primarily to the works themselves – their significant themes, governing ideas and formal procedures; biographical and other background information will thus be employed secondarily, to illuminate these aspects of the writer's work where necessary.

The emergence in the twentieth century of black literature in the United States, the Caribbean and Africa as a distinct corpus of imaginative work represents one of the most notable developments in world literature in modern times. This series has been established to meet the needs of this growing area of study. It is hoped that it will not only contribute to a wider understanding of the humanistic significance of modern literature from Africa and the Caribbean through the scholarly presentation of the work of major writers, but also offer a wider framework for the ongoing debates about the problems of interpretation within the disciplines concerned.

Already published

Chinua Achebe, by C. L. Innes
Nadine Gordimer, by Dominic Head
Edouard Glissant, by J. Michael Dash

NADINE GORDIMER

DOMINIC HEAD

School of English
University of Central England

CAMBRIDGE
UNIVERSITY PRESS

Published by the Press Syndicate of the University of Cambridge
The Pitt Building, Trumpington Street, Cambridge CB2 1RP
40 West 20th Street, New York, NY 10011–4211, USA
10 Stamford Road, Oakleigh, Victoria 3166, Australia

© Cambridge University Press 1994

First published 1994

Printed in Great Britain at the University Press, Cambridge

A catalogue record for this book is available from the British Library

Library of Congress cataloguing in publication data

Head, Dominic.
Nadine Gordimer / Dominic Head.
p.   cm. – (Cambridge Studies in African and Caribbean literature: 2)
Includes bibliographical references and index.
ISBN 0 521 43361 4 (hardback)
ISBN 0 521 47549 x (paperback)
1. Gordimer, Nadine. – Criticism and interpretation.
2. Politics and literature – South Africa – History – 20th century.
3. Postmodernism (Literature) – South Africa.
4. South Africa – In literature.
I. Title.   II. Series.
PR9369.3.G6Z685   1994
823–DC20   94-5833 CIP

ISBN 0 521 43361 4 hardback
ISBN 0 521 47549 x paperback

To Tricia

Contents

Preface

Gordimer's writing career to date has run in parallel with the era of apartheid in South Africa, an era in which the racist organization of South Africa was systematically intensified through legislation and brutal state control following the election to power of the Nationalist Government in 1948. Apartheid (separateness) was a political programme of separate development supposedly justified by the perception of Africans as a distinct subspecies of humanity, inferior to whites, and who had no historical claim to the territory of Southern Africa. Despite the manifest contradiction of biological, archaeological and historical evidence contained in these underpinnings, the political programme might appear, at least, to have had its own coherence; even this, however, is rapidly dispelled by the manipulative machinations of apartheid and the contradictory way in which it buttressed itself through the attempted control of individuals. Prominent measures of early apartheid rule (especially for Gordimer) include the prevention of inter-racial relationships, and the arbitrary division of black Africans into ten separate 'nations', each confined to a designated 'homeland'. (Selected key events in modern South African history, including those mentioned or alluded to in Gordimer's fiction, are listed in the chronology.) On the face of it, apartheid is now at an end, a stage apparently marked in 1990 by the release from prison of Nelson Mandela and the unbanning of the African National Congress; it is tempting to see the award to Gordimer of the Nobel Prize for Literature in 1991 as an affirmation of her own role in creating a literature to challenge apartheid, since the consolidation and ultimate dissolution of the political ideology occurs alongside the publication of the fictions (1949–90) discussed in this book. At a sufficient historical distance this kind of salutary judgement and sense of closure may be possible; for now there are indications that the progression to a post-apartheid state will be tempestuous, as the different factions called into being by South Africa's long history of racial discrimination and prejudice contest the constitutional basis of the new state.

Given the historical and political context of Gordimer's work and my account of it here as a successful intervention in this context, there is an apparent contradiction in the structure of this book: the dynamic of successive chapters is to show how the development of Gordimer's work is characterized by an increasing literariness and stress on textuality. This emerging emphasis, however, is properly seen as a working out of the *politics* of textuality and, consequently, as an appropriate way for Gordimer to define *how* her fictions offer their intervention.

In the first chapter I discuss Gordimer's literary identity and the related recurring themes and issues in her fiction. South African literary identity, in Gordimer's conception, is really a quest to construct a hybridized cultural expression, a fusion of African culture and European literary form. Such a hybrid represents a way beyond the limitations of South African society where apartheid, by preventing different groups from knowing each other, restricts narrative possibilities. Gordimer is only able to achieve such a fusion to a limited extent, but there are recurring themes in her fiction – two in particular – which facilitate the transgression of these imposed limitations: first, her own micropolitics, or politics of the body in which trans-racial relationships challenge the fundamental principle of apartheid; and, second, her (allied) preoccupation with questions of space, an extended fictional deliberation on the geopolitics of apartheid and its policies of spatial control. The second chapter offers extended discussion of Gordimer's first three novels which are often undeservedly neglected by comparison with her later novels: this chapter shows how Gordimer's characteristic themes are evident from the beginning of her novel-writing career. The first two chapters, taken together, form an extended introduction to the book and to Gordimer: subsequent chapters show, through close readings of the remaining novels and selected short stories, how Gordimer develops her major concerns in a writing career marked by an increasing stress on textuality. The final chapter pursues the implications of this development, considering how the work, especially in its late self-reflexive phase, might be said to form a contribution to postmodernist fiction; Gordimer's preoccupation with distinctly postmodernist issues may represent a re-centring of political engagement in an era of atomization and uncertainty.

One notorious feature of apartheid was its division of the South African populace into four 'racial groups': White, Coloured, Indian and African. This presents obvious problems for the interpreter of South African culture since one is sometimes obliged to employ a racist terminology in order to convey how particular legislation operated: where it has been necessary to use it, I place the term 'coloured' in inverted commas, to designate it as an artificially imposed label. In common with other recent critics I have made use of the term black African to identify the numerically dominant and most systematically persecuted and dispossessed demographic segment; one should also be sensitive to the broader concept of black culture and black identity to describe a less divisive and more communal impulse amongst non-whites in South Africa.

June 1993

Thanks and acknowledgements are due to: Abiola Irele for helpful comments and suggestions on the manuscript; the editors of *The Journal of the Short Story in English* for permission to print some reworked material on the short stories that first appeared in their (1990) special issue on Gordimer; and to the Faculty of Computing and Information Studies at the University of Central England for a grant which released me for study leave for the second semester of the 1992–3 academic year, during which period this book was completed.

Abbreviations

Abbreviated references in the text are to the following editions of Gordimer's work. The initials given here are followed by a page number, both in parentheses:

BD   *Burger's Daughter* (London: Cape, 1979)
C   *The Conservationist* (London: Cape, 1974)
FF   *Face to Face* (Johannesburg: Silver Leaf Books, 1949)
GH   *A Guest of Honour* (London: Cape, 1971)
J   *Jump and Other Stories* (London: Bloomsbury, 1991)
JP   *July's People* (London: Cape, 1981)
LBW   *The Late Bourgeois World* (1966; London: Cape, 1976 (reissue))
LC   *Livingstone's Companions* (London: Cape, 1972)
LD   *The Lying Days* (1953; London: Cape, 1978 (reissue))
MSS   *My Son's Story* (London: Bloomsbury, 1990)
OL   *Occasion for Loving* (1963; London: Cape, 1978 (reissue))
SN   *A Sport of Nature* (London: Cape, 1987)
SOT   *Something Out There* (London: Cape, 1984)
SS   *Selected Stories* (London: Cape, 1975)
SVS   *The Soft Voice of the Serpent* (London: Gollancz, 1953)
WS   *A World of Strangers* (London: Gollancz, 1958)

Chronology

1923   Gordimer born at Springs, near Johannesburg.

1948   Afrikaner National Party wins general election and comes to power in South Africa: the apartheid regime commences.

1949   Prohibition of Mixed Marriages Act (together with Immorality Act) makes marriage and sexual relations illegal across the colour line; Gordimer married to G. Gavron; *Face to Face* (short stories), Gordimer's first book published.

1950   Immorality Act; Suppression of Communism Act; Group Areas Act (with subsequent amendments) divides urban areas into racially-exclusive zones; Population Registration Act classifies people by race.

1952   Passive resistance campaign launched by African National Congress (ANC) and South African Indian Congress (SAIC).

1953   Publication of *The Lying Days*.

1954   Gordimer's second marriage, to Reinhold Cassirer.

1955   Sophiatown 'rezoned'.

1955   Congress of the People convened. Freedom Charter adopted at a rally broken up by police.

1955–6   1,156 members of Congress Alliance arrested and tried for treason. Protracted court case – Treason Trial – ensues.

1957   Alexandra Bus boycott.

1958   H. F. Verwoerd becomes Prime Minister; publication of *A World of Strangers*; Africanists break away from ANC and form the Pan-Africanist Congress (PAC).

1959   Extension of University Education Act prohibits universities from accepting black students without special permission.

1960   PAC inaugurates national campaign against the pass laws. Sharpeville massacre occurs at one anti-pass demonstration: police open fire on crowd outside Sharpeville police station, killing 67 Africans and wounding 186. Signals end of non-violent resistance; Philip Kgosana arrested after leading mass protest march in Cape Town; African political organizations banned.

1961   South Africa becomes a republic and leaves British Commonwealth; Gordimer wins W. H. Smith Literary Award.

1961–4 Period of resistance through bombing campaign of sabotage, involving Umkhonto we Sizwe (Spear of the Nation), militant wing of ANC; Poqo (Pure), militant wing of PAC; and the multi-racial, but largely white African Resistance Movement (ARM).

1962   Arrest of Nelson Mandela.

1963   Seventeen Umkhonto leaders arrested; publication of *Occasion for Loving*.

1964   Several ANC and PAC leaders, including Nelson Mandela, are sentenced to life imprisonment.

1966   B. J. Vorster becomes Prime Minister; publication of *The Late Bourgeois World*.

1968   Steve Biko founds the exclusively black South African Students Organization (SASO). (SASO becomes instrumental in the promulgation of Black Consciousness through the 1970s.)

1969   Gordimer awarded Thomas Pringle Award.

1970   –Publication of *A Guest of Honour*.

1971   Gordimer awarded James Tait Black Memorial Prize.

1974   –Publication of *The Conservationist* (joint winner of the Booker Prize).

1975   Gordimer awarded French Grand Aigle d'Or prize, and South African CNA Literary Award.

1976 Thousands of black school children in Soweto protest against compulsory use of Afrikaans in teaching. Two students are shot dead by police and nationwide protests result. By 1977, 575 people are dead, according to official estimates.

1977 SASO banned; Biko arrested and killed by police.

1978 Vorster resigns. P. W. Botha becomes Prime Minister.

1979 Publication of *Burger's Daughter*.

1981 Publication of *July's People*.

1984 New constitution gives Asians and 'Coloureds' (not Africans) limited participation in government. Botha now state president.

1985 Gordimer awarded the Italian Malaparte Prize, and the Nelly Sachs Prize from West Germany.

1986 Pass laws repealed; indefinite nationwide state of emergency proclaimed. Gordimer receives the Bennett Award (USA).

1987 Publication of *A Sport of Nature*.

1989 F. W. de Klerk succeeds Botha as state president.

1990 Release of Nelson Mandela; unbanning of ANC and other outlawed organizations; publication of *My Son's Story*.

1991 CNA Award, South Africa. Gordimer awarded the Nobel Prize for Literature.

CHAPTER I

Gordimer and South Africa
themes, issues and literary identity

Nadine Gordimer, a white South African, is her country's most famous writer, and in that particular conjunction – of national identity and literary fame – lies the tension which is the determining feature of her career: her position as a consistent, and increasingly radical, critic of apartheid is a position located, to some extent, within the power-group it would challenge. Yet if there is an inevitable (unwanted) complicity for Gordimer as a white, middle-class South African citizen, it is due only to her refusal to exile herself that she has been able to articulate the nature of that complicity, and this is the focus of her extraordinary achievement: her oeuvre – the sequence of novels in particular – comprises the most significant sustained literary response to apartheid extant.

Gordimer was born on 20 November 1923 at Springs near Johannesburg, the daughter of immigrants: her mother, Nan Myers, was born in England, and her father, Isidore Gordimer, was a Jew who emigrated from Lithuania at the age of thirteen. Gordimer was brought up at Springs and attended the University of the Witwatersrand in Johannesburg for one year. Her first marriage was in 1949, and she was married again in 1954 to Reinhold Cassirer.

Gordimer has travelled widely, especially in Africa, but Johannesburg has remained her home. She has been a visiting lecturer at a number of universities, including Harvard and Princeton, and her fiction has won many prestigious awards, including: the James Tait Black Memorial Prize; the Booker Prize (joint winner, 1974); the French Grand Aigle d'Or Prize; the Italian Malaparte Prize and the Nelly Sachs Prize from

West Germany. She was awarded the Nobel Prize for Literature in 1991.

One event in Gordimer's childhood has received much critical attention: the invention, by her mother, of a heart condition in the young Nadine that restricted her childhood activities (dancing in particular, which she loved) and sent her to books for diversion and self-definition.[1] Beyond this, however, there is little in the life that stands out as of necessity a primary feature in the interpretation of Gordimer;[2] her career, rather, is one in which private and public realms are intertwined – both for the author and for her fictions – and this returns us to the most remarkable fact about her oeuvre: its massive historical and political significance as a developing and shifting response to events in modern South Africa, spanning over forty years and reaching into six decades, from the 1940s to the 1990s. Her responses to political events in South Africa are manifest in a continuous development and innovation in literary form rather than through detailed historical reference. This conjunction – a sustained response to a vital episode in twentieth-century political history, made through developments in fictional form – makes Gordimer's work of seminal importance for sociological approaches to literature, and for considerations of the form of the modern novel in the era of postmodernism.

Gordimer's oeuvre, in fact, spans the entire period of apartheid in South Africa (her first collection of stories was published in 1949, the year after the first Nationalist Government was elected to power). Robert Green makes explicit the claim that this correspondence invites:

Finally, when the history of the Nationalist Governments from 1948 to the end comes to be written, Nadine Gordimer's shelf of novels will provide the future historian with all the evidence needed to assess the price that has been paid.[3]

Here, however, we need to tread with caution, and be sure to separate out, at least initially, fiction and history, and the disciplines of their analysis. Gordimer's shelf of novels will certainly provide the future literary historian with more material on the apartheid era – its impact on creative imagination and literary form – than will the work of any other single writer. This, however, will form merely one aspect of a future historical assessment, and not its full complement. Moreover, the way in which literary production registers the effects of history requires a specific mode of exegesis, attentive to the uses of literary form.[4] In the 'Introduction' to the *Selected Stories* (1975) Gordimer does display an implicit understanding of the relativity and mutability of her own historical consciousness; she acknowledges that in her writing she acts upon her society, while, in this relationship of mutual influence, history is acting upon her, affecting her styles and forms – her 'manner of . . . apprehension' (*SS*, 12–13). This book is primarily concerned with the question of 'manner of apprehension'; it is written from a conviction that Gordimer's fictional output as a whole is best approached by charting how this consciousness evolves, and is reflected in shifting, and increasingly sophisticated, utilizations of fictional form. However, such a development – though discernible – does not indicate a lack of sophistication in the early work. Gordimer's first three novels, for example, contain remarkably mature dialogues with (rather than merely passive reflections of) the forms and techniques of the European novel; indeed, the seeds of Gordimer's most sophisticated literary gestures – in her most recent novels, *A Sport of Nature* and *My Son's Story* – are contained in *The Lying Days*, her first.

The lack of a simple, linear development in Gordimer's career is confirmed by the persistence of her major concerns. A fundamental issue for Gordimer is the question of her national identity, a subject which has been a consistent preoccupation, and which has direct implications for her own literary tradition and, consequently, her identity as a writer. If Gordimer's formulations concerning these questions of identity have passed through several stages, one thing has remained constant: her conviction of her nationality in terms of simple geographical belonging. In interview Gordimer has explained that exile has never been a realistic possibility for her because of her sense of belonging 'completely' to her country.[5]

There is an obvious ambivalence about Gordimer's historical position, as a privileged white attacking the social system that she is inevitably in complicity with to some degree, and this is a dilemma which all white South African writers have had to face. Gordimer's position with regard to this dilemma is, essentially, that despite the 'self-disgust' the situation might sometimes evoke in whites, the necessary task of historical transformation is really best served by working from within the nation, rather than from a position of self-imposed exile (if one has the choice).[6] This is also an expression of the need to accept one's national identity, however uncomfortable that may be. For Gordimer, however, the difficult problem has been to formulate her literary identity through a shifting sense of her national identity, and this has proved problematic.

In several of her essays and interviews Gordimer considers the materials that comprise a South African literary tradition (sometimes taking the idea of a sense of national identity as her starting point), and in these accounts one can detect subtle but significant shifts in her position.

Writing on William Plomer's *Turbott Wolfe* in 1965 Gordimer considers the novel to be the only one of 'poetic vision' produced in South Africa since Olive Schreiner's *The Story of an African Farm*.[7] Gordimer is in tune with other commentators in seeing Schreiner's novel as the earliest significant South African novel, and this is a view she has repeated several times in her essays. Subsequent considerations, however, suggest that Gordimer's engagement with other novels since Schreiner's has extended both her notion of 'poetic vision' and of the composition of South African literature. Especially significant here is Gordimer's growing awareness of the importance of an emergent black novel in South Africa – with writers like Thomas Mofolo and Sol Plaatje – which has been consistently repressed by apartheid. Of course, the emergence of a black novel, as Gordimer perceives, represents already the imposition of a colonial culture, of a European literary form onto an oral literary tradition; but Gordimer is keen to pursue the positive potential of hybrid forms in her discussions of South African literary culture, and it is a growing understanding of how a literary tradition needs to evolve through cross-fertilization that underpins the direction taken by Gordimer's thinking on her nation's literature.

In a talk given to students of the University of the Witwatersrand in 1967, Gordimer articulates clearly how censorship legislation in South Africa was then obstructing the possibility of a national literature, by enforcing a

silence where the African creative imagination was being and should be heard, in South African literature. It is a mockery even for me to stand up here talking of South African literature in English, and for you to listen, when out of the small number of writers this country has produced, neither you nor I may read Mphahlele, Nkosi, La Guma, Brutus or Modisane. Since they may not be quoted, we could not even discuss, in our consideration of South African English literature today, works of theirs that we may have read before they came under ban. So much for the future of literary criticism in South Africa, let alone a creative literature.[8]

Two important convictions are implicit in Gordimer's concern, and these are convictions which have figured consistently, in evolving forms, in her subsequent writings about a national literature. The first conviction is that a South African literature in English, embracing the work of African writers, is both possible and desirable; the second is that the 'national' literature that emerges under apartheid will be a jaundiced and corrupt phenomenon which cannot be read or discussed innocently – without a consciousness of the silences around it. Here, then, are two fundamental convictions, one Utopian – recognizing the need for cultural cross-fertilization in the national literature – the other pragmatic – acknowledging that the literature of the interim period will be distorted and corrupted by political repression.

A crucial phase in Gordimer's quest for her literary identity is marked by the publication in 1973 of *The Black Interpreters*, a work of criticism which examined South African poetry and, in a broader context, African fiction. Though it is a work of criticism, *The Black Interpreters* is also revealing about Gordimer's sense of her own identity. It indicates an attempt to align herself with the literary culture of the African continent at large: the following definition of African literature, for instance, is one which would clearly accommodate her own work: 'My own definition is that African writing is writing done in any language by Africans themselves and by others of whatever skin colour who share with Africans the experience of having been shaped, mentally and spiritually, by Africa rather than anywhere else in the world. One must look at the world *from Africa*, to be an African writer, not look *upon Africa* from the world.' This is a reasonable definition of African literature, but it should be acknowledged as a broad one, in its formulation of a single 'Africa-centred consciousness'.[9] Some definitions of African literature would not allow space for a white South African writer with Jewish parents, one English the other Lithuanian. Here it may be helpful to employ Abiola Irele's identification, within the more general field of African literature, of work displaying what is termed 'the African Imagination': for Irele white South African writers such as André Brink, J. M. Coetzee and Gordimer do not betray the latter. They do display a 'heightened sense of involvement with the particular experience of the black community' in South Africa, an involvement which justifies their 'claim to be considered African writers, even if their expression has no connection to the African imagination in the sense in which this implies a sense of immediate involvement with an informing African sensibility'. The distinction is based on the relative importance of European literary models, which play a lesser role in the literature of the African imagination where the 'distinctive mark is the striving to attain the condition of oral expression, even within the boundaries established by Western literary conventions'.[10] For Gordimer her European literary heritage is *predominant* as a formative influence, even though she has continually problematized this heritage and tried to find ways of 'voicing' African experience more directly. This conflict between the European literary heritage and the underlying African experience is, in fact, a productive tension in much of her work; her definition of African writing does not, perhaps, register fully this tension of cultural influences.

If Gordimer can be seen as an African writer in the broader sense – though unable to express Irele's African imagination – she also belongs to the subset of South African writers, and here further ambiguities arise. Indeed, it is unclear whether the notion of a national literature in South Africa can have any meaning where black expression has been artificially repressed for generations. Yet, if the artificiality of the category is acknowledged, Gordimer can be described as a South African writer in that her imagination and literary expression have been shaped by the national context.

John Cooke has argued that *The Black Interpreters* marks the rejection of Gordimer's early enthusiasm for a national literature: with the silencing of black writers in the 1960s Cooke argues that Gordimer turned to African literature and was also inspired by the reformulation of colonial experience in the work of Afro-Caribbean intellectuals, and that a consequent greater engagement with African culture results in an increased identification with her environment in the later novels.[11] Cooke's argument is persuasive, indicating an important strategy which has had ramifications in all of Gordimer's subsequent work. The South African situation, however, has demanded other strategies at other times, and has prevented a straightforward engagement with African culture. The Black Consciousness movement (rejecting all co-operation with whites) – which flourished in the 1970s before and after the Soweto riots of 1976–7 – provoked Gordimer into a narrowing reformulation of her national identity: as a white South African complicit with a repressive system. This, really, is the essence of the 'white consciousness' which emerged in response to the separatist philosophy of Black Consciousness, and which Gordimer was interested in for a time. She later expressed disapproval of the separatist philosophy, indicating a conviction that it was a strategy with a particular historical expedient, and this kind of flexibility – sensitive to the requirements of specific contexts – characterizes her position: that of a white South African writer, an experience which requires an acceptance and a working-through of certain complicities that will determine the scope and nature of her literary production.[12]

One consequence of this experience has been Gordimer's attempt to work out her relationship to African culture at appropriate times, and there is a more frequent expression of the importance of African culture in the later fiction, but this expression is often combined with suggestions that this importance may not be fully recognized, and, more crucially, may not be fully *expressed* in the literary forms available to Gordimer, though her experimentations represent a continual attempt to by-pass these restrictions by infusing old forms with new meanings. The dynamic of such experimentation, however, is that of persisting tension between the felt restraint and the something beyond, and this, in a sense, is another way of formulating a duality – a tension between detachment or standing apart, and identification or involvement – that Gordimer has identified as the hallmark of the writer.[13]

In an important article from 1975 Gordimer develops these ideas in a consideration of *cultural identity*, following a definition of such an identity as a kind of free and full meeting of self and other. In this account genuine cultural identity and national literature – generated by a sense of the social whole – is impossible where racial separation is enforced.[14] In the same essay Gordimer speculates on the reasons for the failure of significant black writers to emerge in the 1930s and 1940s, a failure to emulate Mofolo or Plaatje and their ability to combine their cultural origins with their present position.[15] The failure to build on this integration of cultural origins and current situation – of self and other – is the key issue. Gordimer's speculation that the racist legislation of this era and the inequalities it produced led to frustration and a consequent creative apathy may not tell the whole story of how repression can deny certain kinds of cultural expression. Black South African writers have not produced a flourishing novel tradition, and have tended to work more convincingly in the short story and in poetry. There was a brief resurgence in the black novel after the Soweto riots of 1976–7, but this was not consolidated.[16] In *The Black Interpreters* (1973), significantly, Gordimer devotes her section on South African writing to poetry.

The limitations on black South African writers have been various. The impoverished situation of would-be writers inevitably curtailed creative possibilities, and the censorship laws silenced much that was produced; indeed censorship, in concert with other repressive laws, interrupted many a writer's career through incarceration and exile: many leading black writers were forced into exile in the 1960s (and late 1950s), including Can Themba, Lewis Nkosi, Bloke Modisane, Es'kia Mphahlele and Alex La Guma. Black literary production may also have been restricted, as a UNESCO report of 1972 speculates, by the tastes of an impoverished township readership desiring escapist romance and thriller narratives. In this regard the magazine *Drum*, deliberately aimed at the township audience, can be seen to have played an ambivalent role. *Drum* is generally (and rightly) seen as a focus of black opposition in the late 1950s, creating a vital outlet for black journalists and writers; an inevitable consequence of its policy to appeal, however, may have been to foster a formulaic tradition of sentimental stories and detective fiction.[17] What is significant is Gordimer's prescription for the African's contribution to a South African literature: a mode which will combine a re-affirmation of origins and a use of a present situation. Subsequent developments of this idea indicate that Gordimer has in mind a mode which combines traditional with present literary culture, a fusion of a European literary heritage with elements drawn from an African tradition.

Gordimer's thoughts on how such a fusion might best be achieved have developed over the years. An important stage in her thinking on this issue is recorded in a round-table discussion from 1979 with André Brink and Es'kia Mphahlele. At one point in the discussion Gordimer pursues Mphahlele with an insistence that the English literary tradition is the heritage of every writer, black or white, writing in English, and that this must be acknowledged. Mphahlele's response is to argue that the African tradition adapts the materials of an English literary heritage resulting in new forms. Gordimer does not concur with this, claiming that in Africa nothing original in form has appeared. Gordimer and Mphahlele appear to agree that this is the case, but that a new form is striving to be born, though Gordimer seeks to round off this aspect of the discussion with her own affirmation that this emergent form is too young because the tradition in Africa is an oral tradition. Gordimer goes on to make an appeal for African writers to contribute to the major developments of the European novel, something which André Brink, citing Achebe, Ngugi, Awoonor and Soyinka, quietly indicates has already occurred. Gordimer takes the point, but a revealing slippage in the terms of the discussion has occurred: the discussion's touchstone had been 'the position of the writer in South Africa today', but the writers find themselves drawn to make conclusions in broader terms relevant to the continent as a whole. This may well be an understandable and necessary response to the imposed distortions of South African literary culture, but it also indicates that Gordimer's caution may indicate the more appropriate assessment of the question of the national literature, narrowly defined.[18]

Yet if Gordimer is right about the failure of traditional African components to contribute to the development of the novel in South Africa, she is still sanguine – in 1979 – about the scope of the English and European heritage for appropriation by Africans. This is not, however, a view which advocates the *desirability* of cultural imposition, as indicated in this extract from a 1981 interview:

Our fathers' culture – white culture imported from Europe – never had a chance in the South African context. It wasn't indigenous; it wouldn't blend. All it did was to harm black culture. In missionary days, blacks had their own rich oral tradition – *we* superimposed foreign literary forms upon it. In the process we suffered more than they. At least, today, blacks are expressing themselves in those forms; we, however, never appropriated anything from them. We've woken up to it rather late – can we now strike roots in what has been debased by us?[19]

Cross-fertilization is now something which Gordimer sees – with an element of wilful optimism – as occurring principally in black writing. It is also tacitly presented as a way of redeeming a situation of cultural colonization. In an interview published in an excerpted form in 1984, Gordimer identifies fully with this call for a hybrid between the rich pre-colonial oral tradition of South Africa, and the imported European tradition, announcing herself as committed to the 'truly new indigenous culture' that would result.[20] This perception, enacted in the fiction, gives her work a crucial significance as a bridge between white and black writers in South Africa, between the dominant influence of European literary forms, and the indigenous sources of African culture.

The underlying commitment to cultural fusion is more or less constant in Gordimer's reflections: what changes – according to context – is her view on how it is best to be achieved. A more recent statement on this question was published in 1992, where Gordimer is reflecting on how an African literature for the twenty-first century can be realized. The context of this discussion – concerning the literature of a continent – is, of course, different to Gordimer's earlier specific discussions of South African literature. But it may, nevertheless, be possible to detect a shifting position, a loss of faith in the possible efficacy of the hybrid mode – or, at least, a new belief in the need for literature in African languages to take the lead in producing the cross-fertilization, and to become 'the major component of the continent's literature'.[21] This may be a lead to be taken by South Africa's neighbours, but a lead that the literature of South Africa would need to respond to. Just as her fiction is a continually evolving response to political realities in South Africa, so, clearly, have Gordimer's views on the role of a national South African literature evolved in response to a shifting situation; and this is at one with her sense of her South African identity, as 'a constant state of response to demands; continuing and changing demands';[22] a continuously mutable phenomenon, responsive to political change.

Gordimer's concern with the need for the hybridization of cultural forms bespeaks an understanding of the political affiliation of different modes of representation, and her own continual experimentation with literary form can be seen as a felt need to resist particular complicities. This is the concern behind the distinctive contribution she has made to the development of modern fiction.

A very significant characteristic of Gordimer's fiction is its metafictional quality and its (associated) connection with contemporary intellectual trends. In particular, issues central to her novels have often paralleled developments in poststructuralist critical theory. In one sense this simply indicates the

sensitivity of the author to contemporary intellectual trends;
but, since such parallels do not necessarily imply particular
direct influences, Gordimer has also contributed something
original and innovative to the form of the modern novel. She
has, for example, been working out her own micropolitics,
based on a politics of the body, and has betrayed a growing
preoccupation with the importance of human geography; these
are two areas which have become central sites of critical
theorizing and postmodernist expression.

However, in addition to these contemporary parallels,
Gordimer's work is transitional in that it has affinities with a
pre-modernist trend of realism.[23] The influence of Georg
Lukács upon Gordimer's work is crucial, here. It is an important influence, but it can be overstated, especially if used
simplistically as a way of defining the style and form of her
novels. Some critics consider that the novels continue the
Lukácsian tradition of critical realism, and some of Gordimer's
non-fictional statements would seem to lend weight to such an
idea. In *The Black Interpreters* Gordimer considers Lukács'
discernment of 'three main trends in modern world literature':
the first is experimental modernism, condemned by Lukács 'for
its subjectivism, its static view of the human condition, its
dissolution of character, its obsession with pathological states
and its lack of a sense of history'. The second trend, socialist
realism, is 'criticised for its over-simplification, its failure to see
the contradictions in the everyday life of society, and its view of
history – "Utopia is already with us" under communism'. The
third, contrasting trend is critical realism, in which 'the human
condition is understood dynamically, in an historical perspective'.[24] The context of this extract must be borne in mind:
Gordimer is trying to theorize about the importance of the
developing fiction of black African writers, and finds the
model of critical realism – as inherently progressive – to be
amenable for this purpose. She also presents Lukács' ideas
rather schematically: it is a familiar version of the Lukácsian
condemnation of modernism, but the comments on socialist
realism may correspond more closely to Gordimer's own resistance to partisan writing than they do, for instance, to Lukács'

call, in *The Meaning of Contemporary Realism*, for a combination
of critical- and socialist-realist modes.[25]

Gordimer's perception of a writer's treatment of politics may
have come to her from Engels' perception of realism, especially
via Lukács. In *Studies in European Realism*, Lukács considers
Engels' appreciation of Balzac, and his ability to expose systematically the weaknesses of royalist feudal France, even
though he was a loyalist himself.[26] In her essay 'A Writer's
Freedom', Gordimer offers a similar (though inverted) formulation, insisting that a writer's integrity depends upon resisting
the pressure to write in a way which conforms 'to an orthodoxy
of opposition'. Here, what Gordimer appears to have gleaned
from a standard Marxist critique of realism is put into the
context of the political struggle in South Africa, and the
problem for black writers who must resist the internationally-
derived 'jargon of struggle', appropriate for the public plat-
form, but 'not deep enough, wide enough, flexible enough,
cutting enough, fresh enough for the vocabulary of the poet,
the short story writer or the novelist'.[27] This is the formulation
of an aesthetics of language which must deal with politics in a
complex way; interestingly, it seems very close to Irving
Howe's concept of the political novelist as someone who must
build in oppositions to 'his own intentions' and 'allow for those
rocks against which his intentions may smash but, if he is lucky,
they may merely bruise'. In Howe's brief discussion of South
African writers this formula has a particular significance
because 'in circumstances where evil appears to be so complete, a triumph of good might end in a new kind of evil'
coupled with 'a moral imperative to accept that triumph'.[28]
This, it seems, is the same understanding which underpins
Gordimer's aesthetic, produced for a particular time and
place, and which addresses – and attempts to counter – the
potential for new kinds of repression in a society on the verge of
dramatic political transition.

The strongest parallel with Gordimer's fiction is the Lukácsian emphasis on the realization of individual characters
coupled with an understanding of the historical dynamic, a
realization of public and private realms in which one is not

subordinate to the other: the process of realization involves, rather, a dialectical interaction between public and private realms. Such an interaction is certainly a major, and enduring feature of Gordimer's fiction, a feature which can be elucidated by Lukács' notion of typification in the characterization of a novel – for it is this idea that underpins the value assigned to the Lukácsian novel of critical realism. For Lukács, character has to be both the representation of individuality and typicality. This correspondence between Gordimer and Lukács has led several critics to see her as another heir of the critical realists.[29] As Clingman has pointed out, however, Gordimer's preoccupation with the relationship between private and public worlds does not originate from her reading of Lukács, which, as she has confirmed in correspondence with Clingman, commenced in 1968.[30]

In other areas affinities between Lukács and Gordimer are not so obvious. Returning to her account in *The Black Interpreters* of the differences between critical realism and other modes, it is clear that not all of her works fall easily into the former category. *The Late Bourgeois World*, for example, could be criticized for its avant-garde properties: a dissolution of character, and a preoccupation with pathological states is evident in this novel, and in the later *The Conservationist*, even though both do clearly convey a sense of history. Of course, Gordimer's position in this regard would be that a personal dissolution is a seminal feature of contemporary South African history, and so is essential to its portrayal. But there are other modernist features in these two novels which make it impossible to classify them easily according to the Lukácsian taxonomy. One can also see how *A Sport of Nature* could be placed in the category of socialist realism: this, in fact, is a novel which has been criticised for its over-simplification, in its portrayal, at one level, of a Utopia 'already with us'. If there is no direct application of a Lukácsian prescription here, there is still a reaction to his ideas. One aspect of *The Conservationist* is clearly a metafictional consideration of how the modernist features impugned by Lukács can be infused with new meaning, while *A Sport of Nature* conducts a similar debate concerning the categories of socialist and critical realism: one level of the significance of these multi-layered novels is their implicit debate with, and attempted extension of, the Lukácsian credo which Gordimer had found so suggestive in the composition of *The Black Interpreters*.

Gordimer's experimentation with what the Lukácsian critic would call typicality is evident in the novel sequence, in which there is an increasing emphasis on the interdependence of public and private realms. *Burger's Daughter* represents one peak in this experimentation where the life of the central character, Rosa Burger, runs in parallel with the history of modern South Africa; Rosa becomes representative of white South Africa both in her complicity and her final position as a political subversive, a stand which, so the novel implies, is required of all the people of her race. *A Sport of Nature* represents a further (and perhaps ultimate) peak in Gordimer's development of typicality: here the representativeness of the protagonist Hillela is a metafictional matter, a re-investigation (at one level) of the implications of typicality in the previous novels.

Another important feature of Gordimer's fiction may be explained by recourse to Lukács, for whom, according to Fredric Jameson, 'literary realism . . . comes, following the title of one of Lukács' finest essays, to be characterized by narration rather than description'.[31] In 'Narrate or Describe?', the essay to which Jameson alludes, Lukács differentiates between the novelistic impetus of the realists – among whom he numbers Walter Scott, Balzac and Tolstoy – and the impetus of the naturalists, such as Zola and Flaubert. The realists' dynamic impetus to narration, he finds, has been displaced by the naturalists' static habits of description: 'involvement' and 'experience' have been replaced by 'observation'. Lukács' reasons for favouring the principle of narration over that of description include an aspect of the organicism contained in the notion of typicality: in the realist novel events and their settings are inextricably bound up with the histories of both individual characters and of their societies, whereas described scene and event in the naturalist novel can only build into a series of tableaux. History, in effect, is inherently built into the process of narration, 'the general social significance emerging in the unfolding of the characters' lives', whereas description, which 'contemporizes everything', effaces history. This is the case even in the descriptive 'novel of disillusion' because the process of 'capitulation . . . before capitalist inhumanity' is left out, because it has already occurred.[32] For Lukács the existence of a proper historical dimension is made possible by the presence of an ideological orientation: 'The significance of ideology . . . is that it provides the possibility of viewing the contradictions of life in a fruitful, ordered context . . . observation and description are mere substitutes for a conception of order in life.'[33] This formulation privileges the presence of a narrating persona with an ideological orientation which can give narrative shape to the materials of history, a narrative voice with, as Eugene Lunn puts it: 'the cognitive ability to uncover the construction of economic and social life through human interaction'.[34] For Lukács, modernism in literature is a principal villain, here: it is precisely this kind of cohesive narratorial presence which the relativism of the modernists had done much to undermine. Much of importance about Gordimer's writing is suggested by her position in relation to these views of Lukács: it seems clear that her fiction does benefit from the ideological orientation implicit in an overall narrative stance, even though Gordimer also learned much from modernist narrative technique, and has made use of a relativity of narrative perspective. This suggests a significant divergence from Lukács' (very vulnerable) account of modernism: for Gordimer there is clearly something purposive in the narrative relativity associated with modernist fiction. Narrative relativity, that is to say, need not preclude the presence of a pointed orientation.

The extension of narrative possibilities in Gordimer's work, in fact, is a crucial aspect of her quest for a literary form appropriate to her situation, because the cultivation of narrative relativity, of a plurality of voices, is a way of conveying the complexity of the historical situation. It is also a way of deconstructing the authoritative monologic perspective sometimes associated with colonial literature. At one end of this scale of experimentation narrative voice can be used for progressive Utopian ends. Cooke, for example, feels the development of a greater range of perspectives in Gordimer's third-person narration in the novels from *A Guest of Honour* through to *July's People*, resulting in a more authoritative portrayal of a diverse black society.[35] The innovative use of narrative perspective is not always so auspicious, however; indeed, it can be used to explore the restricted inwardness of the white psyche, as in *The Conservationist* where the interior monologue of Mehring encapsulates a limited white point of view, an internalization and appropriation of the experience of Africa. If this extended use of interior monologue implies a necessary limitation to the white South African perspective, the novel supplies an alternative voice – that of Zulu mythology – to imply future possibilities.

There are, however, limitations to what a writer can achieve through the use of narrative perspective: the parameters are set by the cultural situation of the writer, as Gordimer has herself observed. In interview she has spoken of how key areas of both white and black experience are self-contained in South Africa. This inevitably restricts what she can authentically narrate: although she may have created many black characters, and may sometimes have 'dared to do it from a black point of view', she would not attempt, for example, to narrate the experiences of a fifteen- or sixteen-year-old living through the experience of the Soweto riots, knowing 'it would be false'.[36] Apartheid, by restricting the social connection of inter-racial mixing, hampers the potential for narrative fiction to authenticate the inter-racial moment. For Gordimer the restriction is particularly harmful in *artistic* terms, because the natural development of a South African literature depends upon an intercultural mixing, a hybridization of influences and conventions, which is denied. The political implications of this are important, because hybrid cultural forms – combining 'black' African culture and 'white' European culture – will represent not merely a direct challenge to the apartheid ethos of separate cultural development, but tangible proof of its irrelevance. The

principle of narration can be seen as a primary channel for this
literary transgression, a progression beyond imposed limits.

In her review of J. M. Coetzee's *Life and Times of Michael K*,
Gordimer's understanding of the two Lukácsian principles
discussed here – typicality and narration – is revealed. Gordimer recognizes the stature and importance of Coetzee's novel,
but discerns in it an important historical exclusion. Perceiving
Michael K as representative of the victimized black population
of South Africa, Gordimer feels his passivity is historically
unfaithful: Coetzee 'does not recognize what the victims, seeing
themselves as victims no longer, have done, are doing, and
believe they must do for themselves'. This flaw is explained by
recourse to Lukács: 'The organicism that George Lukács
defines as the integral relation between private and social
destiny is distorted here more than is allowed for by the
subjectivity that is in every writer. The exclusion is a central
one that may eat out the heart of the work's unity of art and
life.'[37] Assuming a validity in Gordimer's reading of resistance
in 1984 South Africa, *Life and Times of Michael K* does not meet
the Lukácsian prescription, narrowly applied. Gordimer is, in
effect, identifying the lack of the kind of ideological perspective, as ordering principle, which structures her own fiction;
the assumption of her criticism is that such a perspective will
naturally result from presenting 'the integral relation between
private and social destiny'. This 'integral relation', however, is
surely already bound up with a particular interpretation or
ideological perspective in the writing, and this element of a
prior ideological perspective may be an addition to the principle of narration which is needed to account for Gordimer's
own work.

Gordimer's selective engagement with Lukácsian precepts
suggests an attempt to appropriate the ideas of critical realism,
and to construct, quite self-consciously, a core to her writing
suitable for the articulation of her concerns. Lukács is only one
of many influences on Gordimer, however, but her use of
Lukács is typical of how she has tended to appropriate her
influences, which have been various.[38]

Gordimer's interest in increasingly dialogized narrative

forms accords with her political orientation which has shifted through her career from an initial position of liberalism to one of increasing radicalism. In her fiction she has pursued her political analyses primarily through her own brand of micro-politics or politics of the body, in which questions of sexual expression and transgression are closely linked to racial consciousness. This exploration of sexuality has made Gordi-mer's work of much interest to feminist commentators, though there are problematic areas here.

In a number of interviews Gordimer has expressed im-patience with the feminist movement, an attitude which might seem strange in a writer whose fictions are particularly sensi-tive to the problems of women's oppression. The following is a representative comment, taken from a 1982 interview:

The white man and the white woman have much more in common than the white woman and the black woman, despite their difference in sex. Similarly, the black man and the black woman have much more in common than the black man and the white man . . . The basis of colour cuts right through the sisterhood or brotherhood of sex. It boils down to the old issue of prejudice and the suppression of blacks of both sexes . . . the loyalty to your sex is secondary to the loyalty to your race. That's why Women's Liberation is, I think, a farce in South Africa.[39]

Gordimer is clear here, as elsewhere in her non-fictional state-ments, that racism is the primary issue and sexism a secondary one. This represents an important difference from some femin-ist formulations which reverse this priority, and see racism, and other oppressive social structures as products of sexism, of pervasive patriarchal thinking. For the specific situation in South Africa, Gordimer has argued for the reverse causal relationship: that specific instances of sexist behaviour amongst blacks are directly produced by racist organization. In another 1982 interview (published with the one just cited) Gordimer explains that black women feel their exploitation by black men is 'a consequence of the exploitation by whites'. As an illustra-tion, she describes the familiar situation of a black man from one of the homelands having to move to find work, without being given permission to bring his wife and children with him.

The frequent result of such an enforced separation is that the man finds another woman and has children by her. In such a situation the wife left in the country will often find herself abandoned. The example indicates how instances of acute exploitation of black women are invited, if not completely caused by, white economic exploitation.[40] Yet this does not fully negate the argument that sexism begets racism. It may be that racist structures, initially conceived by sexist thinking, reproduce, in turn, sexist actions: the abandoned black wife and mother inhabits the inner site in a chinese-box system of hierarchical oppression, a model which highlights the problems of a simple causal explanation for social repression. Pertinent here are Karen Lazar's remarks on how a socialist feminism would differ from Gordimer and her hierarchical analysis of the relative importance of racism and feminism:

> A socialist feminism would ... depart from Gordimer on two counts. Firstly, it would argue that sexual oppression is by and large comparable in gravity and extent to other forms of oppression, and, where possible, must be fought concurrently with other struggles. Secondly, socialist feminism would, to use Althusser's terms, stress the 'relative autonomy' of sexual oppression, arguing that, although it is partially constituted in form and mediated by other types of oppression, it has a distinct and 'material' existence that cannot be explained away as a mere facet or ancillary of other forms of oppression. This distinct and material existence calls for distinct modes of analysis and opposition.
>
> Gordimer has not, to my knowledge, expressed any coherent recognition of these aspects of feminist thought.[41]

The invocation of Althusserian 'relative autonomy' is helpful in that it leads us away from simplistic linear causal models of oppression, and also from the hierarchical differentiation between racism and sexism that Gordimer has herself made. Lazar's appeal for specific and equivalent modes of attention to different forms of oppression also has a resonance in connection with Gordimer: it may be that she has offered no 'coherent recognition' of this kind of political analysis in her essays or in interview, but in her fiction her various analyses of oppression do amount to a tacit acceptance of the specificity of various forms of sexism and racism. Beyond this, she has also considered, through her fiction, the various positions that are suggested in the debate about her relationship to feminism. In some of her short stories, for example, she has presented white women and black men as fellow victims of white male oppression. Dorothy Driver notes how, in some of the stories, Gordimer has presented as comparable the oppressed position of women and blacks, though Driver also notes how, at other points in the fiction, such an idea is treated ironically, and, at others, subverted.[42]

Gordimer, then, examines the complexities of racism and sexism by taking up various positions in her fiction to consider these issues. One of her most important and consistent stances stems from the differentiation she makes baldly in her non-fictional comments. Robin Visel succinctly sums up how economic privilege separates white from black women in the later novels: 'While the native woman is truly doubly-oppressed or doubly-colonized, by male dominance as well as by white economic and social dominance, the white settler woman can best be described as half-colonized. Although she too is oppressed by white men and patriarchal structures, she shares in the power and guilt of the colonists.'[43] The argument here is that white patriarchal society supplies a niche for the white woman, based on the requirement of her sexuality, which is subservient, but nevertheless an integral part of the colonising structure: thus the white woman is enticed away from a feeling of affinity of oppression with black men and women. But this position is more than a mid-ground of semi-corruption, as Visel makes clear in another essay on Gordimer's colonial heroines:

The white woman is not allowed to claim innocence; nevertheless, she is increasingly prevented by the social and political conditions of apartheid from *acting* upon her responsibility. Furthermore, she is increasingly cut off from blackness, both by government decree and the rising hostility of her black brothers and sisters . . . the ambiguous, self-divided figure of the white girl or woman is the site of the hesitant, fraught rapprochement of white and black. She is the site of connection, while she is made to realize the impossibility of connection.[44]

This is a more sympathetic account of the white woman's position than it seems at first. The lack of innocence turns out to result not from a free choice, but from an imposition: the ruling ideology interpellates her as a colluder in oppression, yet, through her own oppression she inhabits the site of *rapprochement* which the situation denies. This is an invidious position which is really blameless, even if not 'innocent' in its associations. The only way beyond such a restrictive position is to resist the way in which one is interpellated by the ruling ideology. This, following Visel's argument, is really what Hillela represents in *A Sport of Nature*. By continually breaking taboos – especially socially constructed rules concerning sexual behaviour – Hillela resists being interpellated as a white colonial woman, and is free to achieve the full *rapprochement* the other heroines never attain. For Visel, Hillela seems to represent a failure as much as an achievement: 'she is a symptom of her creator's desperate hope rather than a believable personality. She is evidence of Gordimer's frustration, not so much with the limits of the realist genre, as with the political stalemate for whites in South Africa'.[45] It may be that the perceived need to break free from the constraints of realism – or to extend them – maligns those constraints, since the gesture coincides with the most propitious conclusion to a Gordimer novel. Here Gordimer could be said, at one level, to be aligning herself with the position we have seen her condemn elsewhere – that sexism begets racism – for it is through her resistance of sexual repression that Hillela embraces blackness and black political freedom, although there are other ideas in the novel which conflict with this quite self-consciously.

Gordimer's formulation for an authentic cultural identity – based on inter-racial communication and understanding – represents a conviction which is expressed through sexuality in her fictions: just as the interaction of self and other is presented as the basis of cultural identity, so do the personal interactions in the novels reveal broader political lessons. If this is sometimes seen as an extension of Forsterian liberalism – especially in the early novels – it might also, and perhaps more appropriately, be seen as the foundation of a more radical personal micropolitics. A conversation with Susan Sontag, published in 1987, is interesting in this connection. Here Gordimer takes issue with Sontag's speculations about power and who is best equipped, socially and historically, to write about it. Sontag argues that contemporary middle-class writers do not have access to the ruling classes in the way that, for example, Flaubert and Proust did, and, consequently, cannot write so effectively about social power and its real sources. Sontag distinguishes between these 'real sources', and the 'private situations' that good contemporary writers concern themselves with. Gordimer does not see this distinction: she feels that it is possible for contemporary writers to write about power, that this is a subject that interests her greatly, and that she feels she *does* write about it.[46] For Gordimer private situations are very clearly sources of power.

Foucault's work has been taken as the source of a micropolitics in some branches of critical theory, and the signs are that this will continue to be an expanding and productive area for the theorizing of social change. Gordimer's own micropolitics has a great deal in common with this development in critical theory, and this correspondence has two principal significances. First, it represents a primary example of Gordimer's fictional formulation of ideas that parallel contemporary intellectual developments. Second, it indicates that a focus on the activities and experiences of individuals does not necessarily involve a restrictive cultivation of individualism. Such a focus can most definitely form the basis of a thorough-going political novel.

A summary of the general significances of Foucault's thought locates the accepted divergences between his analyses of power and those commonly associated with theories of social change. These divergences also form the bases of the micropolitics implicit in Gordimer's work. An important point of divergence is Foucault's challenge to the idea that power is something which is possessed; instead of this idea Foucault formulates a model of power as exercised: the focus of the model, rather than on the subjects related through power, is on the power relations themselves. This denial of the pre-existing nature of subjects related through power leads directly to a second key point of divergence, the conviction that power is *productive* rather than *repressive*. Foucault shows how subjects are produced through certain institutional and cultural practices: his focus here has been on the practices of disciplinary power which are created with the development of the human sciences in the nineteenth century: for Foucault, disciplinary practices establish binary divisions – healthy/ill, sane/mad, legal/criminal – which accrue authority and can be used as a means of social control. Such divisions have a pervasive effect in society, conditioning the way individuals label themselves and each other according to established norms. These controls also involve the actual physical segregation of the population through (for example) incarceration.[47] There is an evident connection, here, with the ideological practices of apartheid. The actual incarceration of blacks under directly repressive measures is suggested, and, beyond this, so too is apartheid ideology, which demands a consciousness in individuals of their racial separateness; of course, this is an ideology promulgated by the discourses of political dogma rather than those associated with the human sciences, but the effect is that of a disciplinary practice designed to produce 'normalized' subjects fearful of transgressing a particular binary division, especially through inter-racial sexual contact.

The productive nature of power has profound implications for how it can be resisted, and here we meet with the most positive aspect identified by some commentators of Foucault: the idea here is that rather than attempting to identify centralized sources of power, there are localized instances of it which individuals can address themselves to. This is not to deny that such a thing as state power exists, but rather to insist that effective resistance can be mobilized by locating the pervasive power relations which obtain in the lives of individuals, at the microlevel of society. This conception of power and the appropriate arenas for its resistance inevitably involves questions of sexuality and sexual behaviour. The individual body becomes the smallest unit or focus of productive power and, simultaneously, the smallest identifiable site from which resistance can emerge.

For Foucault, however, the *definition* of individual sexuality is a primary route of disciplinary power. The problem here is not that sexual expression has been denied, but rather that it is channelled and normalized in particular ways, circumscribing not only sexual behaviour, but also the terms in which it can be discussed. This means that the expression of sexuality is not *per se* evidence of progressive political activity; but it does indicate that the transgression of particular sexual taboos can represent a challenge to restrictive ordering practices. This has certainly been a primary feature in Gordimer's novels in which the racist apartheid ideology is often shown to be effectively challenged – at the level of micropolitics – by trans-racial sexual liaisons. Gordimer also seems to perceive the necessity – as does Foucault – of resisting the existing discourses of sexuality. Hillela in *A Sport of Nature* is a practical demonstration of this conviction, since her sexuality leads her into some predicaments that appear to present her as the victim of patriarchal control: at one level the uncertainties of the book seem designed to challenge such preconceived judgements.

Trans-racial liaisons are not always salutary in Gordimer's novels, however, and this has much to do with the insistence on difference they usually uphold. For some commentators such an insistence is counter-productive since it courts the danger of replicating and upholding racist divisions. Despite this danger, Gordimer usually insists on focusing on racial difference in her presentation of progressive trans-racial relations. On one level this insistence represents solidarity with the political promotion of black South African identity. It can also be seen as a strategic inversion of apartheid ideology – the racial division is not challenged, but the evaluation of it is; this, perhaps, is an appropriate response to the disenfranchisement of a demographically dominant racial group. It is also a promotion of difference which suggests a further parallel with Foucault. This is especially so when we bear in mind the ambivalent presentation of inter-racial contact in Gordimer's work: Foucault's presentation of difference is marked, also, by an ambivalent attitude to the liberatory potential of difference, a recognition that difference can supply a source of resistance and potential change, but that it can result also in social fragmentation. The promotion or celebration of racial difference does not, apparently, square fully with Gordimer's prescriptions for advancement through cultural cross-fertilization; but there is also a general salutary principle in Foucault's prescriptions for preserving difference, the sites of marginalized voices from which effective resistance can emerge, and this does locate one positive element in Gordimer's presentation of difference.

In helping to identify and empower 'sites' of marginalized voices, micropolitics is closely allied to another recent, and very important, trend in critical and cultural theory: the increase in attention given to questions of geography and topography – or simply 'space' in some formulations – as a way of explaining key questions of power and social organization. Gordimer's fiction displays an ongoing, and developing understanding of the importance of space, and here, as in other respects, the fiction parallels contemporaneous thinking.

Gordimer's growing interest in the political aspect of the individual's relationship to his or her environment chimes with a radical re-orientation in critical theory with respect to its conception of time and space. These fundamental categories have conventionally been placed in a hierarchical relationship in social theories which privilege time over space, in the process making space a contingent aspect of human activity.[48] The original perception of the social arena, however, requires a more complex formulation, as recent work in the field of human geography has shown. This new formulation suggests that the dichotomy between space and time is erroneous in the first place. Space, in fact, is created through social relations and should be conceptualized as a focus of power, a site of contesting social forces. Essentially, this is an approach geared to the better understanding of the operations and functions of capitalism in the period of postmodernity. This is a conviction that 'a substantial nexus of social power' in capitalist society is produced through the intersection of money, time, and space.[49]

John Cooke has offered the most sustained discussion of Gordimer's treatment of space, arguing that all of her fiction can be approached by a consideration of the respective landscapes upon which her novels are centred, and which reveal a

changing perception of her environment, from the Witwatersrand mining community in the opening of *The Lying Days*,
through an increasing preoccupation with Johannesburg, up
to her most recent preoccupation, with the veld, the South
African landscape in general, from *A Guest of Honour* onwards.
For Cooke, this third stage is the most significant, for this
emphasis on landscape allows Gordimer to focus on the resurgence of African culture, and it is this which facilitates her
attainment of a historical sense and, at the same time, a
Lukácsian critical realism for her own time and context. The
fates of the protagonists in the novels from *A Guest of Honour*
through to *July's People* are, argues Cooke, 'fundamentally tied
to the landscapes they inhabit', landscapes which embody the
cultural situations of these characters.[50]

Cooke's concentration on landscape can appear overstated,
but it is a reading which fills an important gap in criticism of
Gordimer, suggesting the relevance of a politics of space to her
work. In one of her 1982 interviews Gordimer shows how the
issue of land and ownership crystallizes the South African
situation. A question is posed concerning the different
treatment of landscape to be found in the work of white and
black South African writers, respectively: black writers,
Terence Diggory speculates, identify with the people rather
than the land, in contrast to the preoccupation with landscape
in the work of white writers, a speculation which Gordimer
takes up:

I think there's something very interesting there. I think that whites
are always having to assert their claim to the land because it's based,
as Mehring's mistress [in *The Conservationist*] points out, on a piece of
paper – a deed of sale. And what is a deed of sale when people have
first of all taken a country by conquest? ... Blacks take the land for
granted, it's simply there. It's theirs, although they've been con-
quered; they were always there. They don't have this necessity to say,
'Well I love this land because it's beautiful, because it's this, that, and
the other'.[51]

This is a significant idea: that colonial history has generated a
racial divergence concerning spatial perception. And if South
Africa's colonial origins produce this geopolitical tension, it is a

tension which has been subsequently promoted in extra-
ordinary ways by the apartheid system, which was predicated
on the establishment and control of spatial zones. Underpinning this mechanism was the initial apartheid ethos of
racial separation, which conceived of South Africa as compris-
ing four 'racial groups': White, Coloured, Indian, and African.
Also fundamental to the apartheid system of spatial control (in
addition to absolute control for whites) was the idea that
whites in South Africa formed a single nation, while Africans
belonged to several distinct nations. The single white nation
comprised both English- and Afrikaans-speaking whites; the
African 'nations' or 'homelands' were eventually ten in
number. This geographical designation made the white nation
the largest single nation, and also set up spaces – the homelands
– to which black South Africans would (so the government
intended) be largely confined. Blacks were accepted as workers
in other areas while their labour was required, but were
otherwise expected to return to their designated homeland.
This, in effect, was an attempt to restrict urbanization, and the
pass laws were set up to enforce this, allowing the arrest of
blacks resident in towns for longer than seventy-two hours
without a permit. In rural areas outside the homelands efforts
were made to remove Africans from land they occupied or
owned.

In urban areas the government was equally systematic in its
attempts at spatial control. There were many 'petty apartheid'
measures which affected the daily lives of people through the
provision of separate amenities. On a larger scale there were
thorough 're-zoning' strategies: in the cities non-whites were
frequently moved from land they occupied and were re-
situated in newly-established, segregated townships. The
Group Areas Act of 1950 (with its many later amendments)
was a vital piece of legislation for spatial control: it designated
urban areas as the sole province of specific racial groups. In
practice this invariably meant the eviction of blacks from
desirable areas now re-designated as for whites only. Despite
all of these measures, however, non-white (especially African)
population of the towns continued apace.

The policies of the apartheid regime illustrate the inter-dependence of rural and urban control in spatial politics, a point which is seminal to theorists: for Henri Lefebvre, the notion of urbanization assumes a centrality; as Edward Soja points out, Lefebvre's idea of urbanization stretches beyond the confines of cities: it becomes a metaphor for the spatialization of modernity, the way in which capitalism reproduces its relations of production.[52] Commentators on the human geography of South Africa have stressed the centrality of urban development to major social and political developments, though the experience of South Africa incorporates 'unique' urban phenomena: new forms of urbanization have arisen, denying a rigid division between city and country; this is especially evident in the expansion of informal 'fringe' urban settlements, the urban phenomena which challenge conventional definitions.[53] The specificity of South African urbanization suggests not only a challenge to conventional descriptions, but also the existence of sites from which energies for social change might emerge. Foucault's concept of 'heterotopias' helps explain how such a possibility can be conceived: Foucault's heterotopias are sites which stand in a pointed relationship to other social spaces. They have 'the curious property of being in relation with all the other sites, but in such a way as to suspect, neutralize, or invert the set of relations that they happen to designate, mirror, or reflect. These spaces ... which are linked with all the others, ... however contradict all the other sites'.[54]

The concept of heterotopias can identify the sites of social experience and hence of social struggle. The black urban experience in South Africa – especially township life – is a manifestation of dispossession and repression. Yet it also contains a seed of something more positive, as (in its later manifestations) an implicit challenge to governmental control of urbanization. In this sense one might talk of black urbanization as a heterotopia, a socially created spatiality (albeit within strict confines) which maintains a contradictory link to all the other sites of South Africa, to which it is the required source of exploitation as well as the banished site of repression.

For Soja the heterotopia is 'concrete and abstract at the same time', and this articulates very accurately the nature of black urbanization, the concrete embodiment of a counter-culture, and, by virtue of this, also the means of articulating and harnessing abstract ideas of racial identity and solidarity.[55] Gordimer has been consistently sensitive to this ambivalence and potential of black urbanization. In the introduction to the collection of essays on the apartheid city, David Smith quotes a description of a township from Gordimer's *Burger's Daughter* in which she identifies several issues which are explored in Smith's collection. Gordimer, at one point, raises the question of how the 'urban' can be defined in this context: 'is this conglomerate urban or rural?'. She goes on to broach the subject of inequality hinging on the conjunction of power and space: 'is this a suburb or a strange kind of junk yard? The enormous backyard of the whole white city'. She also can see how this special kind of urbanization contains within it, for all its deprivation, the seed of a social possibility beyond that which has been imposed on its inhabitants: 'a "place"; a position whose contradictions those who impose them don't see, and from which will come a resolution they haven't provided for'. (*BD*, 149–51)

Smith finds Gordimer's description significantly perceptive in its presentation of these geopolitical issues, a description which 'captures something of both the life and the landscape of apartheid'. Smith also indicates, in effect, how Gordimer has located the 'heterotopic' quality of township life: her account

hints at the central significance of urbanization under apartheid: that those places imposed by the white government on the black majority have taken on a life of their own, rebounding on the system to its discomfort and ultimate demise. Very simply, urbanization under apartheid, no matter how carefully the state contrived to control it, has undermined apartheid itself, bringing South African society and its cities to the brink of significant if still uncertain change.[56]

Urbanization in South Africa, despite the deprivation and squalor that invariably accompanies it, does identify both a challenge to, and a contradiction emerging from, the policies of the apartheid regime. On the one hand the expanding settlements indicate the failure of the strategies of strict spatial control; on the other hand, the presence of blacks in townships adjoining cities is tacitly required since these people comprise much of a city's required workforce. There is a self-defeating element in this contradiction.[57]

Indeed, this contradiction has come to undermine the functioning of apartheid, even though the government has made attempts to embrace the trend to urbanization within its own practices; through, for example, a new policy of 'orderly urbanization', as set out in the 1986 White Paper on Urbanization. The intention, evidently, was to harness and control the marginalized masses into an authorized workforce, although the government has resisted bearing the burden of new housing costs.[58] In short, recent government policy has colluded with an ongoing resistance to the spatial rigidities of the apartheid state, resulting in urban phenomena which challenge the foundations of apartheid society, even while they graphically embody its contradictions. Gordimer's continuing preoccupation with the significance of human geography, consequently, has an enormous historical significance, as a fictional investigation of a determining feature in the dissolution of apartheid.

Clearly, the heterotopias of urban South Africa return us to the micropolitics of the body: heterotopias are places created for individual bodies to resist the organized spaces of incarceration or surveillance and to establish their own spaces of consciousness and freedom. Urbanization, like sexuality, is thus a form of transgression for Gordimer, of a social development beyond the limits of apartheid. In this sense urbanization and sexuality, through their transgressive potential, are two key routes for the fashioning of the cultural hybridization that Gordimer has identified as the necessary future for South African literature.

The issues discussed in this chapter provide the context of Gordimer's fiction: she continually pursues the question of literary identity and appropriate form, a crucial post-colonial matter; sexuality is utilized to supply a focus of trans-racial contact, and the source of a post-apartheid micropolitics; the treatment of social space extends this micropolitics into a consideration of urbanization which, as geographer David Smith has shown, represents the locus of apartheid's self-contradiction and the source of its demise. These issues are ever-present in Gordimer's fiction – sometimes in complex interrelationships – and they represent a pervasive contextualization. The fiction also includes references to particular historical events and people (especially in the early novels) and some aspects of Gordimer's development can be defined as specific responses to key historical events. The resolution of *Occasion for Loving*, for example, can be seen as a response to the implications of the Sharpeville massacre, which occurred during the writing of the novel. Similarly, the dynamic of *Burger's Daughter* responds to the events during and after the Soweto demonstration and riots in 1976–7: in both cases acts of brutal state repression result in black withdrawal from white assistance in opposition, and this is registered and acknowledged in these novels. Aside from these immediately arresting causal connections, however, the fiction is more properly defined as a slowly evolving series of reflections on the broader issues I have been describing, and the focus of this study is how these issues are treated.[59] One can see the novel sequence – on which I concentrate – as a continuum in which constant concerns are developed. In charting this development there are no clear breaks to be found, but there are discernible phases, and these phases provide the rationale for my chapter divisions: in chapter two I discuss *The Lying Days*, *A World of Strangers* and *Occasion for Loving*, and show how these early novels – which are more significant than is sometimes allowed – introduce issues which determine the structure of later work; the next phase is one of dominant transtextuality and is covered in chapter three, where readings of *The Late Bourgeois World*, *A Guest of Honour* and *The Conservationist* show how textuality begins to assume a central importance in Gordimer's developing political vision; chapter four considers how *Burger's Daughter* and *July's People* extend Gordimer's preoccupation with discursive practices through examinations of the construction of individual identities; the most recent phase in the novel sequence – characterized as one of literary self-reflexiveness – is described through discussions of *A Sport of Nature* and *My Son's Story* in chapter five; chapter six situates the short story oeuvre in relation to the curve of increasing literariness discerned in the novel sequence. The concluding chapter considers the extent to which the foregoing account makes Gordimer a postmodernist writer, and how her textual politics can be seen as a genuine source of historical intervention.

CHAPTER 2

The early novels: 'The Lying Days', 'A World of Strangers' and 'Occasion for Loving'

Gordimer's first three novels, *The Lying Days* (1953), *A World of Strangers* (1958) and *Occasion for Loving* (1963) form a distinctive group: in their forms they appear more traditional than the later novels, and this initial greater reliance on novelistic convention seems to marry with the liberal vision of political opposition in the 1950s, which Gordimer shared, prior to the Sharpeville massacre in 1960 (which occurred during the writing of *Occasion for Loving*). Yet this view of the early novels, though helpful in broad terms, can be taken to suggest a polarization between Gordimer's early and later novels, and this is inaccurate: there are discernible phases in Gordimer's career, but there are no clear breaks, and these early novels incorporate important preliminary challenges to, and innovations in, novelistic form; elements which are taken up more radically in later work. The early novels also treat *thematically* issues which become central to the formal and structural ordering of the later novels, and even here such themes have an impact, at times, on form and structure. In various respects, then, these three novels have an importance that cannot be overlooked.

THE LYING DAYS

The Lying Days concerns the partial growth and acquisition of race consciousness of its first-person narrator, Helen Shaw, through adolescence and young adulthood. The book has an autobiographical element, especially in its descriptions of landscape and town – many of these details are drawn from

34

Gordimer's memories of her youth.[1] It is thus tempting to draw parallels between the novelist and the novel's protagonist, Helen Shaw: the novel details Helen's search for (and confusion over) her social and political identity, just as this first novel has Gordimer beginning her search for her own artistic identity, and an appropriate literary form. The question of beginning to fashion an appropriate *form* is crucial, however, and actually reduces the relevance of any straightforwardly autobiographical reading of the novel; it is not merely that the biographical resonances are dispersed and concealed:[2] more significant is the fact that the novel questions certain features of the novel of development and learning – the *Bildungsroman* in particular, but also the nature of identity in autobiographical writing – and makes this element of formal questioning a principal focus.

The problem surrounding the identity of the novel's protagonist is a problem of narrative voice and perspective in this first-person novel. Michael Wade has perceived the primacy of this issue in comparing the novel to Joyce's *A Portrait of the Artist as a Young Man*:[3] just as in Joyce's novel, in Gordimer's we have to distinguish between different versions of a self, as Helen Shaw matures and develops, and this means distinguishing between the character and the narrator, whose perceptions are often at odds. The ironic discrepancy between the perceptions of character and narrator is a determining factor in interpreting the novel, and a factor which gives the novel a metafictional quality, especially over the central thematic issue of personal growth and development. The novel is consequently more artful than one might assume, especially as this is a first novel which is sometimes seen to be limited in the political conclusions it offers.[4]

There are limitations to *The Lying Days*, particularly concerning the extent to which the liberal heroine is able to break out of her bourgeois background, and here the novel clearly relates to the development of Gordimer's own political consciousness: her critical examination of the liberal white South African mind-cast begins here, even though no purposive conclusions for appropriate political action are offered.

This results in an indeterminacy and ambiguity about the stage Helen Shaw reaches at the novel's end. This air of uncertainty affects the formal effects and devices of the novel itself, indicating that Gordimer is already making headway in her pursuit of appropriate forms to encompass her message of requisite cultural and political change: rather than being imprisoned by the restraints of the *Bildungsroman* structure, with its notional accretion of wisdom leading to the production of an improved and coherent individual, Gordimer uses certain technical devices to complicate and undermine this kind of structural development. This results in an ambiguous form which appropriately mirrors the state of the character as well as the conclusions that Gordimer is able to offer about the state of the liberal consciousness at this early stage in the history of modern South Africa.

A focus of Helen Shaw's development is her tussle to free herself from the effects of her mother's ethnocentric and racist attitudes, and this tussle often produces a complex narrative texture in which different, conflicting voices can be heard. Early in the novel narrator-Helen offers this description relating to the concession stores used by blacks, which she hasn't yet seen for herself:

There were children on the Mine, little children in pushcarts whose mothers let their nursegirls take them anywhere they liked; go down to the filthy kaffir stores to gossip with the boys and let those poor little babies they're supposed to be taking care of breathe in heaven knows what dirt and disease, my mother often condemned. (*LD*, 18)

The explicit racism of the mother's condemnation concerning 'the filthy kaffir stores' with its assumed atmosphere of unspecified 'dirt and disease' is, to some extent, treated ironically by the suggestion that this is an often-voiced – perhaps unthinking – condemnation. However, the *placing* of the final tag – 'my mother often condemned' – is significant, and reduces the impact of the irony here: the opinion appears, initially, to be offered by the narrator and this is an acknowledgement of the extent of Helen's conditioning: the limited child's consciousness must often accord validity to parental opinions, even those which induce unease. Immediately after this Helen makes her way to the stores and observes 'dozens of natives', some who 'stood about shouting, passed on to pause every few yards and shout back something else. Quite often the exchange lasted for half a mile, bellowed across the veld until one was too far away to do more than wave a stick eloquently at the other.' (*LD*, 18) This description introduces the idea of an alternative kind of discourse which is beyond Helen's understanding: the narrative perspective here is tinged with a wry and superior amusement at the 'shouting' and 'eloquent' stick-waving, which clearly represents a kind of cultural bond and exchange that the delimited white consciousness finds slightly ridiculous; yet there is an implicit acknowledgement that this is an important form of communication, and one which represents a quite other, and (as yet) misunderstood culture. This acknowledgement of the other language emphasizes the inadequacy of Mrs Shaw's account of the 'filthy kaffir stores' with which it is juxtaposed.

In both of the above examples Helen reveals a reactionary ethnocentricity; it is the juxtaposition of 'discourses' which emphasizes the point about cultural difference and misunderstanding. Of course, one might expect a certain tension between different values and opinions in the delineation of a *child's* consciousness, but this kind of conflict is sustained through the narrative, making a clear trajectory of personal growth impossible to trace. There are also several hints of cracks and fissures in the edifice of Mrs Shaw's reactionary bourgeois persona, and these help to complicate the question of influence and reaction. When Helen is at university, but still living at home, she finds her mother adopting her (Helen's) ideas and views to explain to friends how her daughter is developing (ideas to which she is normally hostile) (*LD*, 178). The incident can be explained by social expediency, but it does demonstrate at least a willingness to consider alternative intellectual positions. Another incident, of perhaps greater significance, concerns Helen's childhood reading:

I read the books my mother brought home on her adult's ticket at the library; gentle novels of English family life and, now and then, stray examples of the proletarian novel to which the dole in England in the thirties had given rise. 'It's about the life of the poor in England – but it won't do her any harm if she wants to read it.' – My mother was sometimes a little uncertain about these books. 'I don't believe a girl should grow up not knowing what life is like.' (*LD*, 40)

The mother's choice of books, which helps determine the formation of Helen's literary consciousness, reveals a significant dichotomy: the 'gentle novels of English family life' spiced with 'stray examples of the proletarian novel', suggest a contrast required to fulfil one reader's superficial need for variety, but the two genres imply a social and political connection between bourgeois leisure and the deprivation which sustains it. This contrast has an obvious connection with the Shaws' situation, living in the white Mine community (governed by English culture) isolated from the black community which comprises, essentially, the Mine's workforce and, which, therefore, facilitates the production of the means that sustain the white community in its comfort and isolation. Mrs Shaw is not consciously trying to radicalize her daughter, but her choice does go beyond superficial questions of entertainment in her consideration of contributing something to her daughter's social education – her desire to help her discover 'what life is like'. The important point is that contradictions are rife in the novel, and that they usually relate directly to questions of class and political organization, and that this kind of *productive* contradiction – productive in its exposure of reactionary ideas – can be said to relate even to the character, Mrs Shaw, whom the novel offers as the most reactionary force hampering Helen's awakening political consciousness.

The novel's focus on personal and political development (even if only partial) through the exposure of contradictions embraces two thematic areas crucial to Gordimer: her treatment of the body and sexuality, and her consideration of the implications of space. The two areas are of central significance in this first novel; subsequently they will determine the structure and form of Gordimer's fiction more overtly.

The experience of the body has an obvious importance in a novel of personal growth which includes the awakening sexuality of its protagonist; and the broader implications of bodily experience – the connection with particular aspects of political expression and repression – are made quite explicit. At the concession stores Helen is profoundly affected by the sights and smells of a different (impoverished) social environment – a sudden exposure to an array of cultural difference – which she cannot immediately make sense of, and her reaction is registered bodily: she holds her 'buttocks stiffly together', and feels that her eyes are not quick enough to take everything in; she feels a simultaneous need to suppress a giggle, or 'long squeeze of excitement' (*LD*, 20). The stiffened walk – a gesture of withdrawal – represents a protective response to what is frightening, yet still intriguing and desired: Helen cannot take in the experience as fully as she desires, and her further impulse is to repress a kind of hysteria that threatens to overtake her. At several points in the novel Gordimer associates laughter with repression, fear or hysteria: the unmotivated laughter at the tennis club, for example, seems a kind of hysterical unease at the privilege the club represents (*LD*, 25). Helen's physical attraction, and early responses to Ludi Koch are also marked by helpless laughter, before they have kissed for the first time (*LD*, 58). An important detail in this connection occurs early in the novel when we read of 'an unwritten law' that little girls must not be left alone because of the 'native' boys; this un-articulated fear of black sexuality is a collective fear which is instilled into the children of the white community before they can understand its implications (*LD*, 14).

By this chain of associations the novel connects individual with broader social repression, and here one can see something positive in the novel's concern with personal experience, which some critics have seen as representing a withdrawal from questions of political and historical commitment:[5] this is not a fully fledged micropolitics, but Helen's experiences do teach her that the individual body is the smallest identifiable site of both political repression and political growth.

It is in Helen's relationship with Paul Clark that the connections between sexuality and politics become clearly visible. Another dichotomy – that of a mind/body split – orders Gordimer's thinking here. The novel has a preoccupation with the

necessity of balance between intellectual and physical com-
patibility. This is rather crudely signalled in a conversation
Helen has with a fellow train passenger, Ian Petrie, who
explains that his marriage, void of intellectual equality, is
based purely on physical companionship (sport as well as sex)
and that this is the important thing (*LD*, 106). The same
dualism presents problems for Helen's two important relationships; her (eventually failed) affair with Paul Clark, and her
platonic (but ambiguous) friendship with Joel Aaron. Helen's
relationship with Paul founders when she begins to voice
doubts about their political complicity and they begin to lose
their intellectual common ground. Helen perceives a different
dualism for Paul, caused by his work for the government
department responsible for 'Poor Relief' and 'Housing', the
minimal efforts of which are directed towards the black under-
class (*LD*, 239). The work, as Paul clearly understands,
inevitably compromises him in his more radical political activities: mixing with African Nationalists by night, yet doing the
bidding of the government they contest by day. Helen and
Paul's relationship fails, by degrees, as the impossibility of
purposive political action, working within the system, becomes
clearer; and, for Paul, there is the danger (articulated by
Helen) of becoming 'schizoid' (*LD*, 281). After the Nationalist
Party's election victory of 1948 one early effect of apartheid
legislation, following the Prohibition of Mixed Marriages Act
(1949), is registered in a resonant image which also conjoins
the ideas of sexuality and repression as they impinge on Paul
and Helen. Paul recounts to Helen the experiences of an
elderly 'mixed' couple, disturbed in their bed by the shining
torch of a policeman, enforcing the new ban (*LD*, 259), an
image recalled as Helen and Paul lie in bed with the headlights
of cars playing over their heads (*LD*, 261).

As this invasion of the most intimate of personal spaces – the
bedroom – indicates, the novel's focus on personal politics is
related to its preoccupation with space. In later novels (such as
The Conservationist) space becomes an integral part of the poetic
design of work which is also principally concerned with the
social and political uses and appropriations of space. While

there is not quite this tight unity of novelistic form and social content in *The Lying Days*, there is, nevertheless, a spatial component to the novel's design which is crucial to how it is interpreted. The novel is written in three sections, each with a different setting which, ostensibly, acts as a kind of background to key stages of Helen's development: part one, 'The Mine', establishes the industrial situation of Helen's upbringing (and suggests a submerged political consciousness), while part two ('The Sea') presents the possibility of an apolitical white escapism, expressed through Helen's adolescent sexual awakening with Ludi Koch on the coast. The final (and longest) part is 'The City' where Helen's political awakening begins. The tripartite structure, looked at schematically, seems designed to parallel the process of *Bildung*, yet the structure seems also to reject such a design once having entertained it: the final section crystallizes how place is intimately bound up with individual lives; the city contains the sites of real and complex lived relations, a fact which implicitly discredits the notion of setting as illustrative background for the development of one individual.

Specific details throughout the novel also serve to discredit the idea of setting as background. The most arresting spatial images represent Helen's developing 'racial consciousness'. These begin with her childhood recollection of first venturing out from the isolated white Mine community to the forbidden concession stores which the blacks use. Helen's fascination and amazement at the jumble she sees in the shop windows, and at the bewildering array of sensory experiences that greet her, represent a significant culture shock, or encounter with this 'other', so close, yet usually concealed from her view (*LD*, 19–24). As Helen begins to make her way home again, she observes a Mine boy urinating in the street and reports that 'a sudden press of knowledge, hot and unwanted, came upon me'. She senses 'a question that had waited inside me but had never risen into words or thoughts because there were no words for it' (*LD*, 24). The sudden knowledge, and the question, can both be taken to indicate a young girl's emerging consciousness of male physical difference, but beyond this naturalistic explanation of the reaction there is a resonant suggestion of an emerging political consciousness, a 'knowledge' that material situations differ, even the provision of facilities for essential bodily functions, and a 'question', as yet not properly articulated, concerning why this should be so. The importance of the scene is emphasized by later considerations of the provision of toilet facilities, the most basic and necessary of public spaces. At the university Helen has one of her first talks with Mary Seswayo, the black student she tries to befriend, in a cloakroom (*LD*, 130–2), a setting which seems insignificant enough. Yet Helen has first encountered Mary in a cloakroom at the university, at which point the narrator pauses to remark how rare it is to find somewhere where a black girl can wash her hands in the same place as a white girl (*LD*, 105), a point reinforced later when the narrator, reflecting on the restrictions which hamper Mary, observes that there are no public toilet facilities for blacks at all in the Johannesburg shopping centre (*LD*, 169). The detail that Helen is forbidden by her mother to use certain public conveniences (*LD*, 23), now clearly represents a luxurious disdain and adds a further poignancy to this motif, and to the implication that not only general notions of power, but basic facets of human dignity are bound up with the control of space; and all of this is incipiently present in the child Helen's reaction to the Mine boy urinating in the street. With hindsight the original fear of the sexual other is exposed as a spectre constructed and perpetuated by apartheid and its 'petty' measures of enforcement.

Helen's concern with the idea of spatial provision/deprivation as a political issue is crystallized through her (often over-paternalistic) concern for Mary Seswayo. The scene in which Charles and Helen drive Mary home to the Mariastad location in which she is staying involves a culture shock for the two whites which is analogous to Helen's reactions at the concession stores. The narrator articulates the whites' shock at the sensory experience of the township:

All above the crust of vague, close, low houses, smoke hung, quite still as if it had been there for ever; and shouts rose, and it seemed that the shout had been there for ever, too, many voices lifted at different times and for different reasons that became simply a shout, that never began and never ended. (*LD*, 173)

The spatial compression of the township gives the illusion of permanence, despite its architectural insubstantiality. The images focused on to express this paradox are significant: the polluting smoke is a permanent feature, and the impression of the many voices of the township forming a single shout suggests the disorder and incoherence of compression and squalor (at least to the whites, with a more privileged notion of personal space and communication). Paradoxically, the single voice also suggests a coherence and unity, the unity of a common experience of repression, and there is a clear sense here of the unity required for political action, even though we see only the raw material of this mobilization: an (as yet) unarticulated, but nevertheless unified, 'shout'. This is an embryonic version of the heterotopia – discussed in the opening chapter – which is suggested by the township description in *Burger's Daughter*. It is significant that, in contrast to this single shout, Charles and Helen are both reduced to silence by the experience of the township: they both 'stopped talking, as people do when they feel they may have lost their way' (*LD*, 173). This is a suggestion of guilt, of a tacit awareness of white complicity in the material manifestation of repression. Perhaps these images are a little clumsy, especially the suggestion of an emerging black political voice which silences the whites; but the politics of the geography give the scene an extra dimension and importance. When Mary disappears into one of the houses, Helen is able to imagine the inside of Mary's house (which she hasn't seen) simply because the location is uniform in its squalor and compression (*LD*, 175).

The theme of Mary's domestic space is developed through Helen's concern over Mary's exam revision. Having discovered that the house in which Mary is staying is too cramped and chaotic for study, it occurs to Helen that Mary could stay with her and her parents: not in the house exactly, but in the 'cooler', a storeroom originally built for keeping food, and which would be 'neither inside the house, nor out in the yard with Anna [the servant], but something in between' (*LD*, 187).

The compromise solution – the creation of a makeshift space which is neither inside the domain of the whites, nor outside where the black servants are billeted – is clearly symbolic. Yet Helen's compromise, designed primarily to placate the racist concerns of her mother, also indicates the literal dilemma of spatial provision for blacks.

Spatial images and references are rife in the novel and there is room here to mention only a handful of the more significant instances. There is, however, one further important aspect of this motif, involving the character Joel Aaron, who acts in the novel as a kind of moral conscience for Helen, helping, in key scenes, to nourish Helen's developing political consciousness. In one studiedly symbolic scene Helen and Joel take a drive to a beauty spot known as Macdonald's Kloof, and here Helen reflects on questions of racial difference, making the crucial 'discovery' that Mary Seswayo 'is a girl . . . like me' (*LD*, 142). Joel traces, on a rock, a 'map' which represents a version of the world, based specifically on an awareness of political geography:

'Here's a whole group of islands, with a warm current wrapped round them, so they're the coconut-palm kind. The people sing (you would find out that they've got hookworm) and they sail about – all over here – in the hollowed-out barks of trees, with figureheads like ugly sea monsters. Over this side is a huge, rich country, an Africa and America rolled into one, with a bit of Italy thrown in for charm – ' (*LD*, 145).

This symbolic scene, which crystallizes a key moment in Helen's awakening, contains also (and seems implicitly connected to) this resonant image of global spatial politics, presented ironically by Joel's observation of the 'cocktail' of privilege, embracing resources (Africa), capitalist clout (America) and cultural and aesthetic credibility (Italy). This last ingredient – 'a bit of Italy thrown in for charm' – is one of several parodic allusions to Forster to be found in Gordimer's early novels. The resonance of this scene, and the centrality of the idea of mapping to it, are elements which indicate the importance of questions of space even at the beginning of Gordimer's novelistic career. The scene resurfaces in a dream

of Helén's immediately following a moment in which the
headlamps of cars shine into the bedroom of Paul and Helen,
reminding them of the police with flashlights enforcing the
Mixed Marriages ban (*LD*, 261). Here the Kloof episode, with
its broader implications about geopolitics, is explicitly linked
with localized measures of racial and spatial control.

A more fully worked-through spatial issue is represented by
Joel: he is training to be an architect, and it is clearly appropriate that this character, whose function has a direct bearing
on the novel's political vision, should be studying the provision
and organization of social space. The question of architecture
and urban design is one which recurs in Gordimer's work. At
one stage we learn that Joel's future plans include the possibility of building houses for blacks (*LD*, 157), and, in the final
scene, we see Joel sailing for Israel, a symbolic return of the
Jew-architect in 'the hope of realizing a concrete expression of
his creative urge, in doing his work in a society which in itself
was in the live process of emergence, instead of decay' (*LD*,
366). This remark, by narrator-Helen, occurs in the final
chapter of the novel, in which the narrator now explicitly
identifies herself as the writer of the novel, and here she is
considering whether or not the process of fictional composition
is comparable to the positive expression of Joel's 'creative
urge': the example of Joel's intended active participation in the
construction of a new society. The implication is that this
should be the goal of the novelist, especially in South Africa,
and the novel's preoccupation with spatial politics indicates an
intention to contribute to the building – in a sense literally, as
well as metaphorically – of a more equitable society. Yet, as the
novel indicates, this is a society in decay and the narrator is
equivocal in her conclusions about what the novel has been
able to achieve: Helen's hopeful conviction that she will return
– that she is not running away from her country's problems – is
described as 'the phoenix illusion that makes life always possible' (*LD*, 367). The idea of the phoenix illusion – almost the
final image of the novel – suggests, rather than a condemnation
of Helen, a realistic understanding of the limits to what a novel
can achieve in contributing to an alternative political future at

this time. In these final pages the ironic distance between Helen as narrator and Helen as character (more mature at this stage in the narrative) is less marked, but the distance remains, preventing an unequivocal assertion of personal development or formal resolution.

The novel's engagement with political events is not pronounced, and this may seem surprising since the novel covers the period which includes the 1948 election victory of the Nationalists, and the early effects of apartheid legislation. With hindsight it is easy to condemn the novel for not displaying a more explicitly outraged attitude to these developments, and critics are probably right in identifying an element of unregenerated liberalism in the novel's tone: the narrator's use of the term 'native' in passages offered as objective analysis may be just the most obvious example of an unconscious ethnocentrism. Nevertheless, there is also a strategic principle behind the novel's lack of urgency in its treatment of political events, a principle which ironizes the impercipience of the white characters: prior to the election, the common view amongst Helen's friends is that the Nationalists, tainted in the public mind by their war-time support of the Germans, don't stand a chance of coming to power (*LD*, 235). This misreading of the outcome by a group identified, to some extent, as belonging to a Left intelligentsia, reveals a certain complacency in an unmotivated opposition, a lack of urgency emulated in the novel's narrative. There is, therefore, a kind of shock tactic in the novel's lack of political urgency, and not merely a limiting liberalism; clearly this shock tactic, which both mimics and criticizes political complacency, is more effective with hindsight, but it can still quite properly be ascribed to the novel's own formal techniques: structurally, the novel is concerned with perceptions before and after the 1948 election and in its latter phases with the need for a clear commitment of some kind. Helen's understanding of the equivocation of her own position is in tune with a post-1948 sense of frustration which includes a personal critique and acknowledgement of complicity.

In the section which details some of the early measures of

apartheid, one paragraph lists a number of crucial measures including the Mixed Marriages Act, the Suppression of Communism Bill and the machinations of the Nationalist Government to remove 'coloured' voters from the electoral roll (*LD*, 255).[6] These are extremely important instruments of apartheid oppression, and are glossed over by the narrator. However, it is the attitude *represented* by the 'gloss' which the narrator focuses on: she attempts to account for the complacency of South African whites, a complacency based on a philosophy of public commitment through private experience: 'when the impact on individual lives, personal lives is not immediate and actual, political change does not affect the real happiness or unhappiness of people's lives, though they may protest that it does.' (*LD*, 255) This observation has the air of an authorial statement, and its logic stresses the difficulty of connecting the private with the public. It is followed by an account of how the narrator sees herself and Paul as being closer to political commitment than most concerned whites, as a result of Paul's first-hand experience of individual suffering: the anecdote of the elderly 'mixed' couple – caught under the Mixed Marriages ban – is offered apparently to demonstrate how an empathy with individual suffering is more affecting than abstract political outrage (*LD*, 259). Gordimer's later novels suggest that this is a false distinction: throughout her novelistic career Gordimer insists on the necessity of arriving at the political through the personal, but, in later work, as the logic of the connection is developed, there is no sense, as there is here, of two discrete realms.

A WORLD OF STRANGERS

Gordimer's second novel, *A World of Strangers*, suffers from some of the same restrictions as does her first – principally, restrictions of political vision resulting from the same climate of liberal commitment which was to prove an inadequate response to the brutal oppression of the (still developing) apartheid system. Yet, like *The Lying Days*, the novel has a significant value above and beyond these inevitable historical limits. Both are novels of learning and in each case the learning process is delineated in the personal progression of the central protagonist, who also narrates the novel. Both novels are, to some extent, critical of their respective protagonist at certain points, but this principle is more significant in *A World of Strangers* than it is in *The Lying Days*. The suggestion of auto-biography in the earlier novel is missing in the second, and this denies any simplistic reading of the character-narrator, Toby Hood, as a mouthpiece for the novel's political programme. It is true that neither Helen Shaw nor Toby Hood function in this way, but Gordimer's self-conscious understanding of the various possibilities and ambiguities surrounding her central character are more pronounced in *A World of Strangers*, and this indicates that the inadequacies of the novel are less severe than is sometimes claimed.

Like *The Lying Days*, the novel is carefully structured to make pointed revelations. The apolitical Toby Hood comes from England to South Africa on assignment for his family's publishing house, and proceeds to lead a dual life dividing his time between the townships and white high society. Toby's personal relationships help focus the nature of these unbridge-able 'worlds of strangers': his kindred black bachelor friend, the similarly apolitical Steven Sitole, takes him into the town-ships; by contrast, his prejudiced lover Cecil Rowe (from whom Toby conceals his friendship with Steven) epitomizes the attraction he finds in privileged white society. By the end of the novel Cecil has married someone else, Steven has been killed (in a car crash, pursued by police) and Toby leaves South Africa, promising to return, his eyes having been opened to political reality.

Criticisms of *A World of Strangers* concentrate on the empha-sis placed on personal development which displaces, so the argument runs, any clear prescription for purposive political opposition. What is worse, the presentation of the developing individual consciousness of Toby Hood is usually taken to represent political advancement on a broader scale, which must progress, so this reading of the novel suggests, by an extensive process of personal growth and awakening. This emphasis on the personal also corresponds with the political milieu of a novel which, according to Clingman, 'falls within the discourse of a liberal humanism, and relates to the fullest flush of the last great moment of that ideology in South Africa'.[7] This locates the political ideology which governs the novel's historical context, and which also characterizes the thinking of much political opposition to apartheid in the 1950s. In certain ways, however, *A World of Strangers* appears to distance itself from a liberal ideology. The important interpretive point concerns whether or not Toby can be seen to *represent* this imperfect moment of liberal humanist commitment at the novel's conclusion; critics have sometimes assumed that he can, as Robert Green does in stating that Toby's 'engagement, the novel asks us to believe, had come to him through personal relations, rather than through ideological struggle or political involvement'.[8] It seems to me that the novel remains sceptical about Toby's political 'growth', and does not present him as representative of a positive oppositional force; the novel is equivocal about him, sometimes presenting his assimilation of his South African experience as hopeful, and sometimes implying quite contrary conclusions about his perceptions: at times there are clear affinities between the psyche of Toby Hood and the institutionalized mind-set of the apartheid regime.

A question that remains to be considered is whether or not an emphasis on *personal* awakening and development, even if it is only partial, can be said to be adequate. There is also a distinction to be made between the emphasis which Gordimer places on individual experience and Toby Hood's own commitment to it, which is clearly satirized. Early in the novel Toby expresses a crass impatience with political questions: 'I want to take care of my own relationships with men and women who come into my life, and let the abstractions of race and politics go hang.' (*WS*, 34) This emphasis on the personal is quite distinct from the way in which the novel examines the 'abstractions' of race and politics in South Africa through key personal experiences.

Toby does develop as the novel progresses, but it is important to realize that the novel continues to condemn his attitudes. In particular, his attitude to women, which remains essentially static, complicates his notional development: throughout the book Toby views women purely as objects of desire, and not as potentially equal partners. After a disturbing encounter with the blind racism of one of his office workers, Toby finds himself unwilling to share his feelings of anger and confusion with his lover, the superficial Cecil. Rather than finding an opportunity to articulate and develop an incipient moral outrage, he finds, in his lover, the offer of a distraction, and reflects: 'I had, I supposed, an Eastern equation of women with pleasure; I fiercely resisted any impingement on this preserve.' (*WS*, 141) This reduction of woman to an object for personal gratification is, in Toby's mind, a 'preserve' to be 'fiercely' protected, and this metaphor establishes a link between an individual male desire, and what one might call the institutionalized male desire of the state, which also employs a sanctioned violence, a 'fierceness', to establish 'preserves' for whites. This is the first occurrence in Gordimer's novels of a connection which is given extensive treatment in her fiction: the connection between egocentric male desire, and the illegitimate political appropriation and control of social space. At one point Toby insists on leaving the light on when making love with Cecil: 'she argued about the light, but I wanted to see her face, to know what she was feeling. (Who knows what women feel, in their queer, gratuitous moment?).' (*WS*, 146) Here, again, female sexuality represents the unknown 'other' for Toby, who asserts control over the available technology in a futile attempt to record in his memory the nature of this other. He also displays the classic male confusion about and (implicit) fear of the female orgasm, which he desires to examine in a space he controls.

Later on in the novel, at a club run by Indians, Toby witnesses the singing of a beautiful Indian girl, and sees her as a 'creature' made to please (*WS*, 182). Toby expresses a similar attitude towards the end of the novel, when dismissing the thought of marriage for himself: 'for me, the exoticism of women still lay in beauty and self-absorbed femininity, I would choose an houri rather than a companion.' (*WS*, 249) Even allowing here for a degree of mocking self-irony, the attitude expressed confirms Toby's reactions to the Indian girl: in both cases there is an evident commodification and reduction of woman to an exotic other for personal use; this is precisely the way in which the forces of colonial imperialism view the potential of exotic 'other' places and populations. In short, the confused sexuality of the novel's narrator produces an attitude which parallels the world-view of the apartheid regime, a regime with its roots in an appropriating colonial past.

This important equivocation surrounding Toby is developed in his relationship with Anna Louw, the novel's only evidently socialist character. Anna Louw is diametrically opposed to Cecil, who has no political consciousness whatever, and does not represent a potential distraction. The relationship between Toby and Anna is brief and insubstantial, but it does involve a sexual encounter, which is significant in a novel in which (as is typical of Gordimer) sexual responses are also an index of the public self. Toby's advances, significantly, are produced through fear: he records his feeling of being 'suddenly afraid of her', and that 'pleasure came to me as if wrung from my grasp' (*WS*, 174–5). Toby's involvement in this sexual act seems motivated, once more, by a need to control the object of fear, but he can establish no such control over Anna. The fear of the 'other' produces the desire to control and oppress.

If Toby's confused sexuality parallels aspects of the racist order he witnesses – and the parallel persists throughout the novel – clearly there is a problem in seeing the novel's central character as exemplifying an awakening political conscious-ness. In some senses, however, this *is* his function, and so an ambiguity surrounds his role, and this determines the novel's formal effects. These effects can be seen as a deliberate part of the novel's design since the problematizing of Toby is an integral aspect of the novel's larger purpose, even if local instances of confusion cannot always be associated with the grand design. The choice of a recalcitrant subject as the focus in a novel structured, notionally, as one of inner development presents a clear paradox; and the result is an impression of the *difficulty* of individual progression in the political context described. The difficulty is appropriate to the novel's theme, and the paradox offers an implicit comment on how inner development is charted in a novel: there is no easily identifiable *Bildung* in *A World of Strangers*, and this indicates a crucial technical problem in this first-person novel, a problem of narrative voice. Toby's narrating voice reveals, as we have seen, stasis rather than progression in key areas, and this suggests that there might be an alternative voice embedded within the narrative to imply how Toby does develop. One must not overlook the element of a development that does not surface into full consciousness – there clearly is a partially articulated, semi-conscious progression for Toby – but at times this needs to be articulated for the reader in a way that, for consistency's sake, cannot come from Toby. The result is a co-existence of two voices: Toby's, and the accent of a hidden third-person narrator which acts as a kind of conscience for Toby, or, more accurately, as an inner voice that articulates his semi-conscious understandings. This dialogic quality explains the apparent paradox of a character-narrator who appears to be inconsistent about the effect his experiences have on him. An indication of this dialogism is given in various passages describing Cecil. In chapter seven, Toby gives his typically approving appraisal of her superficial qualities: 'I was delighted to see how she looked every inch the hard-riding, hard-drinking bitch, just as, in the Stratford [bar], she had unconsciously assumed the spectacular narcissism of the mannequin.' (*WS*, 130) The delight Toby takes here in Cecil's unthinking ('unconscious') adoption of different roles – roles which emphasize the facade of a certain type – is at one with his commodification of women as objects of desire, a tendency which persists throughout the novel. It comes as some surprise, therefore, to read a far more lucid analysis of Cecil in the very next chapter:

She seemed to have no doubts about the worthwhileness of the things she attempted, whether she wanted to be a mannequin in Rome or a champion show jumper; but like a bloodhound that has had no nose bred into it, she was guessing at the trail, and ran helter-skelter, looking back inquiringly all the time, uncertain if she were going the right way about her pursuit, and in the right style. Nothing came naturally to her. (*WS*, 142)

Now the narrative voice – ostensibly Toby's – sees Cecil's pursuit of different roles as entirely aimless, as divorced from a 'natural' role, as indicated in the analogy of the ill-bred blood-hound. This is not a lucidity that is representative of Toby, nor is it something he can sustain; of course, one can distinguish between different moods – a reflective one, and a less rational mood governed by sexual desire – and this would account for the discrepancy. But perhaps the more plausible explanation, given the persistence of this kind of tension in the novel, is the one adduced above: here we might see an alternative accent which breaks into the narrative to articulate clearly that which Toby's experiences should enable him to see, but which he cannot focus on consistently.

This principle of dialogism, discernible explicitly in the narrative here, can be said to relate also to the design of the novel in various ways. Particular scenes, for example, are structured to imply a lesson learned for Toby, even though there is often confusion in the way he articulates this lesson: again different perspectives co-exist (here at the structural level), which locate Toby's own vacillation.

There are further instances of a dialogic tension at localized points in the narrative which reveal a crucial aspect of Toby's partial progression. These are moments that relate to Toby's overall world-view, the way in which he interprets the 'reality' before him. His personal debate about 'reality' – a direct, political question – has also a metafictional aspect to it as it coincides with a parallel debate about literary realism, and the adequacy of this mode for serious political analysis.

Stephen Clingman considers the novel to be, formally, a work of realism, but one which also extends this mode in order to reinforce it. This is seen as a partial failure, because just as the mode of realism is challenged, yet ultimately reinforced, so is the interpretation of political 'reality' in South Africa chal-lenged, but not displaced. For Clingman, the novel's formal project represents a parallel in this regard with the strategies of the opposition movements of the 1950s; the Congress Alliance, 'which virtually constituted the opposition to apartheid in the 1950s', despite its challenge to South African political reality, ultimately reinforced its framework, which the Alliance didn't offer to displace.[9] The historical context has a crucial bearing on the adequacy, or otherwise, of the political vision one can ascribe to *A World of Strangers*. Before considering this, however, there is more that needs to be said about the novel's engagement with questions of 'realism' and 'reality', and these questions are best approached through a broader consideration of the novel's literary self-consciousness.

The novel begins with a kind of prologue section prior to part one, and this prologue is a Forsterian pastiche. Toby Hood's first encounter with Africa is mediated by the limited and limiting opinions of the upper-middle-class English people in whose company he finds himself on his voyage (just as, for example, Lucy Honeychurch is prevented from an encounter with the 'real' Italy by her cousin Charlotte in the opening chapters of *A Room With a View*). But such parallels are patently absurd, and reveal a dark irony in the novelist's view of her literary antecedent: in contrast to Forster's characters, there can be no enriching personal growth for Toby through an unfettered encounter with the foreign. The process of understanding is one which must uncover personal hypocrisy and complicity, rather than merely realizing personal potential. It is significant that the most sustained allusion to Forster is confined to this prologue, in which Toby is at the height of his egocentricity: the ironic allusion is used to reinforce the characterization. The conclusion, in which Toby and Sam Mofokenzazi are forced apart by the separate stairways of petty apartheid, is, as has often been pointed out, an obvious echo of *A Passage to India* where Aziz and Fielding are forced apart by the Indian landscape at the novel's close. Again, the allusion embodies a barbed irony: Gordimer supplies the motivation (apartheid) for the separation of her characters, a pointed supplement to the anthropomorphic moment from Forster which is her model.

There are a number of other literary allusions in the novel, and some of these appear to characterize Toby as someone who is bookish and out of touch – as being 'too literary by half', as Judie Newman puts it.[10] Toby, for example, compares himself to Sinbad the Sailor at one point (*WS*, 18), and describes his personal appearance as coming 'straight out of Dickens' at another (*WS*, 10). Yet if these references identify the limited and inadequate frame of cultural reference which this Englishman brings to Africa, he also seems aware of this inadequacy at times. When he is befriended by the embittered Steven Sitole, the novel's principal black character who, in apparent despair, has opted out of direct political opposition, Toby describes their drinking spree in these terms: 'Like Alice plunging after the White Rabbit, I went with Steven into the townships, the shebeens, the rooms and houses of his friends.' (*WS*, 122) There is a manifest irony here: for this sexist Englishman to imagine himself as Lewis Carroll's Alice is only marginally less absurd than the description of the cynical black man, seeking refuge from the oppression of apartheid, as the White Rabbit. In this moment Toby seems to acknowledge the absurdity present in the discrepancy between his new experiences and the cultural baggage he brings with him. But there remains an ambiguity, another instance of dialogism, perhaps, the co-existence of two voices representing different stages of the narrator's development.

The literary self-consciousness of the novel is something which also affects its allegiance to, or dependence upon, realism as a literary mode. Clingman, following Barthes, sees the novel as a work of 'classical realism' since 'its fundamental motivation is to undertake a reading of social reality in apparently as objective a manner as possible'. This objectivity is bestowed upon the novel by Toby who is offered by the novel as 'the epitome of disinterested objectivity'.[11] As my discussion so far has indicated a quite different view of Toby is possible, one which denies him this position of disinterested objectivity. The associated definition of realism – as a mode which maintains a stable, identifiable focus on the social world it purports to describe – would therefore not, in my reading, properly account for a novel that is actually showing how the ostensible objectivity of its narrator conceals a complicity which hampers his progression. The debate about the social 'reality' described, in other words, involves, also, a debate about how the interpreting is, or ought to be, done; about what it means to narrate.

It might be that this account of the novel implies a kind of postmodernist sophistication which is not really sustained, and it is true that the metafictional aspect of the book is low-key. But the ambiguity surrounding Toby is, necessarily, a formal problematic, which is definitely utilized by Gordimer. In this connection, it is significant that Toby, at key moments, has cause to reflect on various notions of 'reality'. Soon after installing himself in 'the biggest tourist hotel' in Johannesburg, Toby reflects, thinking of his recent voyage and his English fellow passengers: 'I seemed to have progressed merely from one unreality to another.' (*WS*, 35) Toby's understanding that the two privileged environments he has encountered are 'unreal' is matched by a later realization that Cecil 'belonged to the unreality through which I had fallen' (*WS*, 104). In both cases a partial advancement is implied – beyond the trappings of privilege and the superficial attractions of his lover. In establishing what is 'unreal', Toby has yet to determine where 'reality' lies; when he establishes this, through a comparison with township life, the conclusions he draws do not reveal a significant political advancement:

I decided that possibly life in the townships seemed more 'real' simply because there were fewer distractions, far fewer vicarious means for spending passion, or boredom . . . The reality was nearer the surface. There was nothing for the frustrated man to do but grumble in the street; there was nothing for the deserted girl to do but sit on the step and wait for her bastard to be born; there was nothing to be done with the drunk but let him lie in the yard until he'd got over it. Among the people I met with Cecil, frustrated men threw themselves into golf and horse-racing, girls who had had broken love affairs went off to Europe, drunks were called alcoholics, and underwent expensive cures. That was all. That was the only difference.

But was it? With so much to comfort and distract them, don't people perhaps learn, at last, to feel a little less? And doesn't that make life that much less 'real'? (*WS*, 149–50)

This speculation continues, taking various turns and reaching no conclusions. The important point, however, is that the terms of this speculation are evidently inadequate since Toby seems unaware of the actual implications of the contrast upon which these reflections are based. Structurally, the novel is based on this contrast, this world of strangers: the book offers telling contrasts between the privileged white suburbs (epitomized by the refined High House) and the vibrancy of the black townships, and this contrast emerges from Toby's experiences. Moreover, the very *possibility* of these experiences depends upon Toby's inability to draw clear moral conclusions from what he witnesses, because it is his impercipience that enables him to move so freely between the two worlds without more serious qualms: the book's structure, in this sense, is dependent upon the narrator's impercipience. In the passage quoted above, Toby contrasts the two worlds to determine which betrays the greater degree of 'reality'. The contrast is based on the most extreme material disparity, and, in this sense, the 'reality' which Toby perceives to be closer to the surface in township life must really identify the basic necessities of life, which poverty makes more pressing. Yet his account draws back from this economic implication, and is diluted by a nebulous (and apolitical) consideration of the relationship between 'feeling' and 'reality': an aesthetic notion of human vitality reveals what is to the advantage of township life, thereby obscuring the actual disadvantages that make this 'advantage' possible. This extended consideration of 'reality', then, merely reveals a moral and political lacuna in Toby's (and the book's) narrative perspective, which must be seen as deliberate.

Toby's confusion about issues of economic reality is not Gordimer's: towards the end of the novel she has Sam Mofokenzazi articulate for Toby the economic implications of an administration based on principles of racial discrimination:

'If you know anybody who wants to know what it's like to be a black man, this is it. No matter how much you manage to do for yourself, it's not enough. If you've got a decent job with decent money it can't do you much good, because it's got to spread so far. You're always a rich man compared with your sister or your brother, or your wife's cousins. You can't ever get out of debt while there's one member of the family who has to pay a fine or get sick and go to hospital. And so it goes on. If I get an increase, what'll it help me? Someone'll have to have it to pay tax or get a set of false teeth.' (*WS*, 243–4)

Clingman claims that Sam's political ambitions involve the hope that all his people can become decently bourgeois, though his explanation, here – of the impossibility of the embourgeoisement of blacks under apartheid – suggests also that *individual* material advancement is at odds with the existence of a living community.[12] Sam's explanation implies that the bourgeois advancement of black people can only result from a loss of communal responsibilities, and this would clearly be inimical to any kind of collective opposition. The implications of Sam's personal economic life are subtle, but far-reaching; there is an implicit rejection of any solution that might be identified as a liberal amelioration of material inequality which, so the logic of Sam's account implies, can only dissipate a positive movement for political change.

It must be acknowledged, however, that this tacit realization – which rejects a liberal solution – is only quietly present in the novel. It may be quite legitimate to draw conclusions about the author's own political development on this basis – especially when one bears in mind the more explicitly committed later novels – but in formal terms, the limitations of the novel's politics are determined by the choice of narrator. This choice also demands that a series of personal lessons be presented for the advancement of the recalcitrant Toby, and a lack of density in the novel's direct political and historical reference is the inevitable result of this. The Prohibition of Mixed Marriages Act is mentioned, by Anna (*WS*, 118), but reference to it is really confined to a consideration of her marriage to an Indian, and whether or not she allowed political commitment to determine her personal choice (*WS*, 167). Similarly, we have only oblique references to the activities of the Alliance Congress and the Defiance campaign through a reference to Steven's refusal to have anything to do with either (*WS*, 115). Robert Green has some justification when he claims that the

novel's preoccupation with personal events results in the concealment of important actual political events.[13] Even so, there
is something purposive in this personal focus which the formal
design of the novel dictates. Gordimer is able to suggest something of the *psychological* motivation of particular groups
through this focus. Anna Louw's family, for example, are
passionate Nationalists whose politics, in Anna's account, are
produced through a fusion of hatred and fear (*WS*, 172–3).
Similarly, we gain some psychological insight into the type
represented by the guests at the High House, identified as an
English group preoccupied with their own opposition to the
Afrikaner Nationalists, regardless of the question of black
oppression (*WS*, 198–9). Perhaps the most significant detail of
this more localized kind concerns the network of black contacts
within which Steven operates. Toby observes how Steven
always seems to know 'a fellow somewhere', and that this
comprises a network which facilitates a *practical* neutralization
of adverse legislation: 'the more restrictions grew up around
him and his kind – and there seemed to be fresh ones every
month – the quicker he found a way round them.' (*WS*, 194)
This avoidance of the legislation is also an avoidance of the
political issue, since circumvention is preferred to open opposition. But there is clearly something positive in the fact that
Steven offers a site of individual resistance that links with a
broader movement – in this case the network to which he
belongs – which can generate practical resistance.

The principle of dialogism which surfaces explicitly in the
narrative on occasion, relates also to aspects of the novel's
design. As mentioned earlier, particular scenes are structured
to imply a lesson learned for Toby, even though there is often
confusion in the way he articulates this lesson. In a sense this
identifies the organizing influence of the author above and
beyond the character she has created, but this is not really
precise enough because the learning implied in such scenes is
not fully separated from Toby's consciousness: there is an
element of accretion, of a burgeoning political memory, which
gathers importance through successive scenes. This implies an
understanding on Toby's part of how the progression of his

narrative – in terms of key learning scenes – demonstrates the
advancement he cannot always describe, and this, again, indicates the co-existence of different perspectives which locate
Toby's vacillation.

One of these learning scenes in particular reveals how this
uncertain process of implication operates. In the eighth
chapter of the novel Toby and Cecil come across a deserted
house while out riding. This episode, which occurs immediately after Toby's lucid analysis of Cecil (*WS*, 142), discussed
above, reveals the crucial dual perspective. Toby and Cecil
determine to break into the deserted house, and soon discover
that they are not the first to have done so. Cecil makes the
immediate assumption that out-of-work 'natives' are sleeping
there. This is not an unreasonable assumption given the lot of
the black African, but Cecil's assumption betrays a simple
association between blacks and the dirt and disorder of the
deserted house: she displays 'the confidence of an order where
dirt and chaos went with one side, and beauty and power went
with the other' (*WS*, 145). The actual material implications of
the scene escape her (racist) mind-cast which always and
immediately reduces blacks to a sub-human other, incapable of
inhabiting responsibly her domestic order, and the 'power'
that creates it. It is clear that a different interpretation of this
scene is required, and that Toby does not align himself with
Cecil's. The scene is, actually, the culmination of a series of
descriptions of interior (especially domestic) space, and these
need to be considered together in order to see how Toby's
accreted learning on this subject progresses.

Anna Louw's house is compared to 'a nest or a cave, a
hidden, personal place that exists unperturbed under the
unnoticing eye of the passing world' (*WS*, 111–12). As with
other characters, Anna's domestic space is described in a way
which reveals it to be an index of her public life: Anna's
socialist activities are repressed in this political environment,
yet preserved to continue 'unnoticed', and the nest/cave image
conveys this well. Sam's house, as Toby perceives with Steven's
help, is a kind of showcase of bourgeois black life (the realization of which is a political goal he seems to move away from

as the novel ends) (*WS*, 125). Toby describes the decor of Cecil's living-room as indicating 'a room of many attempts, all of which had petered out into each other' (*WS*, 132), and this indecisiveness is evidently an externalization of her inner vacuousness and, by extension, of the same quality that the High House group share in their superficial existence, oblivious to substantive political issues. Steven, perhaps most significantly of all, has no place to live (*WS*, 126), this fact of domestic dispossession being a key feature of the rootless Steven's political dispossession.

Toby's experiences, then, present a continuing connection between domestic scenes and the external political situation which orders them, and, with this background, the episode at the deserted house, apparently inhabited by black squatters, acquires a crucial significance. The episode epitomizes the fact of material inequality and, at a symbolic level, it also represents the fear of a black uprising in Cecil's mind: the revolutionary desecration of the 'white man's house' in a broader sense. In interview Gordimer has sometimes used this image to describe the process of political maturity for white South Africans, who must first leave their mother's house, and later the house of the white race.[14] The characters' responses to this space – the house of the white race – are clearly crucial: Cecil's indicates the confusion of political naivety as well as epitomizing the irrationality of a partisan political order under threat; Toby's response is less clear-cut, for, excited by her fear, he attempts to seduce Cecil. At first she is merely passive, but is soon recalled to herself and the impropriety of the situation and stops him (*WS*, 145). Again Gordimer asks us to interpret a sexual response in terms of broader political questions, denoted by spatial control. Cecil's fear which excites him is decribed as a fear of herself (*WS*, 145), yet, in the light of the scene's symbolic connotation, this fear can also be taken to represent a wider fear of racial threat. Toby's desire, then, seems to be ignited by this representative fear and by the scene of desecration which has inspired it, and, accordingly, one could interpret his action as a semi-conscious attempt to provoke a corresponding desire in Cecil and to draw her into a more enlightened plane of political response. Yet there is also something evidently repressive about his unsolicited advance, and this makes his actions very problematic. This manifestation of desire in the face of fear might be said to replicate the oppression of the political order which Toby is slowly learning to reject; it might also be said to imitate the threat which Cecil fears from the black community. The ambiguity of Toby's desire focuses the various political impulses, fears and confusions which the scene has thrown into relief. Again there is a discrepancy between the learning which this scene implies for Toby and the confusion which his responses denote: the formal ambiguity persists.

OCCASION FOR LOVING

Gordimer's third novel, *Occasion for Loving*, explores a disillusionment with liberal strategies of opposing apartheid, and for achieving black liberation. The novel also conveys a burgeoning sense of the positive potential of black African roots in South Africa, and this amounts to a preliminary sketch of how a black political mobilization – based on a shared history – might be brought about. This is a provisional idea, surrounded by doubts and ambiguities, but it represents a new and important vision in Gordimer's work.

The novel focuses on a cross-racial affair between the black artist Gideon Shibalo and the young white woman, Ann Davis, who has come to South Africa with her husband, Boaz, who is researching the musical heritage of the black African. This love triangle has many broader political ramifications; the same is true of the relationship of Jessie and Tom Stilwell, the couple with whom the Davises are staying; Jessie's personal quest to make sense of her past, her family life, and her political stance has a partial parallel in Tom's writing of the history of South Africa. Jessie's quest is directly influenced (and enhanced) by her involvement with Gideon and Ann, and the difficulties the lovers encounter.

The plot creates a complex intertwining of private and public realms, in a way that does not allow a clear 'message' to emerge, and this is an aspect of the book's richness as much as it is an indication of an equivocal political stance; the problematization constitutes a serious and detailed debate of difficult issues.

Occasion for Loving reflects its historical limitations in the political analysis and prescription it is able to offer, yet it also represents a new resolve and understanding in the consciousness of the white opposition. Dramatic events in the history of modern South Africa occurred during the writing of the novel, most importantly the Sharpeville massacre of 1960, which made quite clear the futility of peaceful resistance to the apartheid regime. The Sharpeville demonstration was against pass laws which effectively restricted Africans to work in the Sharpeville area on sub-poverty-line wages. This protest – against these vicious spatio-economic controls – ended when the police opened fire on an unarmed crowd assembled outside the police station. Most accounts of the shooting record sixty-seven Africans killed and one hundred and eighty-six injured.[15] Most of these were shot in the back as they fled. This act of sanctioned state violence, together with the banning of black opposition movements, marks a transition to a climate in which opposition can only be expressed through acts of violence. Gordimer had moved in circles of intellectual opposition in the 1950s, especially the circle surrounding the Johannesburg magazine *Drum*; she had been involved, that is, in the activities of the 1950s which generated a hopeful climate of multi-racial co-operation.[16] In the new climate, however, the notion of multi-racial opposition appears naive: racially motivated state violence draws a stark line which necessitates the pursuit of black freedom by blacks for blacks. The failure of cross-racial personal contacts in *Occasion for Loving* reflects a consciousness of this necessity, and so, paradoxically, this is a 'failure' which can be given a positive cast: the personal co-operation of whites and blacks is, at this time, an irrelevance, and the novel's suggestion that political progress requires an acceptance of separation represents a progressive diagnosis of the historical situation.

This ambivalence – a 'failure' which reveals a positive per-

spective – is symptomatic of a novel which is obliged to face up
to a number of historical contradictions, and which, in doing
so, produces a valuable series of complex, and often ambiguous, analyses.

The pursuit of personal history is examined most extensively
through Jessie's quest to make sense of her past, and to establish
her present connections with it, a requirement that is explicitly
stated early in the novel (*OL*, 23). It is interesting that Gordimer is now pursuing a new kind of 'connection' which is
explicitly different from the Forsterian philosophy of personal
contact – 'only connect' – which the earlier novels allude to
parodically. An indication of this perspective is given in one of
several recollections made by Jessie of crucially formative
childhood episodes; as she recollects a sterile Christmas spent in
a resort with her mother and stepfather (as she then thought
him to be), Jessie remembers the sight of a woman, in their
hotel lounge, sewing without any thread, her needle 'flash[ing]
in and out ... empty, connecting nothing with nothing' (*OL*,
44). This image, through its allusion to Eliot's *The Waste Land*,
conveys a far starker analysis of the vacuousness of bourgeois
existence than do the earlier references to Forster, for the need
for 'connection' is, by suggestion, endemic in this kind of white
liberal existence. The 'connection' that Jessie must make
involves more than a reaching out across racial and cultural
boundaries; what is required is a full acceptance of her personal history and, consequently, of her own, unavoidable complicity in white political dominance. The Christmas motif is
used again, a few pages later, to reinforce this notion of complicity: as Tom and Jessie discuss childhood Christmases with
their guest Boaz, Jessie asks him what he was given when he
was fifteen, forgetting, as Tom brashly admits to having done a
moment later, that Boaz is a Jew. It is a casual conversation,
and one in which Jessie is trying to turn the subject, so it is not
given much prominence; but the assumption of a uniform
cultural experience is all the more sinister for its casualness,
and it suggests an element of complicity in the broader political
situation, which, as the novel shows, is in one sense the imposition of one culture on another (*OL*, 47).

Ostensibly, Tom Stilwell is a positive political force; he is an enlightened academic, writing a history of Africa from (as Jessie calls it) the black point of view, or, as he calls it, correcting Jessie, 'the historical point of view' (*OL*, 15). This avowed intent expresses the belief that a disinterested perspective can be achieved, that an objective rendering of history to record the black experience in Africa is possible. The doubts about white complicity, however, also cast doubt on this notion of objectivity, and the notion of academic purity and freedom that underpins it. Later we learn that Tom is involved in a campaign against the Extension of University Education Bill (Gordimer doesn't give the full name (*OL*, 63)). The Bill, designed to close the universities to non-whites, provokes an uncharacteristically violent outburst from Tom, especially where its implications for academic freedom are concerned. (This legislation, when it became an Act in 1959, prevented the established universities from enrolling black students, unless special permission from a cabinet minister was granted.[17]) It is the challenge to academic freedom which this represents that particularly angers Tom, especially as he feels it will be impossible to motivate public opinion in support of this unfamiliar concept:

'Only let there be some noise and broken heads so that people begin to see that academic freedom is something to fight over in the street! People feel it's a phrase that doesn't concern most of them, like "higher income tax bracket". Let 'em understand it's on a level with their right to their weekly pay-packet, the defence of their wife's good name and blood-heating things like that.' (*OL*, 64)

There is a sense in which Tom's preoccupation with 'academic freedom' is treated ambivalently, and this raises further questions about the purity of his historical work. Tom calls, albeit ironically, for a revolutionary uprising in defence of academe, and the way in which he envisages the populace compromises him still further: the 'people' he imagines are all, evidently, men, heterosexual and married, and with a shared notion of proprietorship where their wives are concerned. Of course, this is an *ironic* condemnation of a uniform populace – prompted by Tom's disgust – but his assumption that there is nobody beyond this stereotype to appeal to is indicative of a position of internalized defeat.

Since personal histories and political attitudes are representative of public history and politics, the problematic details of localized moments like this are crucial for any political conclusions the novel can reveal. This is particularly relevant in considering the cross-racial relationship between Gideon and Ann which forms the core of the novel. Here, for the first time, Gordimer focuses in detail on a theme which has dominated much South African fiction.[18] It is clear that Gordimer treats sexual relations between white and black without any residual notion of sin, or broken moral codes; but, nevertheless, there is a preoccupation with the affair, and the attitudes of all the major characters to it, attitudes which do reveal important contradictions and confusions.

Through Jessie's quest to make sense of her past the novel attempts to exorcise the effects of the repression of cross-racial relationships. Judie Newman has written excellently on this aspect, showing how Jessie's initial childhood fears of being assailed in the dark (*OL*, 69) – which are suggestive of an Oedipal fear of/attraction to her father – are shown to be repressed fears of the possibility of attraction to black men; Jessie is able to articulate this herself towards the end of the novel and the exorcism – which rejects the simplistic Freudian suggestion and unpacks the taboo of social conditioning – is then complete (*OL*, 253).[19] This is indicative of how repression is treated in the novel as a whole: Gordimer is not interested in irrelevant and nebulous questions of 'sin' and 'morality', but rather in how this repression has been socially constructed and inscribed.

The construction of individuals has political ramifications which can be discerned in how problems and confusions are manifested *psychologically*. This means that, for example, the affair between Ann and Gideon – which is destroyed by external forces – is also destroyed by forces which have already been *internalized* (especially by Gideon), and these are what Clingman calls, in a resonant phrase, the 'prestructuring effects' of apartheid.[20] Just as Jessie has been 'prestructured' to repress her attraction to blacks, so is Gideon's response to white women determined by the social context, though this is something he is not able to unpack in the course of the book as Jessie is. The representativeness of Gideon and Ann's relationship – and its inherent ambiguity – is made explicit in a passage in chapter seven, where Ann is described as:

that new being – beginning to appear, here and there – for whom the black man in a white city waited. In her, the kicks and the snubs and the vengefulness and the hate met, complemented and merged with each other, two terrible halves of the vicious circle become whole, and healed. She was white, top-class beauty, young; young and beautiful enough for the richest and most privileged white man ... The laws had not changed, the pass was still in your pocket; this simple miracle happened in spite of these things and far beyond them, in a realm where their repeal would have been powerless to release you anyway. It was not worth much – yet it was beyond price. (*OL*, 92)

This is offered as the typical black man's response to a woman like Ann, and there is a significant ambivalence in this response. The cross-racial contact is presented as a way of healing the rift, of by-passing the effects of brutal repression, but this healing of the 'vicious circle' does not eschew politics, because the attraction embraces the idea of social standing: it provides a way of getting what the 'most privileged white man' can get. This may be an anarchic challenge to the racial philosophy which has produced the kind of repression we see in Jessie; but the challenge is presented in the same proprietorial terms: the white man and the black man vying for the right to sexual possession of the 'white, top-class beauty'. In this sense these are indeed two halves of the same vicious circle. The conclusion of the passage given above conceals this common ground by suggesting that, in the black consciousness, the 'miracle' of sexual contact with a beautiful white woman occurs in a realm – an internalized realm – where the facts of repression can be kept at bay. The rest of the passage, however, indicates that the sexual contact is also a political statement, and that this is a statement with negative as well as positive connotations.

The theme of problematic sexual politics is articulated especially through the responses and attitudes of Gideon. It may be possible to view the estrangement of Gideon and his wife as suggestive of a break-up of the bourgeois restrictions of the family unit, restrictions which Jessie fears in her own domestic situation throughout the book; but there is also a child from Gideon's marriage which is supported haphazardly: at one point we learn that Gideon's brother-in-law has taken up this responsibility, unasked, as he owes Gideon money for a car (*OL*, 173). Here the carelessness about the past relationship becomes problematic: the commodification of the needs of the child, reduced to a debit/credit in an unwritten account, suggests a social irresponsibility, though the sense of a collective responsibility of an impoverished community may counter this. The question of female oppression within the black community is a larger problem, however, and is also suggested in Gideon's relationship with Ida: in chapter nine we discover that Ida, a nurse, has been living with Gideon in a casual way for a year, that she knows his commitment to her is insufficient to make them a couple, but that she does chores, such as his washing, for him (*OL*, 130). Again, the potential challenge to the restrictions of the couple-centred social structure is tempered by an imbalance of commitment, which results in an oppression. At the end of the novel, when Gideon's affair with Ann is over, Jessie sees the drunken, maudlin Gideon at a party with a nurse, presumably Ida, though she has now become an anonymous background feature of the novel, just as she is to Gideon (*OL*, 287). The invisibility of the oppressed Ida complicates our view of Gideon's suffering and reinforces the notion of a hierarchy of oppression.

An immediate point of crossover from personal to public history – again presented ambivalently – lies in the cultural and artistic interests and activities of individual characters. The work of Boaz on the African musical heritage is crucial here. An important conversation occurs in chapter eleven between Gideon and Boaz, in which it emerges that Gideon has no contact with the African musical heritage that Boaz is working to preserve. Gideon poses the seminal question to Boaz of whether his studies in music are preserving a 'fossil' or something alive, and Boaz considers he is doing both, because although the instruments may disappear, the need to make music will not (*OL*, 151). The idea of this duality precipitates a vital debate about history and culture in which Boaz considers a possible point of contact between African and Western musical traditions, a parallel which implies a cultural future, rooted in an African past, that represents a fusion of cultures rather than the imposition of one on another: this is the kind of hybridization that Gordimer has called for in South African literature. Gideon is cynical about this idea of fusion, arguing that the white man has eradicated the African past – that an imposition has already occurred (*OL*, 151). The debate is inconclusive, but the fact that there is an African past to preserve has a positive significance, in conjunction with other factors. Even at the scene of the mine-dancing – in which features of an African tribal past are paraded as cultural oddities for a white audience – even in this scene there are glimpses of a positive potential inherent in African tradition. Jessie is horrified at the sight of the dancing: she senses the prostitution of the event, which reduces the dance to a trampling of the past (*OL*, 37). These feelings, however, are determined primarily by the nature of the audience and its responses, rather than solely by the inherent properties of the dance, which are shown to reveal something more positive in the movements of the dancers: 'They pranced, leapt, grovelled and shook, taking on their own personal characteristics – tall, small; smooth, boy's face or lumpy, coarse man's; comic, ferocious or inspired – and then adding themselves to, losing themselves in the group again.' (*OL*, 36–7) Despite the prancing and grovelling, the dance also contains within it the positive potential of a genuine community. It is a deeply buried potential, but it is there in the representation of the patterns of a community which is able to accommodate (without repressing) a whole range of human moods and manifestations, which have room for expression even while they are contained by the general patterns of the dance.

The most important aspect of this connection between personal and public histories is Gideon's role as a painter whose creative energies are reinvigorated by his relationship with Ann. Here the sexual relationship feeds directly into a creative energy which has a broader communal significance, but the ambiguity surrounding the relationship between Gideon and Ann applies also to the creative energy she inspires in him. When Jessie is looking through Gideon's paintings of Ann, she discovers several portraits (apparently all nudes, though this isn't clear) including some in which Ann is black (*OL*, 117–18). The suggestion is that the sexual relationship, which inspires an artistic reverence of the subject, is also a way of establishing an inter-racial *rapprochement* through art: Ann can be envisaged as black as well as white to the recording artist's eye. But there is an ambivalence in Gideon's inspiration, indicated by his reflections when walking through Alexandra township, where the squalor he observes makes him think, with disgust, of his estranged wife. This disgust is articulated as a response to her physical appearance, which he sees represented in the women around him, and which stands in marked contrast to his preoccupation with Ann's physicalness. His reflection begins with a consideration of the 'type' of which his wife is representative:

She could have been one of the women passing him in the street. He was approaching the row of Indian shops at the top of the township, now, and there were some pretty ones about . . . He saw the thickness of their calves and ankles, the selfconsciousness of their plastic smartness. He had in his mind, mixed with the shapes and colours, the coming together of objects and movement that was always working towards the moment when he began to paint – the thin wrists and ankles, the careless style of Ann. Little breasts of a woman who bore no children. Flat belly with the point of each hip-bone holding a skirt taut. Soft thin hands smelling of cigarette smoke . . . A woman without woman's work or woman's ambitions. (*OL*, 175)

This is an important passage because it articulates Gideon's new-found artistic inspiration, which is based on a sexual preference. The preference recalls the earlier summary of the black man's attraction to white women, in that the element of social status helps to determine the response: here it is the privilege of Ann, which removes her from toil and a situation associated with child-bearing, and which enables her to be less self-conscious about her looks, it is this privilege which establishes her attraction. There is also the appeal of the exotic, based on an appreciation of pure racial difference, the thin wrists and ankles (which Gideon has designated as being peculiar to white women (*OL*, 149)); this appeal is something usually associated with the appropriating white male imperialist. The evident ambivalence of Gideon's responses raises important queries about the validity of his artistic expression, which seems to be bound up with a sexuality that is in some ways complicit with the oppressive social order.

A similar ambivalence is evident in Ann's response to a portrait Gideon paints of her in chapter twelve. She is drawn to look regularly at the picture in which she finds 'no surface likeness to provide reassurance' though 'she knew it was the likeness of what he found her to be'. This response indicates the absence of a shared understanding of what or who Ann is, and this communicative failure is reiterated immediately by a description of Ann's comparable failure to perceive Gideon in terms of his social context: Ann has no sense of Gideon in relation to his family, and merely has 'an awareness of him as a single creature unrelated to any other' (*OL*, 160). This image of social rootlessness has a clear resonance, placed as it is immediately after the sense of 'rootlessness' which Ann perceives when looking at her portrait: Gideon's art does not seem, here, to offer the kind of communal possibilities that it does at other times, or which seem to be suggested as potentially present in other aspects of African culture.

The novel, then, uncovers positive potential in both art and personal relationships for the pursuit of freedom in South Africa, and yet reveals pitfalls in both areas, especially where individual activity has been predetermined or distorted to some extent by socializing forces which have been internalized. This suggests a bleak diagnosis of the situation in which a pervasive force of institutionalized repression has tainted even the most potentially efficacious agents. Looked at in these terms the novel appears to be transitional, rejecting the liberal solution of multi-racialism, yet unable to articulate a coherent alternative programme for change.[21] There is, however, another important strand in the book which does suggest the possibility of future progression: Gordimer's preoccupation with landscape becomes, in *Occasion for Loving*, directly linked to a sense of an African history. Cooke has shown how the archaeological discovery, in the early 1960s, of ancient African Kraals marked a significant change in Gordimer's thinking: these ancient ruined cities on the Witwatesrand disproved the colonial assumption that whites had been the first settlers there, and had a rightful claim to the gold it contained.[22] This proof of an African past – which provided an *historical* challenge to the white colonial arrogation of wealth and power – gives a new edge to Gordimer's considerations of environment and social space. It also suggests the source of a black African *living* history which challenges the present. The significance of the musical studies of Boaz is brought into sharper focus by this strand: the duality of his studies – to preserve a past heritage and also to forge links with something living (*OL*, 151) – is a correlative to this sense of space, in which the history of a landscape offers a present political challenge.

The ambivalence of the novel towards the sources of political advancement extends also, however, to the issue of African history. This is indicated in brief references to the Zulu king Shaka (or Chaka) in part three of the novel, in the scene at the beach house. A printed humorous notice in the beach-house lavatory, listing items not to be flushed away, is signed 'Big Chief Shaka' (*OL*, 187). The irony of invoking the great Zulu king is double-edged: it is an implicit apologia for the dogma of the notice, but the self-rebuke for pomposity is implicitly levelled at Shaka also. This is confirmed a couple of pages later when we are told that, from one point in the region, Jessie and the children can see far inland: 'as far as you could see, and further, it was Shaka's country; less than a hundred and forty years ago the black king had trained his prancing armies and spread his great herds of cattle here.' (*OL*, 189) This reference to the kingdom of Shaka, which he created and presided over from 1816–28, invites reflection on the historical precedents for the control and ownership of land by black Africans. The name of Shaka, as Leonard Thompson points out, 'has passed into African literature and the consciousness of modern Africans as a symbol of African heroism and power', following his immortalization in such works as Thomas Mofolo's novel *Chaka*.[23] Gordimer has elsewhere written of the importance of this novel in the development of an African literary consciousness,[24] but her reference here has a critical irony which squares with historical accounts of Shaka. The language used of this king who 'had trained his *prancing* armies and *spread* his *great herds* of cattle here' (my emphases) tacitly acknowledges (and ridicules) the warlike and aggrandizing nature of Shaka's actual rule. The Mfecane wars of Shaka's reign wreaked havoc on southeastern Africa, destroying the basis of this farming society: thousands were killed and thousands more became refugees as communities were destroyed and society collapsed. The long-term consequences for the various African peoples were also disastrous: many Africans impoverished by war were forced to go to the Cape Colony and work for white colonists, while whites were presented with new opportunities for expansion into the eastern part of Southern Africa.[25] This seems to be the subtext of the narrator's ambivalence towards Shaka and his prancing armies: as evidence of African power, but also of a vainglory which facilitated the process of white colonization. This recalls and reinforces the presentation of the mine-dancing in which the participants are seen to 'prance' in a scene in which an ambivalence about African cultural potential emerges (*OL*, 36–7).

Other important scenes in the novel, and the tensions they uncover, are predicated on the struggle for space. It is significant, in this connection, that the squalor Gideon sees in Alexandra is associated in his mind with the wife he has abandoned: the distortion of personal relationships, and the perspective of an individual, can be directly related to the physical manifestations of social inequality. Perhaps the greatest tension which the novel generates occurs in those scenes in which Gideon and Ann are driving, aimlessly, in the African landscape, unsure of where to take their affair. In chapter seventeen Ann is disturbed, sleeping by the road, by a local white farmer. He leaves before Gideon comes into sight, but the fear of discovery provokes a series of nervous spasms in Ann when the man has gone. The fear of discovery is here linked to the political question of the control of space. The farmer has adopted with Ann 'that indiscriminate comradeship that white people feel when they meet in the open spaces of a country where they are outnumbered' (*OL*, 234), and here different tensions collide: Ann's shock of fear, at being almost discovered even in this open country where blacks predominate, suggests an inner realization that there is nowhere to hide, that there is no space beyond the control of racial legislation. The farmer's implicit fear, however, suggests that white control of this space is tenuous, that the logic of numbers creates an ever-present challenge to the monopoly of power and ownership. The tensions are linked, of course: the fear involved in the maintenance of this insecure power is an implicit violence offered to those – such as Ann – who would challenge its codes. Ann's spasms of fear may also suggest a consciousness of a potential imminent disruption to these codes, a fear of being swept helplessly along in a wave of revolutionary change.

The same tension between the tenuous white control of space, and the power of a repressed challenge is suggested over the issue of bathing rights at Isendhla. Jessie overhears a woman in the store discussing the residents' plans to protest against 'natives' using 'our beautiful beach', and to set up a segregated area for blacks. The fear, and the mobilization to assert ownership, have been inspired, apparently, by occasional glimpses of Gideon on the beach. The woman leaves a poster in the store calling a meeting to discuss the matter, and as she leaves she backs into Jessie, 'gasping a smiling apology, as she went. Jessie caught full on for a moment, like a head on a pike, the fine grey eyes, the cheerful bright skin, the full cheeks and unlined mouth of a tranquil, kind woman.' (*OL*, 258) The image is arresting: Jessie, for a moment, imagines the woman as the unwitting victim of violent revolution, a force implicitly called into being by an insistence on spatial control and repression.

As in the earlier two novels, space is a site for political struggle, but is also, now, a potential source of living history, of political coherence, a point most explicitly made in a view of the landscape, and its African inhabitants, seen by Jessie from her car towards the end of the book:

The women slapped at washing and men squatted talking and gesticulating in an endless and unimaginable conversation that, as she passed, even at intervals of several miles, from one kraal to another, linked up in her mind as one. In this continuity she had no part, in this hold that lay so lightly, not with the weight of cement and tarmac and steel, but sinew of the earth's sinew, authority of a legendary past, she had no share. Gideon had it; what an extra-ordinary quality it imparted to people like him, so that others were drawn to them as if by some magic ... a new kind of magic ... the dignity of the poor about to inherit their earth and the worldliness of those who had been the masters. (*OL*, 269)

This passage brings together several strands in the novel, and resolves some of the confusions. The history which Jessie reads in the landscape is a living history in that the conversations of the inhabitants merge to suggest a unified voice of the present. This is similar to the township 'shout' heard by Charles and Helen in *The Lying Days*; the difference here is that the (more articulate) unified voice is based on the authority of the past. Jessie's acceptance that this is a movement that she has no part in is crucial: it marks a full transition away from liberal policies of multi-racialism, and it also suggests that the failure of cross-racial personal relationships in the novel is actually a positve thing, a necessary break, which clears the ground for this mobilization to emerge with clarity. It is also significant that Gideon, surrounded at times by ambiguity in the novel, is presented, in the final analysis, as someone who does possess the quality which this living history can bestow: in Jessie's estimation, here, the potential of history can be tapped into, even by those whose attitudes and activities bear the scars and distortions of the 'prestructuring' of apartheid. The repressive ideology, it is implied, is not, finally, all-imprisoning, and the signs of collective hope can be discerned in particular individuals.

This conclusion might not seem to chime clearly with the

ending of the novel which emphasizes the gulf between Jessie
and Gideon, following his drunken racist rejection of her at a
party – 'White bitch – get away' – and his subsequent failure to
remember the rift, which ensures it remains: 'so long as Gideon
did not remember, Jessie could not forget.' (*OL*, 288) But this is
the phase of separation which has already been diagnosed as a
necessary aspect of political progress.

The first three novels, though partially restricted by the ideology of their age and by the models of Gordimer's literary
heritage, do betray a sophistication that is not usually
acknowledged and which belies their restriction at times. For
Abdul JanMohamed these first three novels constitute Gordimer's 'bourgeois phase', which is succeeded by the 'post-
bourgeois phase' of *The Late Bourgeois World*, *A Guest of Honour*
and *The Conservationist*, and something of this distinction is
evident in many accounts of Gordimer's work.[26] My readings
explicitly challenge this received view, emphasizing the formal
accomplishments of the early novels: *The Lying Days* bears a
dual relation to the *Bildungsroman* structure, which is both
employed and rejected. This formal ambivalence registers
appropriately the situation of Helen, and also the situation of
Gordimer: she is prepared, right at the beginning of her novelistic career, to question the formal properties of the European
literary models upon which her work still partly depends. This
dependence, rather than a limitation, is utilized positively in
The Lying Days as an integral reflection of Helen's position. *A
World of Strangers* is also a sophisticated novel of transition, in
which particular formal ambiguities – in both the dialogic
texture of the novel and its scenic design – are used to characterize a colonial consciousness. In *Occasion for Loving* the
formal ambiguities are used to expose ideological restriction,
and so coalesce into a prescription for the basis of a liberated
political consciousness.

CHAPTER 3

Developing narrative muscle: 'The Late Bourgeois World', 'A Guest of Honour' and 'The Conservationist'

Gordimer's next three longer works of fiction are all unique in their forms and scope, and demonstrate the range of the author's developing narrative skills. These works – *The Late Bourgeois World* (1966), *A Guest of Honour* (1970) and *The Conservationist* (1974) – embody a range of techniques, produced, in part, by Gordimer's desire to react against and build upon previous work. There is also, however, a unifying principle in this group: each of these works is governed by a single, dominant intertextual presence which inspires both the issues treated in each novel, and the manner in which they are treated. These are by no means the only fictions in which quotation from, and allusion to, other texts occurs: the distinctive feature is that each of these novels stands in a transtextual relationship to a single, dominant textual source, and this principle of transtextuality determines a unique period of creativity.

THE LATE BOURGEOIS WORLD

In a 1979 interview Gordimer observed that *The Late Bourgeois World* 'shows the breakdown of my belief in the liberal ideals'.[1] Such a breakdown, as the preceding chapter suggests, was under way in the first three novels; but here it surfaces emphatically in the disruptive form of this arresting novella. In another retrospective interview Gordimer indicates her conviction that this novel marks the beginning of her maturity as a writer of narrative fiction: she feels that her early novels betray narrative weaknesses – they 'fall into beautiful set pieces' – and only with *The Late Bourgeois World* did she begin 'to develop narrative muscle'.[2] The first three novels do contain something important and challenging in addition to (sometimes through) the set pieces, but Gordimer is right to draw this distinction based on narrative form: *The Late Bourgeois World* registers the fragmentation of the liberal ideology, and does so through a skilful disruption of form which is more overt than in her previous work.

The political context of the novella, as Gordimer has pointed out, is the social climate which generated a wave of young white saboteurs in the years 1963–4.[3] This explanation of the book indicates that Gordimer's concern was with the background to the activities of the African Resistance Movement (consisting predominantly of white students and young professionals), a group which played a part in the series of bombings of post offices and other strategic targets, together with the (larger) militant wings of both the ANC and the PAC. All three movements were broken by the government, and this phase of violent resistance was over by the end of 1964 – well before the publication of Gordimer's novella in 1966.[4] Consequently, this was an era of defeat for anti-apartheid movements, in which the first phase of militant struggle was nipped in the bud, and something of this mood of defeat is reproduced in the form of the novella. Yet its stucture, as Gordimer's own remarks imply, is one which registers primarily the mood that gave rise to the campaign of sabotage in the first place, a mood of alienation and doubt concerning the possibility of political progress: these uncertainties are represented in the experimental nature of the novella's form.

The title *The Late Bourgeois World*, as Judie Newman has pointed out, is taken from Ernst Fischer's *The Necessity of Art*, a work in Marxist aesthetics which 'forms a vital intertext to the novel';[5] or, perhaps more precisely, a vital *transtext*. Fischer's preoccupation with questions of form – with regard to both social structures, and the means of artistic expression – seems to have inspired Gordimer's formal project in this work which makes the same connection.

Fischer's book examines the relationship between art and

social reality, concentrating particularly on questions of form and content. Fischer's conviction about the function of art has an obvious relevance to Gordimer's writing: he felt that 'truthful' art, in a decaying society, must reflect that social decay, and yet must also indicate the means of social improvement. *The Late Bourgeois World* examines the possibilities for social change in South Africa, as do all of Gordimer's works to some degree; but this is her first book in which social decay is overtly reflected in the form, as a *sustained* fact of the composition. For Fischer, the way in which art is able to perform this dual function – of both reflecting a situation of decay and also helping to change it – parallels another duality: the paradoxical need to make 'individuality *social*', to establish a connection with something outside, yet essential to, the individual. This is what produces the aesthetic experience of art for Fischer, a combination of being absorbed in reality, and yet feeling the excitement of being able to control it, and these dualities are combined in Fischer's prescription for the permanent function of art towards the end of his book. A further requirement of 'socialist art' is to present a hopeful and broad, historical vision of the future, and this stands in contrast to the vision of the future Fischer associates with the artists and writers of 'the late bourgeois world', which is negative, even apocalyptic. This apocalyptic shadow, the possibility of nuclear devastation, must be offset by the socialist artist offering a different possibility, both rational and humane.[6]

Fischer's discussion of how these goals can be achieved centres on the dialectical relationship of form and content which, again, reveals parallels with important aspects of bourgeois-capitalist social organization. As a generalized frame of reference Fischer characterizes form as being conservative, as representing stasis, and content as revolutionary, embodying change. This formula produces a notion of literary aesthetics in the tradition of subsequent Marxist thinkers: Fischer's notion of the dialectical relationship between form and content anticipates the aesthetics of writers such as Althusser and Macherey, and the critical appropriation of their ideas. To be progressive, form must be mutable, and this applies to social organization as well as to artistic expression: an overemphasis on form can conceal (and buttress) a regressive content, as, for example, the content of a class domination can be hidden by the successful preservation of an outdated social form. For Fischer, the tendency to overlook content has affected the intelligentsia in the capitalist world, producing a 'formalism' in the arts, a phenomenon *complicit* with 'a social form no longer in keeping with the times'. Fischer consequently sees content – the social factor – as being decisive in the fashioning of artistic style. This means that form, driven by content, has a crucial significance from the point of view of Marxist aesthetics: the aesthetic quality is also a moral quality.[7]

The fashioning of a form appropriate to a particular content – a particular social reality – is clearly what Gordimer attempts in *The Late Bourgeois World*: this novella represents an experiment in genre designed to convey the problems of a particular situation. Indeed, there are many points of contact between *The Late Bourgeois World* and Fischer's *The Necessity of Art*, and there are also significant discrepancies which indicate both the idealism of Fischer's aesthetic, and the grim nature of the social reality – the content – which underpins Gordimer's short novel. The book is an exploration which works through and beyond Fischer's aesthetic in order to rationalize the function of art in the South African context.

The duality of the self which Fischer sees as an essential feature of the socializing of individuality is strived for in the novella (as in all of Gordimer's novels), but never realized. The narrative comprises the reflections of Elizabeth Van Den Sandt, estranged wife of the naive revolutionary Max, on the day she hears of his death. Her reflections touch on key personal-political matters: her relationship with her lawyer-boyfriend Graham; the implications of this for her son, Bobo; her attitude to Max's politics (he had turned state witness on his arrest), and the nature of her own emerging commitment. Relationships in the novella are partial, incomplete, especially the affair between Elizabeth and Graham which she considers to be 'not classified, labelled' (*LBW*, 55). Elizabeth is actually suspicious of Graham, especially of his attentions to her son, which she feels represent an attempt 'to move in on responsibility for the child as a means of creating some sort of surety for his relationship with me. It's not for nothing that he has a lawyer's mind.' (*LBW*, 9) This is partly a salutary wariness, a resistance to the self-contained bourgeois family unit that Graham implicitly offers, a resistance, in Fischer's phrase, of 'a social form no longer in keeping with the times'.[8] But the resistance is also a failure of contact, of social definition: this seems to be a time that requires a wariness which can only obstruct the inception of a visionary communal realm.

Despite the failure of contact in the novella, there is also a sense of the need to extend individual contact, and to find points of social connection. In a discussion about 'the age' Elizabeth experiences a significant 'double-take':

Graham said, 'How would you say things are with us?'

For a second I took it as going straight to all that we competently avoided, a question about him and me, the lie he had caught me out with on my hands – and I could feel this given away, in my face.

I did not know what to say.

But it was a quiet, impersonal demand, the tone of the judge exercising the prerogative of judicial ignorance, not the partisan one of the advocate cross-examining. There was what I can only describe as a power failure between us; the voices went on but the real performance had stopped in darkness.

I said, 'Well, I'd find it difficult to define – I mean, how would you describe – what could one say this is the age *of*? Not in terms of technical achievement, that's too easy, and it's not enough about us – about people – is it?' (*LBW*, 112–13)

The confusion between the possible meanings of Graham's question – ostensibly about the contemporary age, but also apparently about their personal relationship – implies that there really should be no distinction between these two realms, public and private. Elizabeth is momentarily silenced by a consciousness of the vacuum that exists in their relationship, and in its failure to find a point of social contact. She is also silenced by the impersonal discourse of Graham, his arch 'judicial ignorance' which represents the compartmentalizing of bourgeois life, depending on a quiet rhetorical deceit that masks what is actually felt or known. It is also a discourse which belongs to the maintenance of a bourgeois society of ownership, quite in opposition to the personal terms of contact that Elizabeth searches for when she begins her answer.

There is, then, a sense of the need for some kind of social definition of the self, but no success in realizing it, and the reason for this is clearly shown to be a discriminatory society which alters the implications of individual actions for blacks and whites. When Elizabeth reflects that friendship is a luxury which only whites can afford (*LBW*, 119), she articulates one effect of a repressive state that bars the way to the social definition of individual behaviour: since blacks are forced to adopt a more utilitarian attitude to friendship than whites there is no common basis from which to proceed; Fischer's prescription appears inadequate for this particular situation.

Overall one can say that the novella fulfils one half of Fischer's prescription that art should reflect decay at the same time as showing the world to be changeable: a clear picture of a society in decay emerges, but a sense of how this situation can be changed does not. There are general indications of the kind of change that is needed, but no clear articulation of them, and this problem is reflected in Gordimer's choice of literary form, and the use she makes of this form.

A particular feature of shorter narrative forms – novellas as well as short stories – is that ideas are expressed obliquely, and there is an ambiguity in *The Late Bourgeois World* that stems from this oblique expression. The ambiguity in a short narrative stems from the effects produced by the technical limitations of point of view, which can be governed, as is the case in Gordimer's novella, by a single consciousness. What we are presented with is a single, alienated consciousness, and this presents difficulties for the writer seeking to investigate ways out of this kind of alienation. This is not an impossible feat in a work of short fiction; indeed, the major modernist short story writers employ a dialogized narrative texture in order to circumvent the problem of a single, dominant voice, and Gordimer has been influenced by some of these writers.[9] A problem with Elizabeth's narrative is that it is inconsistent, although this is actually a key aspect of the characterization: her evolving attitude to Max, involving a progressive acknowledgement of the importance of the basis of his political stance, comprises the central movement of the internal drama; and a certain lack of narrative reliability is an integral aspect of the narrator's slow and ambiguous political awakening. The overall nature of the narrative reproduces a situation of political uncertainty in which the path of progressive action is difficult to determine.

A measure of the ambiguity is suggested in Elizabeth's vision of her domestic future. By ironic contrast with the purposive vision of the future which Fischer sees as an essential feature of socialist art, Elizabeth's narrative imagines, briefly, an extension of the bourgeois life she, and the novella are both resisting:

I began to think about how one day I would buy albums and begin to stick in the photographs of Bobo as a baby that are lying in an old hat-box on the top of the bathroom cupboard. Most of the others – him as a little boy – went along with our personal papers and cuttings in security raids on the old cottage, and I've never been able to get them back. Sticking Bobo's pictures into an album and recording the dates on and places where they were taken suddenly seemed enthusiastically possible, just as if the kind of life in which one does this sort of thing would fly into place around us with the act. (*LBW*, 124–5)

The stability of the bourgeois life is enticing and desirable, but not really possible: just as many of the photographs have been sacrificed in the interests of political commitment, so has Elizabeth lost the requisite political naivety to exist in this way, even though the enticements of such an existence remain. The full ambiguity of Elizabeth's situation is given in a passage recollecting her family origins, and her initial attraction to Max:

The summer I was seventeen, the summer I met Max, I was helping out, for Christmas, in my father's shop. The fancy goods counter . . . Black men lingered a long time over the choice of a watch that, paid for out of notes folded small for saving, would be back within a week, I knew, because those watches didn't work properly . . . The shoddy was my sickening secret. And then I found that Max knew all about it . . . this quality of life was apparently what our fathers and grandfathers had fought two wars abroad and killed black men in 'native' wars of conquest here at home, to secure for us. Truth and beauty –

good God, that's what I thought he would find, that's what I
expected of Max. (*LBW*, 102–3)

This passage shows Elizabeth's understanding of her own complicity in the history of colonial racial repression, and her own
personal involvement in the economic exploitation of blacks,
while working in her father's store. This youthful political
awakening is, quite obviously, associated with a sexual
awakening; and the appeal of Max, specifically, is based on a
need for an aesthetic answer to the shabbiness. Such a solution
would not be unlike the kind of aesthetic solution Fischer
requires, but this 'solution' is here ironically rejected. The
juxtaposition of ideas reinforces the condemnatory tone: the
'shoddy' material facts of economic exploitation render aesthetic solutions irrelevant.

A seminal part of Fischer's condemnation of the late bourgeois world is his rejection of technological advancement, principally as represented by a nuclear age of pessimistic visions of
apocalypse. Another image of this age in which technology is
the enemy of art is that of space travel: the ability to fly to the
moon may render 'moonstruck poets' superfluous.[10] In the
novel's closing pages, Elizabeth flirts with the idea of a tran-
scendence symbolized by the astronauts who have been
walking in space on the day Max has died, and this enticement
is akin to that of the photo-album. The space mission, an
extreme expression of capitalist wealth, stands in clear opposition to Max and the politics he represents, as indicated when
reports of Max's death are displaced in the late final edition of
the newspaper by reports of the astronauts (*LBW*, 152–3). The
question of the apocalyptic vision, and its implications for art,
is taken up in another key scene. This is the scene in which
Elizabeth and Graham observe a sunset (*LBW*, 109–11). Here
we are presented with a summary of the novella's engagement
with and enactment of Fischer's prescriptions:

The super-sunset was still framed there, a romanticised picture that
made the room look drab. He said, 'It's magnificent.'
   'I'm getting used to them.'
   He went on looking, so that I couldn't close the doors, and waited
for him to have had enough, like a patient attendant at a museum.

'I'd like a few cows and lovers floating above Fredagold Heights, though,' he said. He has a Chagall drawing in his bedroom; curious; the way some women have a Marie Laurençin print in theirs. Why not in the living-room? There is some private vision, version of life to which the public one doesn't correspond. Or into which the public is not allowed. And yet he had never been interested in Chagall until a rich client gave him the drawing. Then he hung it in the bedroom.

'Suppose it is fall-out,' I said.

'Well?' ...

'Then it's not beautiful, is it.'

'There's nothing moral about beauty.' ...

I hardly notice these sunsets any more, but his attention attracted mine as one's attention is attracted by someone's absorption in a piece of music one has heard too often and ceased to hear. I said, gazing because he was gazing, following the colour, 'If it is fall-out there's something horrible about it looking like that.' (*LBW*, 109–10)

Graham's interest in Chagall suggests to Elizabeth a separation between private and public lives, indicated by the placement of his Chagall drawing in the bedroom, away from the gaze of visitors. The credibility of such a separation, however, is undermined by the implied superficiality of Graham's appreci-ation of Chagall in whom he had no interest before the gift of the drawing, which he treats as decoration rather than work of art. If Elizabeth's consideration of Graham's aesthetic response implicitly criticizes the separation of private/public, it is still not clear how the connection which will make 'individuality *social*' is to be made, although she is working towards this. Her rejection of a purely personal aesthetic is indicated by her insistence on recognizing that fall-out may have contributed to the effect of the sunset, a recognition of the broader social implications of something presented for aesthetic appreciation. Paradoxically, the way forward, for Elizabeth, is to face the dangers and manifestations of the nuclear age, the apocalyptic view which Fischer requires art to get beyond in offering an alternative vision of the future. Elizabeth, it seems, like the novella itself, is at an interim stage, coming to terms with the apocalyptic vision, while trying to formulate a way beyond it.

The novella ends with Elizabeth apparently coming to a decision – without clearly articulating why – to use her dying grandmother's bank account to channel money for the PAC. This, evidently, would be a crucial subversion of a bourgeois form – the private bank account put to the service of revolutionary ends. At the end of the book, however, this is merely a possibility, and it would, in any case, represent only a minimal act of personal commitment. Elizabeth is presented as someone for whom the avenues and possibilities of public action are severely restricted, and the ending of the novella sees her coming to terms with, and taking stock of, this situation. The form of the work, itself, is also a 'taking stock' which consciously interrupts the sequence of Gordimer's first three 'set-piece' novels: the terse urgency of the form emulates the fragmented identity of its protagonist and encapsulates a historical situation in which repressive legislation has achieved a certain private/public separation; the only available formal strategy for the novella is to register the shock of the separation and to gesture towards a reconnection.

In an essay on the short story, published two years after *The Late Bourgeois World*, Gordimer examines the socio-historical significance of the short story form. The reading of a short story, as Gordimer points out, does not require the conditions of privacy associated with middle-class life (dedicated reading time, space and comfort) in the same way that a novel does, and so, she speculates, the survival of the short story may correspond to the break-up of bourgeois life. This intriguing speculation, though perhaps vulnerable in some ways, clearly has a relevance to *The Late Bourgeois World*, a shorter fiction in which a fragmented form is used to convey the 'late-bourgeois' existence of a South African white.[11] These formal effects of the work are inextricably related to its transtextual reference: the partial application of Fischer's prescriptions is the textual-aesthetic correlate of Elizabeth's interim stage, replicated in the disruptive form.

A GUEST OF HONOUR

Gordimer followed her short exploration of genre, *The Late Bourgeois World*, with an extensive and exhaustive attempt to produce a dense work, in some ways reminiscent of a classic realist novel, which evokes a sustained and detailed sense of political reality; this novel, *A Guest of Honour*, is her longest to date. As in all Gordimer's work, there is a working-through of questions of generic form in *A Guest of Honour*, but this formal project is quite different to that of *The Late Bourgeois World*: now the project is to create a dense political novel that will find a way of interrogating the requirements of Lukácsian critical realism. Gordimer meets her objectives by finding an appropriate point of intertextual reference, in the work of Frantz Fanon. There is much political debate and analysis in the book, and this analysis follows Fanon in defining the nature of the political struggle in the post-colonial African state in which the novel is set: the contradictions inherent in a newly independent state *not* pursuing the socialist implications of its drive for independence are criticized in what amounts to an extended critique of neo-colonialism.

A Guest of Honour begins with the decision of Colonel James Bray to leave the stability of his home in Wiltshire to return to a newly independent African state. Bray had been deported from this (imaginary) country ten years before – by the colonial regime – for supporting the growth and rise of the People's Independence Party which is now in government: while ostensibly a colonial administrator, he had worked in the Party alongside Adamson Mweta, now president, and Edward Shinza, a Trade Unionist. Bray returns to the country for the independence celebrations, and accepts a post as Educational Adviser, a post which takes him, initially, to the Gala district where he had previously resided. The plot revolves around the conflicting ideologies of Mweta and Shinza, and Bray's movement to align himself with the revolutionary aims of the banished Shinza, as he becomes aware of the neo-colonialist nature of Mweta's rule, which appears as a betrayal of the ideals of independence. Related to Bray's new political awakening is a sexual awakening: his wife, Olivia, remains in Wiltshire, despite their original arrangement that she would eventually join him, and she comes to represent the life of stability he has left behind. Bray's affair with Rebecca Edwards represents a personal vitality to parallel the public vitality of Bray's growing political maturity.

The governing PIP, working in concert with the Trade Unions, fails to prevent general industrial unrest, as the workers, inspired by Shinza, come to realize that their government is putting the interests of foreign investors before the interests of its people. Part four of the novel is taken up with the Party Congress in which the rival ideologies of Mweta and Shinza are clearly articulated. Bray now aligns himself with Shinza in the process of lobbying on his behalf. Back in Gala, Bray witnesses violent clashes between the workers and government forces, and finally resolves to fly out of the country in order to try and raise money for Shinza's cause. On the way to the capital, however, he is ambushed and killed by workers who take him for a key member of a riot squad whose violence they seek to avenge. When the novel ends Mweta has restored order with British military assistance, and Shinza is in exile.

The book that informs the politics of *A Guest of Honour*, and its dominant intertextual source, is Frantz Fanon's *The Wretched of the Earth*, the celebrated analysis of anti-colonial struggle, first published in 1961. Explicit reference to Fanon is made in a discussion between Bray and Shinza in which Shinza offers a quote which Bray later looks up (*GH*, 258; 292). The passage quoted introduces one of several ideas from Fanon which order the presentation of issues in *A Guest of Honour*, Fanon's point that the anti-colonial struggle should not be based on racial difference – on a simple rejection of the white colonizer – but on questions of economic exploitation, since it is a *class* struggle.[12] This marks an important phase in Gordimer's presentation of political issues: she is, at this stage, following Fanon's conviction that African unity can be achieved only through a 'people's' movement, led by the 'people', which will defy the interests of the bourgeoisie. For Fanon this class-consciousness is necessary to challenge 'the native bourgeoisie' which, under economic pressure from colonial interests, exercises its new class aggressiveness to control the power and wealth formerly accrued by foreigners, and appropriates existing exploitative structures under the guise of a new nationalism. Gordimer's novel presents a fictional consideration of Fanon's question of whether or not this bourgeois phase can be eschewed – of whether there is any place for ex-colonial 'guests of honour' in such contexts. (The ironic element of the title is particularly pointed in this connection.) The activities of Bray and Shinza concur with Fanon that this question should be answered 'in the field of revolutionary action', and this is the rationale of revolutionary violence which *A Guest of Honour* imports from *The Wretched of the Earth*: for Fanon 'absolute' violence is the only way of calling into question the colonial order, itself established on principles of force. This is the kind of violence which, in Fanon's conception, involves the people, and makes 'social truths' available to them, and without which the struggle for post-colonial independence amounts to no more than 'a fancy-dress parade and the blare of the trumpets'. Bray's detached observation of Mweta's theatrical independence ceremony has the glimmering of this kind of conviction behind it (*GH*, 21). Other important ideas common to both Fanon and the novel concern the nature of contradiction, as both an inevitable feature of bourgeois activity, and as an inevitable aspect of the complex pursuit of national independence. Perhaps the most crucial of Fanon's analyses of the anti-colonial struggle – for *A Guest of Honour* – is the prescribed rejection of individualism, the doctrine of subjectivity (imposed by the colonial bourgeoisie), which must be supplanted through a new commitment to local organization and communal interaction.[13]

Through the career of Bray the novel presents the rejection of individualism as the bedrock of the other ideas imported from Fanon, and this is also the basis of Bray's typicality: the novel traces the dissolution of his erstwhile bourgeois self, and makes this dissolution representative – Bray is an ex-colonial type – of the dissolution of the colonial-bourgeois subjectivity that can encourage neo-colonialism. In this respect the typicality of Bray creates an essential parallel between his personal development and the effective decolonization of a nation in Fanon's terms: the dissolution of individualism connects with a rejection of neo-colonial half-measures, with an understanding of the class basis of the anti-colonial struggle, and with the need to embrace violence in pursuing this struggle. Bray, then, is an agent of revolutionary consciousness. As an ex-colonial (who has always been sympathetic to African independence) Bray also typifies the necessary shift in colonial consciousness in the face of historical pressures for decolonization. In summary, these connected aspects of Fanon's analysis – the rejection of individualism, the critique of neo-colonialism, the recognition of the class basis of opposition, the acceptance of revolutionary violence, the acknowledgement of contradiction – these are the key issues in *A Guest of Honour*.

Gordimer's attempt to deal in detail with questions of political change results in a novel which contains many extensive political discussions, speeches and individual reflections, and Fanon is the pervasive transtextual presence in the treatment of these scenes. The novel's political engagement is complicated, however, by its fictional setting, which is a composite (non-existent) central African country, as Gordimer has explained.[14] Clingman has pointed out that the choice of setting – an imaginary African country having just achieved independence from colonial rule – represents a particular response to events in South Africa: the continuing repression of political opposition in the late 1960s renders the possibility of immediate, particularized change impossible.[15] Consequently, Gordimer creates an imaginary setting in which to investigate the implications of post-colonial African independence, and this creates a potential difficulty for a novel striving for a density of political reference: the avoidance of an actual setting relocates the political investigation at a more theoretical and generalized level. Even so, the issues which are investigated by the novel – the question of African independence, the problems of extrication from the logic of colonial economics and colonial constitution – these are the issues which Gordimer has clearly identified as being crucial for South Africa at some future point; in any case, the fictionality of the book's setting is partly determined by its relationship to Fanon: his prescriptions, even though they draw on specific national examples, are presented as relevant for the decolonization of the African continent as a whole, and Gordimer creates an appropriately non-specific context for the exploration of these prescriptions.

The validity of the political reference in *A Guest of Honour* depends upon the typicality of the characters, and the broader social and historical forces they can be seen to represent. This is especially important in the case of Bray, whose personal development supplies a focus and structural centre for the novel. This does not, in any sense, undermine the novel's broader historical focus since every element of Bray's personal development is emblematic of a required, broader political development. Moreover, there is a crucial element of *impersonality* in the progression of Bray (the loss of individualism in Fanon's terms), and this places the emphasis on his sense of social responsibility, rather than on his personal feelings. This impersonal progression also involves an acknowledgement of the necessity of *contradiction* as an inevitable feature of political life: Bray's eventual acceptance of contradiction at a personal as well as a public level is a clear indication that the novel eschews any simplistic notion of transition. The complex and paradoxical nature of political reality is reproduced at the level of individual action.

The connection between the personal and the political is sustained even in sections of theoretical discussion, and this is principally achieved through the network of tensions between Shinza, Mweta and Bray which provides a framework for considering the key issue of neo-colonialism. Mweta's position is that the colonial economic structure is a continuing hindrance (*GH*, 63), and, as a consequence of this legacy which cannot be surmounted, the country's prosperity depends upon encouraging and co-operating with foreign investors. For Shinza, this amounts to a collusion with foreign exploitation, as he indicates in his second speech to Congress, a Fanonian critique of neo-colonialism, the logic of which, as Shinza makes clear, is to exploit the people of a nation as both workers and consumers (*GH*, 361–2). The opposing positions of Mweta and Shinza are presented to form a stark choice between capitalism and genuine socialism, between a state which exploits its people, and one which is based on their interests. This is also a choice which Bray must make, as he decides where to place his allegiance, and much of the novel is concerned with how his mind is made up in the political choice which also faces the nation at large.

The importance of an impersonal individual response, in a political sense, is revealed in Bray's differing responses to Mweta and Shinza. He has a physical affinity with Mweta, and is conscious of a physical hostility between himself and Shinza, and these polarized responses are in inverse relation to his developing hostility to Mweta and affinity for Shinza in political terms: the physical and the ideological stand in opposition, and this makes a rejection of the physical – the personal response – an essential feature of the appropriate ideological choice. This gives a sharper focus to Gordimer's micropolitics: political responsibility remains a matter of individual choice, but the emphasis is now clearly on intellectual influence rather than personal sympathy. The themes of impersonality and contradiction become conjoined in Bray's eventual acceptance of contradiction as an inevitable fact of social life. This is summarized in the reflections Bray makes when fleeing the country, on his way to try and raise money for Shinza's revolution:

His mind was calm. It was not that he had no doubts about what he was doing, going to do; it seemed to him he had come to understand that one could never hope to be free of doubt, of contradictions within, that this was the state in which one lived – the state of life itself – and no action could be free of it. There was no finality, while one lived, and when one died it would always be, in a sense, an interruption. (*GH*, 464–5)

His experiences indicate that an individual lives in a state of impersonal contradiction, controlled by external forces which deny the possibility of the 'finality' of the contained self. This makes sense of the ambiguity surrounding some of Bray's actions in the quest for social definition, and indicates that a crucial aspect of his typicality is that the paradoxical effects of political reality can be read off in the contradictory fault-lines of his own behaviour and attitudes. The meaning of the 'impersonality' of Bray's final political commitment is suggested in his grim acceptance of the need for violence:

He was aware . . . of going against his own nature: something may be worth suffering for as a matter of individual conviction, but nothing is worth bringing about the suffering of others. If people kill in a cause that isn't mine, there's no blood on my shoes; therefore stand aside. But he had put aside instead this 'own nature.' It was either a tragic mistake or his salvation. He thought, I'll never know, although other people will tell me for the rest of my life. (*GH*, 465)

Here Bray rehearses how he has put aside the remnants of a liberal ideology, and its aversion to violence, which contradicts the logic of his new ideological commitment. The inverted commas around the second occurrence of 'own nature' indicate that this prior conviction was a construction to be cast off. Even in this state of apparent clarity, however, a paradox remains, as Bray realizes he will never know whether his choice represents a mistake or his salvation: the nature of social life remains contradictory, even (perhaps especially) on the plane of revolutionary commitment.[16]

Consistently, the contradictions within are matched by the contradictions without: the complex and paradoxical nature of individual action and motivation can be traced back to the social system which produces these individuals, and this is really the measure of the novel's political realism. Political debate, far from appearing as an extraneous factor, is an integral aspect of the novel's design which creates a dense impression of the interrelationship between public and private life. Bray's comments on the contradictory nature of the colonial system, for example, clearly parallel the paradox within himself, produced by this system, which the novel unravels:

'The apparent contradiction between my position as a colonial civil servant and this belief [in the People's Independence Party] wasn't really a contradiction at all, because to me it was the contradiction inherent in the colonial system – the contradiction that was the live thing in it, dialectically speaking, its transcendent element, that would split it open by opposing it, and let the future out – the future of colonialism *was* its own overthrow and the emergence of Africans into their own responsibility.' (*GH*, 246–7)

Turmoil and change represent an inevitable historical process for colonialism, produced by its own internal contradiction, its progressive feature, once identified. For Bray, the same process continues through the novel: the belief he articulates here – in the idea of independence – is eventually re-formed at another level, of revolutionary commitment, when the ideals of independence are seen to have failed.

Contradiction is also evident in other local details in the novel's fabric, including its symbolic elements. Bray's fig tree, which carries a great burden of symbolic significance in the novel, is a prime example of this. Frequently Bray sits beneath the tree writing, as when he is compiling his education report (*GH*, 201), or when he is writing to Mweta about the workers' dispute (*GH*, 278). On these occasions the tree is associated with inspiration, and seems to symbolize hope for the future. The inspirational motif is reinforced by Rebecca's observation that Bray beneath the tree looks 'like Buddha under the sacred banyan' (*GH*, 209). This association has an ironic resonance given the novel's ultimate rejection of philosophical, meditative approaches to political difficulties; and this ambivalence about the tree's purport is an integral part of its significance, as is clear on its first appearance where it inspires in Bray, who appropriates it as 'his tree', 'an irrational happiness, like faint danger' (*GH*, 95). The feeling is emblematic of a paradox which governs the action: that which is purposive and progressive is also dangerous, and this applies to both political and personal commitment. (It is clearly significant here that Bray and Rebecca frequently sit together beneath the tree.) This ambiguity persists right to the end in the episode where Hjalmar Wentz remains alone in Bray's house, after the flight of his daughter with the right-wing political refugee, Ras Asahe and his consequent nervous breakdown: Wentz wishes to stay in order to finish paving beneath the fig tree, the task he has set himself as a kind of subconscious therapy. Here it is not clear whether Wentz's behaviour symbolizes the blind activities of an anachronistic colonial power, or whether his doggedness represents a hope of rebuilding the future (*GH*, 459–60).

Another measure of the novel's engagement with contradiction is the treatment of sexuality, which, as is typical of Gordimer, affords an index of political maturity, but in an inconsistent manner. The ordering idea here is that sexual and political vitality go hand in hand: Bray's affair with Rebecca accompanies the progression of his political understanding, just as the vitality of Shinza's political ideology in opposition to Mweta is reflected in his marriage to a new young wife and the fathering of a baby. This implicitly involves the destruction of stable bourgeois domestic ties which repress vitality: Bray's affair with a younger woman involves a progressive sense of physical alienation from his wife, Olivia, and the secure retirement in England with which she is associated. When Mweta and Olivia are linked in Bray's mind the regressive political implications of the marriage are underscored (*GH*, 377).

The affair between Bray and Rebecca, however, is itself contradictory, and is not used in any straightforward way to 'illustrate' an intellectual growth. Indeed, the parallel between the personal and the political demands an evocation of paradox in the former, given the novel's consistent indication of paradox in the latter. When Bray and Rebecca make love for the first time Bray is thinking of Shinza, and this clearly emphasizes the equation of sexual and political vitality. Rebecca leaves, however, 'before there was the necessity for some sort of show of tenderness', and Bray realizes 'that he had made love to her without seeing her face' (*GH*, 143). These details can (and have) been interpreted as being both positive and negative: it is unclear whether the lack of tenderness and the anonymity indicate an impersonality which is progressive (by virtue of its distinction from the couple-centredness of bourgeois love), or whether the impersonality is in this case regressive, suggestive of the colonial appetite for conquering new territory.[17] In fact this ambiguity is important and persists throughout the relationship. In a later scene Rebecca stands passively while Bray, finding her passivity 'greatly exciting', caresses her (*GH*, 243). Here it seems that Bray's excitement is aroused by the commodification of the woman, another suggestion of colonial thinking which seems still to taint Bray's subconscious. But this, like the dubious arousal, is an interim stage as is made clear a couple of paragraphs later where we read of 'a growing gap between his feelings and his actions' which amounts to 'a new state of being' (*GH*, 244). This indicates a period of transition – to a new state – which involves a mismatch between feelings and actions in the interim. The ambiguity in Bray's sexual responses indicates a process of development which accompanies the gradual change in his political stance, the gradual progression away from conciliation to revolutionary commitment. This commitment is never explicitly articulated and, in the same way, the sexual relationship between Bray and Rebecca is never free of ambivalence.

The interweaving of sexuality with the presentation of political issues is an indication of Gordimer moving beyond the transtextual inspiration of Fanon to extend her own concerns. The same extension occurs over the issue of language. When Bray reflects on the state of life, and its contradictory nature, he considers death to be an 'interruption' to this state (*GH*, 465), and, when he is killed his final thought is 'I've been interrupted, then–' (*GH*, 469). The interruption has a metaphoric connotation, but relates also, in this specific scene, to Bray's inability to remember any word of Gala to speak to his assailants: his mind is blank of the language in the crisis. The ability to speak is the prerequisite of social involvement, which also means that language is an expression of power, a fact reinforced by the association made between language and repression. When Shinza informs Bray that a young worker in the fish-meal factory has been detained and tortured – whipped – he says 'they put their questions on his back' (*GH*, 124). Later Bray challenges Mweta with this account of imprisonment and torture, and goes on to discuss the terms under which the fishing communities are working, while 'Mweta listened with that flickering of the eyelids of a man to whom words are whips, blows, and weapons, taken on the body and given on the bodies of others' (*GH*, 169). This identification of language and repressive power is largely symbolic in this description of a head of state, but the association occurs elsewhere, and contributes to the novel's investigation of the complexity of individual actions.

We have already seen how the novel cultivates an ambi-

valence surrounding sexual activity which can be seen as both
regressive and progressive, and in one of these ambivalent sex
scenes the issue of language as power becomes the central focus.
One morning, when her husband is visiting her, Rebecca slips
over to Bray's house to resume their affair, temporarily interrupted by the presence of the husband. The scene culminates
in an act of fellatio in which Bray's climax is presented as
having symbolic significance: 'In an intensity that had lain
sealed in him all his life (dark underground lake whose eye he
had never found) barrier after barrier was passed, each farthest
shore of self was gained and left behind, words were reunited
with the sweet mucous membrane from which they had been
torn.' (*GH*, 279) Ostensibly, the sexual release appears to
represent a symbolic healing which is also an articulation of
identity for Bray, a discovery of personal power signified by the
'reuniting' of words with the sexual expression of the self. But if
the episode is read from Rebecca's point of view, a quite
different interpretation irresistibly presents itself. The basic
feminist notion of language as a phallocentric construct which
silences women can clearly be said to be symbolized by this
scene in which a literal phallus does the silencing. The 'reuniting' of words with the 'mucous membrane' of sexual expression
is now double edged: what is a linguistic gain for Bray appears
as the silencing of Rebecca, and this reinforces the ambivalence
of language introduced in the notion of Mweta as one who can
both receive and dispense the violence of power through words.
This ambivalence also surrounds the appropriation of Bray's
educational report after his death. On the one hand there is an
evident irony in the appropriation by the state, for its own
ends, of the words of someone who had begun to work for its
overthrow. At the same time, however, it is true that Bray's
voice lives on after his death, and that, consequently, his work
may have some purposive role to play.

Perhaps the most crucial 'contradiction' – or disruption of
form – is to be found in the overall structure. Elaine Fido
considers that, through an 'emphasis on the character and the
final tragedy of Bray, Gordimer is following a Western tradition of fiction. Furthermore, by examining the relationship of

masculinity to power and therefore to politics, Gordimer shares concerns with a growing number of feminist writers'. This suggests a connection between a Western fictional tradition which concentrates on personal history, and the novel's examination of how 'politics seem to grow naturally out of the sexual nature of men'.[18] The logic of Fido's reading is to implicate the European tradition of realism – with its assertion of the self – together with the colonizing tendency of masculine political structures. One impetus of the novel is, I think, to raise the possibility of such a connection, and this is what is implied in the negative connotations of Bray's sexual reawakening. Yet this reawakening, as we have seen, has a positive side also, and this is indirectly reinforced by a structural shift in the novel, which disrupts the focus on a personal history. There is an inevitable, but crucial shift in the novel's narrative focus following the death of Bray: the narrative, which has relied on his perspective up until this point, now shifts to the point of view of Rebecca.[19] Admittedly, only the short final part six of the novel remains, but the section is long enough to establish the new focalizer, and to consolidate the effect of the formal shock of the transition. Bray's tragedy now becomes Rebecca's tragedy: the novel ends in the daze of Rebecca's attempts to pick up the pieces of her life, while Bray's activities have become a part of the history of the new country's political process. Ironies surround the assimilation of Bray's efforts but, in formal terms, there is a disruption of the presentation of the personal history, and a concomitant presentation of the broader political significance of the life. This withdrawal is actually facilitated by the new personal focalization: Rebecca's state of shock demands an uncoloured presentation. Ultimately, all of the ambivalences and contradictions do contribute to a coherent overall design, because the texture of the novel replicates the progression of Bray towards an impersonal revolutionary political commitment, and a simultaneous acceptance of the complex and contradictory nature of political reality. The crucial narrative shift, following the death of Bray, might be said to be a novelistic enactment of a Fanon-inspired rejection of individualism; here, perhaps, as in *The*

Late Bourgeois World, Gordimer uses her transtextual principle to make an important formal point: the dissolution of Bray is emblematic of the final dissolution of the colonial world with which he was once affiliated, a world predicated on individualism for Fanon. Consequently, it might be seen as quite appropriate for Gordimer to disrupt the effect of Bray's individual dominance in the novel, and in doing so she acknowledges, perhaps, a 'colonial' impulse in a Western tradition of fiction, an impulse her work courts, then explicitly rejects.

THE CONSERVATIONIST

In *A Guest of Honour* Gordimer intertwines her investigation of the typicality of a main protagonist with ideas drawn from a dominant intertextual source, and this same combination appears in a different conjunction in Gordimer's sixth novel, *The Conservationist*, joint winner of the Booker prize in 1974. The narrative strategy of *The Conservationist* is complex, and involves an equivocal treatment of the prediction of political change, the nature of a benighted white consciousness and the idea of conservation itself. These issues are examined through a sophisticated use of transtextuality – involving allegory and prophecy – and the modernist narrative technique of stream of consciousness.

The transtextual element in *The Conservationist* creates a brooding subtext, through a series of references to Zulu mythology – which gradually undermines and dissolves the coherence of the principal narrative of the central protagonist Mehring, the white 'colonizer'. In this sense, the novel – through its style – is an enactment of political transition, a decolonization presented as an historical inevitability, and articulated in a 'decolonization' of the novel's form. With the emphasis on style and form there is little in the way of plot to recapitulate: the novel, like many modernist novels, is presented as an internal drama. The focus is on the dissolution of the colonizer, a process put into effect by the presence of a black body discovered on his farm and buried on the spot by the police. The body assumes a symbolic significance as

Mehring's 'other', and eventually resurfaces after a storm, displacing Mehring in a gesture of symbolic decolonization. In Gordimer's micropolitics this is her most extravagant extrapolation, in which a single body – a corpse – is 'disinterred' in a development which symbolizes the end of black African dispossession.

Mehring's attitude to his farm, and the validity of his position as farmer are undermined in various ways: he is emblematic of a class of wealthy city businessmen whose farming is an indulgence of 'a hankering to make contact with the land'. The dilettantism that this implies is crucially confirmed by the fact that farming losses are tax deductible, which makes success or failure for 'farmers' like Mehring unimportant (*C*, 20). Another important motive for Mehring in acquiring his farm is his desire to secure a place to take a woman (*C*, 38), and this exacerbates the dilettantism, and also indicates a parallel between geographical and sexual acquisition and power, a parallel which supplies a seminal feature of his character.

These impressions are complicated, however, because Mehring also exhibits some concern for and understanding of agricultural and environmental needs, if only from his own capitalist point of view. His conviction that only a productive farm can be beautiful is a mercenary view, but also one of efficient husbandry (*C*, 64). In accordance with this pragmatism, Mehring displays concern for the ecosystem of his farm after fire damage, articulating a concern for the interdependence of flora and fauna which, he feels, escapes his black farm workers who believe (so Mehring feels) that the threat of damage is passed once the land is saved from the fire (*C*, 90). This complicates any straightforward notion of the care of the land passing from whites to blacks. Mehring also lays plans for the future in planting oaks (*C*, 140) and European chestnuts (*C*, 210), and this is emblematic of his ambivalent position: the planting of *non-indigenous* varieties is both conservation and colonization. Mehring's 'conservation', then, is condemned in the novel, though an ambivalence does surround it: there is a sense in which his desire for the land is synonymous with his exploitative habits in sexual and economic spheres; yet there is a residual (though apolitical) pragmatism in his attitude to his farm, and this means that the idea of Mehring as conservationist, though ironic, is not simply or straightforwardly so.

The possibility of a black inheritance of the land and of the responsibility for its cultivation is undermined in the novel, at least at the realistic level: there is no black pastoral to supplant Mehring's story. Such a pastoral would depend upon the emergence of a dormant African cultural heritage, a heritage which has been lost, as many details suggest; for example, when we read that the rural workers no longer know how to make drums in the traditional manner, but use oil drums instead (*C*, 150). It is true that Jacobus manages the farm capably in Mehring's absence after the storm, but his capabilities merely imitate the individual control and dominance of the white Master: he drives the other black workers to make repairs about the farm, and administers medication to a cow with mastitis by imitating the vet (*C*, 224). There is no real suggestion, here, of an incipient black self-sufficiency, rather this is a working unit which pulls through to fulfil white requirements.

The subtext of Zulu mythology, however, implies the existence of a *submerged* heritage of African ownership and continuity. This subtext consists of ten quotes from the Reverend Henry Callaway's *The Religious System of the Amazulu*, the transcription of first-hand accounts of Zulu codes, customs and beliefs made by this British missionary in the nineteenth century.[20] Michael Thorpe has shown how the Zulu cult of the ancestor – recorded in Callaway's book – contributes to the important ancestor motif in *The Conservationist*[21]. The specific context of the quotes from Callaway can, perhaps – as Thorpe suggests – reinforce their significance in the novel. The first two quotations, for example, come from a section on the sacrificial slaughter of a bullock, and indicate appropriate prayers offered to the *Amatongo* (spirits of buried ancestors that can influence the living). The context of these prayers is not given in the novel, and this is not strictly necessary: an impression of a culture which has the surety of faith and known religious practices is clearly given. The effect of a later scene, however, might be enhanced by a knowledge of the context of the sacrifice and its appropriate practices: this could be said to provide a benchmark against which to measure the evidently debased ritual of the sacrifice of a goat by the black farm community in the novel (*C*, 162–4). The general effect of the subtext is usually evident without reverting to Callaway, though the source of the transtextual references amplifies and enhances the effect. The quotes which are particularly important are those that discuss the *Amatongo* (*C*, 155, 183) and the question of the ownership and occupation of Africa (*C*, 201, 233). The *Amatongo* are clearly linked to the eventual 'resurfacing' of the corpse buried on Mehring's farm (*C*, 225–6). One quote (*C*, 183) includes a comment from one of Callaway's informants whose exposure to Christianity has compromised or 'overlaid' his certitude in the mythology of his own culture, a negative development which the logic of the irruption of the subtext reverses. The final (tenth) quote from Callaway implies historical continuity for black Africans, and challenges the eighth quote (*C*, 201), in which white opportunism in Africa is incorporated in a myth of origins.[22] In interview Gordimer has indicated her intention that the resurfacing of the body should symbolize a recovery of ownership of the land: when the body 'comes back', there is an intended reference to 'Mayibuye', the ANC slogan which exhorts: 'come back Africa'.[23]

The novel stages a conflict between its subtext and the predominant narrative line of Mehring's consciousness. The eventual overthrow of the predominant narrative style is an implicit repudiation of Mehring and the world-view he represents. Mehring's exploitative nature is brought clearly into focus through his sexual predacity: in a recollected conversation with his mistress Mehring confesses to the 'special pleasure' he takes in buying a woman, a process she describes as 'sexual fascism' (*C*, 71, 96). A similar impulse of exploitation obtains in Mehring's frequent erotic imaginings about young women and girls, as when he discovers he desires the young daughter of a dinner hostess (*C*, 27–8), or when he meets the daughter of a male friend in a coffee bar and tries to commence a seduction (*C*, 178–82). In his final monologue, when

Mehring has been lured off the road by a female hitcher, he begins to fear that he is either going to be mugged, or that he is being entrapped into a cross-racial relationship (he is not entirely sure of the woman's ethnic origins). As he plans to run, leaving the woman to be raped or robbed, he considers it won't matter to her because 'coloured or poor-white, whichever she is, their brothers or fathers take their virginity good and early' (*C*, 250). Mehring's blanket condemnation ostensibly affirms both a class and a racial difference between himself and 'coloureds' and 'poor-whites', a difference which supposedly justifies his selfish impulse to self-preservation. This constructed difference actually locates an important feature of Mehring's *own* psyche, since he is a man whose desires turn frequently to young girls that could well be his own daughters.

The most important scene of this kind occurs on a business flight when he interferes with the young Portuguese girl in the seat next to him. In this scene landscape is elided in Mehring's mind with bodies as objects of sexual desire. Mehring's sexuality, his predation of young girls, and his exploitative attitude to the land are all associated in this section. It is significant, too, that the young girl does not actually speak throughout the process of Mehring's surreptitious probing of her beneath her blanket, yet the contact is described as a narrative, and the bodily responses are described, metaphorically, as speech and communication. This is Mehring's narrative – an exploration of the young body presented in his stream of consciousness – and the 'communication' is that which he desires. Through the night, we read, 'now and then, quite naturally, he encountered the soundless O of the little mouth that made no refusal' (*C*, 124). The girl's 'soundlessness' confirms that this is Mehring's narrative, that the power of speech belongs to him; the silent 'mouth' of her vagina is his focus. As he passes through immigration control, however, Mehring is seized with a fear of discovery, of the girl finding her voice and denouncing him; he fears the interruption of his narrative which the book as a whole rehearses. The episode on the plane is a kind of vacuum: it is 'happening nowhere' (*C*, 123), and this is an emblem of Mehring's own vacuous nature, socially and politically. In this 'nowhere' – this exploiter's utopia – he displays a capacity for exploitation which is an intensification of his usual behaviour. The form of the episode also reveals the nature of the psyche that is exposed: it is written as a self-contained piece, cut off from the rest of the novel. Interestingly, this self-contained episode was also published separately as a short story.[24]

The association in Mehring's mind of landscape and objects of sexual desire reveals the irony of his putative position as 'conservationist', and there are other instances which confirm this ironic undermining of such 'conservation'. Mehring's neighbour, old De Beer, is the exemplary Afrikaner landowner, a man whose size bespeaks prosperity and power: 'Old De Beer is a handsome man, his clothes filled drum-tight with his body ... The retaining wall of belly and bunch of balls part the thighs majestically. Oh to wear your manhood, fatherhood like that, eh, stud and authority.' (*C*, 47) This is Mehring's view which, though evidently ironized by a co-existing authorial accent, is apparently sincere: the overt presence of assertive male sexuality in the archetypal landowner is something of which he approves. The clearest association of male sexuality and a use of the land implying exploitation and violation occurs in Mehring's final monologue. Having picked up the woman who lures him off the road with the promise of a sexual encounter, Mehring reflects on a mine dump which they pass in the car:

There: has it not even a certain beauty? ... This is a firm dump, that the rain has not softened in substance and outline, but that the wonderfully clean sunny air, sluiced by rain, gives at once the clarity of a monument against the glass-blue sky and yet presents curiously as a (remembered) tactile temptation ... the imagined sensation of that lovely surface under his hand (the tiny snags of minute hairs when a forearm or backside cheek is brushed against lips) – that produces ... not what the doctor calls a 'cold erection' ... It's more like warmth coming back to a body numbed by cold or shock. Subliminally comforting. (*C*, 238–9)

The dump, of course, is the product of industrial exploitation of the land, something which has an obvious resonance for Mehring whose money has been made in pig-iron; it is something which (as Mehring acknowledges) would usually be seen as an unsightly industrial by-product, but it inspires in Mehring an erotic arousal which supplies an unequivocal link between exploitation of the land and male sexuality. This extract helps extend our understanding of Mehring's inappropriate responses, linking the mind-cast of the spatial and sexual exploiter with the psyche of the industrialist.

A potential difficulty with the representation of sexuality in *The Conservationist* is that it checks a predominant significance it has had in previous Gordimer novels, where, if political and sexual awakening do not go hand in hand, there is usually the possibility at least that they will: here an assertive and exploitative sexuality is straightforwardly condemned as an index of a politically benighted consciousness. As we have seen, there is an ambivalence in Gordimer's treatment of sexuality in her previous novels, but there is a drive towards an open sexuality emblematic of political freedom, a state which Irene Gorak has called 'libertine pastoral', in which liberated sex unites radical politics with private relationships, resulting in 'a vision of South Africa as a place of freely interpenetrating white and black bodies'; this libertine ideal is seriously undermined by Mehring in *The Conservationist* because these are his values.[25] Gorak's complaint, though perhaps not sufficiently sensitive to the ambivalence of Gordimer's treatment of sexuality, does highlight a problem which is consciously present in *The Conservationist*: Mehring has a vision of sexual freedom which is very close to Gorak's characterization of the libertine ideal, and he espouses it in a misogynistic monologue directed against his mistress:

Yes, that's the deal, the hopeful reasoning of the impotence of your kind, of those who are powerless to establish their millennium. The only way to shut you up is to establish the other, the only millennium, of the body, invade you with the easy paradise that truly knows no distinction of colour, creed and what-not – she's still talking, somewhere, but for me her mouth is stopped. (*C*, 154)

Mehring here envisages a code of free sexuality which is not merely apolitical, but which will represent a way of silencing unwanted political views: this is an envisaged assertion of power and dominance, political and sexual, which extends the concept of sexual fascism detected in Mehring by his mistress, Antonia, and which recalls Mehring's preoccupation with the 'soundless O' of the Portuguese girl he abuses.

Another major difficulty with *The Conservationist* is its technique, especially the modernist-style stream of consciousness which dominates the narrative, and through which Mehring's psyche is presented. The difficulty stems from the self-consciousness of the method, the creation of a narrative style to embody that which the novel condemns, and here Gordimer produces a semi-parody of modernist narrative to represent and ironize the self-absorption of the principal character. One has to be clear that Gordimer is not offering final conclusions about modernism, but that she is deliberately developing a particular tendency that can be seen – in the manner of Lukács – as an integral feature of modernist writing. The perceived distancing from reality that Lukács complained of in modernism is cultivated in Mehring's monologues, producing the semi-parody which serves Gordimer's particular ends here.

The principle of the stream of consciousness in *The Conservationist* is to present a psyche in confusion, and Gordimer has chosen a very economical method for this: the fluidity of the technique allows subconscious and subliminal connections to be made immediately, as in the passage concerning the mine dump above. Mehring's final internal monologue represents an instant recapitulation of the issues that have accrued around his character through the novel:

He's going to run, run and leave them to rape her or rob her. She'll be all right. They survive everything. Coloured or poor-white, whichever she is, their brothers or fathers take their virginity good and early. They can have it, the whole four hundred acres. She'll jump up and scream after him, sobbing and yelling, and they'll come at him at the same time, that one will tackle him round the legs, grabbing him as he passes, holding fast from the ground like a fist out of hell, and bring him down to them ... no no no. No no, what nonsense, what is there to fear – shudder after shudder, as if he were going to vomit the picnic lunch, it's all coming up, coming out. That's a white tart and there was no intent, anyway, report these gangsters or police thugs terrorizing people on mine property, he's on

a Board with the chairman of the Group this ground still belongs to
... No, no, no. RUN.
– Come. Come and look, they're all saying. What is it? Who is it?
It's Mehring. It's Mehring, down there. (*C*, 250)

Mehring is obviously the focalizer in this passage which
presents a psyche in confusion: it associates Mehring's sexual
and geographical habits of exploitation, and his underlying
insecurity, a fear of being discovered, of being forced out of his
cocoon of self-absorption. His worry at being discovered com-
mitting a sexual misdemeanour produces the immediate
impulse to give up the farm – 'the whole four hundred acres' –
as recompense. The fear of being held by the 'fist from hell'
obviously calls to mind the black man's corpse with which
Mehring is continually identified, and which heralds his down-
fall. The above passage ends, still apparently with Mehring's
monologue, imagining or hearing the voices of friends looking
down upon his beaten body: his final monologue ends with an
exteriorized view as the cocoon is destroyed.

Mehring's stream of consciousness is finally ruptured as
much by internal as external forces, and this suggests that the
mentality he represents contains the seeds of its own destruction, just as the intensified stream of consciousness appears to
spiral endlessly in a kind of narcissistic vacuum. Quite crucial,
here, is the coincidence between the final breakdown of
Mehring's narrative, and the re-emergence of the body associated with the subtext of Zulu mythology. Mehring's idea of
being viewed as from above places him in the position of the
body buried in his third pasture, and since the body has
resurfaced Mehring here symbolically changes positions with
it. Accordingly, the final chapter is free of Mehring's focalization: the modernist stream-of-consciousness narrative has
been exorcised from the novel along with Mehring, and the
final chapter extends, instead, the logic of the subtext.

The novel ends with the formal burial of the black man.
Mehring has now disappeared from the farm (he is phoned at
his office concerning money for the coffin), and the black
workers perform the ritual that has so far been denied the dead
man: he has no name, no member of his family is present, yet

'he had come back. He took possession of this earth, theirs; one of them.' (*C*, 252) The fact that no one present is related to this anonymous dead man is significant, given the novel's evocation of Zulu mythology: continuity has been shown to be a matter of familial descent in Zulu culture (*C*, 233). Thorpe's account of this turn of events is instructive; he indicates that there is no obligation in custom to someone who is not a family member or a revered elder. The murdered man, in fact, has dubious associations with the shanty town and may well be a casualty of gang rivalry. Despite this, Jacobus and his community, rising above their superstitious fears, bury the man and, in doing so, embrace him as one of their own. Here Gordimer moves beyond a strict application of Amazulu ancestral rites. The acceptance of the dubious stranger by Jacobus' community can be seen as symbolic of the acceptance by Africans of the darker side of their identity; and this acknowledgement may form a sound 'moral' basis for their repossession of the land from an 'amoral' white order.[26] This reading does, I feel, locate the positive emphasis of the novel's conclusion (though it is possible to overemphasize this): previously the loss of contact with Zulu culture – the failure to adhere strictly to it – has suggested an irony directed against the Africans running the farm. Now this impetus is reversed: the failure to adhere strictly to traditional rites indicates a more communal impulse.

Gordimer here acknowledges the limitations of the Zulu heritage, as she had done in *Occasion for Loving*, implying that if its communal potential can be extricated from its mystifications then the African cultural heritage can provide elements to be combined purposively into appropriate future social models. As in her two preceding longer fictions, Gordimer uses a transtextual principle to structure a formal innovation: here she stages a direct confrontation between a dominant feature of modernism and an account of African culture. Mehring's internalized stream of consciousness is an intensification of the literary individualism rejected in *A Guest of Honour*, and it is duly supplanted by the novel's subtext, though this is also subject to a revisionist treatment. Clearly the novel embodies a clash rather than a *fusion* of cultural sources, though this may

related to Rosa's personal relationships: in part one of the novel she is affected by her lover Conrad and his egocentric world-view which stands in contrast to the (for him) sterile commitment of the Burger family. In part two Rosa pursues her attraction to cultivate her personal, sensual side. This she does in France – withdrawn from the South African political scene – under the auspices of her step-mother Katya, Lionel Burger's first wife, who long ago fell foul of (and herself became disillusioned with) the mechanisms of the Communist Party. In the final section, part three, the terms of Rosa's return and recommitment are given. The narrative form of the novel is crucial in the tracing of the progression. The novel includes in each section third-person narratives juxtaposed with Rosa's first-person narration, which is presented for different address-ees: for Conrad in part one; for Katya in part two; and for Lionel in the third part. This sequence of addressees facilitates Rosa's developing reflections on her situation.

There is an apparent dialectical structure to the novel, though this is not as clear cut as it might at first appear. Critics of *Burger's Daughter* have often detected a Hegelian-dialectic structure to the novel – the tripartite organization of thesis-antithesis-synthesis – in which the original thesis of political commitment – Rosa's heritage – is challenged by its antithesis in the form of the solipsistic world-view represented by (especially) Conrad and Katya.[5] A synthesis then emerges, following this view, in which Rosa 'humanizes' radical com-mitment by importing into it a new-found sense of the per-sonal. The notion of a 'synthesis' in the working out of Rosa's commitment is helpful in one sense, because it locates the novel's focus and the nature of its central debate. However, Rosa's career is not as programmatic as the thesis-antithesis-synthesis model might suggest: the dialectic involves vacillation and uncertainty, and Rosa's 'synthesis' establishes an unfixed and potentially changeable response, one deemed appropriate to a particular historical situation. The search for the terms of the new commitment does involve the fundamental elements which Peck suggests are opposed in the dialectic: private/ public, and future/present, for example.[6] But there is no real binary opposition in the way these elements are considered since the dialectical interaction is complex.

In part one the general tendency of the 'argument' is to explore Rosa's repressed need for self-expression, a need to develop a sense of self independent of the programmatic life-style of the committed Burgers, and it is her relationship with the egocentric Conrad that affords her a view of this alter-native, self-centred way of engaging with the world. Conrad is the addressee of Rosa's narrative in this section which is written as a kind of open 'diary confession', offered to the (now dead) Conrad. Rosa, reflecting how she had felt comfortable with the undemanding Conrad in his cottage, after her father's death, examines the phrase 'now you are free', which, she states, came from being with Conrad (*BD*, 40). The phrase has an obvious metaphysical connotation, being addressed to some-one deceased, but it also condenses a crucial debate about the idea of 'freedom', either as a political or a personal concept. Much of Conrad's reported speech in this section is critical of Rosa's upbringing, of how a 'natural' individual response, in his view, is repressed in her, especially at times of emotional crisis: he observes that she failed to cry when her father was sentenced, and considers this to be evidence of conditioning, even brain-washing (*BD*, 52). The self-contained demeanour which Conrad condemns is, of course, a reasoned public response to repressive political opposition, and the question of conditioning really concerns whether or not Rosa has had the opportunity to accept this reasoning for herself. Rosa finds grounds to 'accuse' her parents on this score (*BD*, 66), par-ticularly over the visits she is required to make to the political prisoner, Noel de Witt, posing as his fiancée: for Rosa the pretence is supplanted by an actual adolescent infatuation, so that her visits and encoded love letters, used to pass on essential communications, are a torment of deceit for her. Her actual feelings remain hidden, as her parents inadvertently distort her personal development.

The business with Noel de Witt appears to justify some of Conrad's critique, and is merely the most extreme example in Rosa's general re-evaluation of herself and her past, the impetus of which is succinctly expressed in this new estimation of the claims of public and personal needs, again addressed to Conrad: 'Whatever I was before, you confused me. In the cottage you told me that in *that house* people didn't know each other; you've proved it to me in what I have found since in places you haven't been.' (*BD*, 171) Rosa indicates here that her encounter with Conrad suggests to her a new conception of personal relationships which the Burger household does not encompass, and which is beyond Conrad, too. But this is no rejection of the Burger household; Rosa goes on to articulate and defend the Burgers' conception of the personal:

The creed of that house discounted the Conrad kind of individualism, but in practice discovered and worked out another ... they made a Communism for 'local conditions' ... people in that house had a connection with blacks that was completely personal. In this way, their Communism was the antithesis of anti-individualism. The connection was something no other whites ever had in quite the same way. A connection without reservations on the part of blacks or whites. The political activities and attitudes of that house came from the inside outwards. (*BD*, 171–2)

This passage is a significant one because it states, early on in the novel, the kind of conclusion that the book as a whole seems to endorse: a genuine *and* politically motivated ethos of personal interaction is the securest foundation of an anti-racist opposition. This Communism for local conditions is rooted in a personal ethos fitted to the South African situation; and in cultivating this idea of commitment coming from the inside outwards – the private route to public responsibility – the book is typical of Gordimer.

The two passages I have just quoted offer a perspective of hindsight, and anticipate the movement of the novel's dialectic as a whole. The matter of perspective is complex, however, and appears to involve contradiction and vacillation at local points in the narrative. Confining ourselves to Rosa's narrative for the time being, the problem is really that there are different focalizers presented in juxtaposition – different versions of Rosa with differing experiences and orientations to the world. When Rosa speaks, addressing Conrad, of what she has 'found since in places you haven't been' (*BD*, 171), this is clearly the Rosa who has visited Europe – the Rosa who has lived through part two of the novel. But when, on the following page, Rosa announces 'I have lost connection', we return to a notional present in the narrative (*BD*, 172). This Rosa is disillusioned with the actuality of political opposition and finds herself unable to engage with it: this is Rosa before arriving at the rationale of the Burger way which is summarized in the preceding paragraph. This juxtaposition of focalizers – of Rosa at different stages of her development – creates an effect of uncertainty and vacillation which a closer reading, taking on board the matter of temporality, disproves: it is not that Rosa is confused, but rather that, ultimately, she is not. A resolution is anticipated in the juxtaposition, but this does have the effect of interfering with the perceived dialectical structure of the novel: Rosa's preliminary disaffection with her heritage is already signalled as an incomplete response, by these proleptic suggestions of her later re-engagement with it, and this really dismisses the simplicity of the underlying thesis-antithesis-synthesis design.

The vacillation can be appropriately illustrated from the last few pages of part one. Rosa, having secured a passport to travel abroad, attends a women's political meeting, a possibly 'dissident' act which could result in the rescinding of the passport. Her initial feeling about the meeting – or at least the reaction given first – is one of condemnation: she reads into the meeting an assumed sisterhood that ignores the fact of class difference (*BD*, 204). Arguably, this is Rosa analyzing the event with hindsight, but a contrary reaction, located as belonging to the narrative present, is given on the following page, where Rosa feels she can identify her direction in life, as a result of the meeting; as a consequence, the passport loses its significance, and seems irrelevant to Rosa's actual experiences (*BD*, 205). Although reported with hindsight, by an older Rosa 'try[ing] to sort this out in some order, now, of present and future' (*BD*, 205), the response, so it is stated, belongs to the past; moreover, it is a response which reveals an incipient need to be involved with group action, a need which pushes aside the desire to travel and any thoughts of the value of a passport (which has been hard to obtain for the daughter of two famous dissidents). This need, however, is not properly articulated in the present of the narrative's action, a point confirmed by Rosa's reaction in the crucial donkey-beating scene that follows; here her growing need for a personal basis to her involvement is confronted with, and confounded by, a scene of individual cruelty. Rosa comes across a black peasant family on a donkey-cart ahead on the road; the male driver is engaged in a ferocious whipping of the animal, with a terrified woman and child looking on. Rosa, as we know, is searching for the personal root to the political, and this is what this scene supplies for her, in a wholly negative way:

I had only to career down on that scene with my car and my white authority ... with my knowledge of how to deliver them over to the police ... I could formulate everything they were, as the act I had witnessed; they would have their lives summed up for them officially at last by me, the white woman – the final meaning of a day of other appalling things, violence, disasters, urgencies, deprivations which suddenly would become, was nothing but what it had led up to: the man among them beating their donkey. (*BD*, 209)

Rosa interprets the personal scene as being emblematic of the broader political situation, and in making the public/private link she tries to perceive a way in which she can make a purposive intervention. The dilemma for Rosa is that the only intervention she can make would be politically negative, at once a denial of the political reality and a confirmation of the hierarchy she detests: Rosa understands her complicity with the system, and that her only recourse is to a law which can only punish symptoms and ignore causes. As an individual she is helpless, she cannot act, and this reaffirms her decision to go to Europe: she states that she does not know how to live in her father's country (*BD*, 210).[7]

In the briefer second part of the novel Rosa's European sojourn is detailed in which, under the influence of her step-mother Colette – 'Katya' – Rosa is able to pursue a personal life free of her customary political obligations.[8] One aspect of this is a cultivation of her aesthetic sensibility, and this intro-

duces a sideline debate about the nature of aesthetics, which is
resolved in part three. The basic design of part two is to chart
Rosa's withdrawal from, and subsequent rediscovery of, poli-
tical commitment. A brief, flirtatious exchange with the young
Frenchman Michel Pistacchi ends with her turning the conversation from politics – and his condemnation of the French
Communists – in order to encourage him to speak of the family
home he is frightened of losing to the Communists' ideals.
Instead of arguing the point about property and ownership,
Rosa fishes for an invitation, which is forthcoming, to visit this
small 'farmhouse-cum-villa'. A brief rural idyll ensues in which
Rosa expresses approval for this inheritance (*BD*, 254). This
scene represents a deliberate turning away from the Burger
lifestyle, a kind of obstinacy which Rosa explains in her
summary of why she goes to France. She is in pursuit of the
world outside her father's vocation, and the knowledge of how
she can 'defect' from him (*BD*, 264). In the main this notion of
defection is shown to be a misnomer: Rosa's pursuit of her sense
of self necessitates the reinterpretation of political commitment
hinted at in part one, and reinforced in this second section
when Rosa turns an abstract political discussion to the question
of how political organization – specifically, repressive laws –
affects individual lives (*BD*, 296). This sense of the personal
basis of political commitment, already anticipated in part one,
lies behind Rosa's return and new sense of purpose in part
three.

The structure of the book suggests that part two is crucial for
Rosa's personal development, for it is this section which details
Rosa's sojourn in Europe, her period of release from the reality
of South Africa. With Colette in Nice, Rosa finds herself in a
withdrawn, cocoon-like environment in which she can explore
her personal wants, pleasures and emotions. This would
appear to be a crucial stage of development in which attention
to the self facilitates a growth that is preliminary to a successful
return to the social world. Liscio argues (illustrating this point
which, she points out, is fundamental to feminists such as
Cixous and Irigaray) that Colette's nurturing is important in
just this way, because pleasure in the self creates the ability to

move freely toward someone as a genuine other, rather than from a motive of self-need.[9] However, this straightforward reading of the function of part two does not account for certain complications. One such complication is presented through Rosa's relationship with the married Bernard Chabalier which, despite its apparent intensity, can only really lead into a one-sided domestic situation while Chabalier remains married. There is a sense in which Rosa appears to grow through and beyond this relationship, so that when she tells Chabalier that she feels he can make everything possible for her, there is a suggestion that their relationship has released the power of Rosa's emotional response that will be put to more productive use elsewhere: it is, simultaneously, an acknowledgement and a rejection of their bond.

More important, perhaps, is Rosa's response to Marisa Kgosana which appears to conjoin the sensual and the political: Marisa personifies this conjunction that is so central to the novel's implicit conclusions. As Leeuwenburg suggests, Marisa is a character who functions on different levels: as an individual, as a type, and as a symbol of African continuity. For Leeuwenburg she is clearly based on Winnie Mandela, and this actual historical allusion supplies a bridge between world and text for the personal/political conjunction. At a larger historical-symbolic level, Leeuwenburg sees Marisa as representative of Mother Africa, in her sunny self-confidence and proud sexuality.[10] Marisa's significance for Rosa is made quite clear in part one of the novel, and this, again, reduces the function of part two in the dialectic: the potential of Rosa's sensual response is apparent before her sojourn in France which, consequently, cannot be said to develop aspects of herself which lie dormant. There remains, however, the problem of perspective which can confuse the precise chronology of Rosa's progression. Here is the first description of Marisa, presented in Rosa's narrative in part one:

Leaning on her elbow at the cosmetic counter opposite I saw the half-bare back of a black woman dressed in splashing colour which included as overall effect the colour of her skin. The boldest, darkest lines of blue and brown, ancient ideogrammatic symbols of fish, bird and conch were extended in the movement of two rounded shoulder-blades from the matt slope of the neck to their perfect centring on the indented line of spine, rippling as shadowless store lighting ran a scale down it. The cloth suggested robes but was in fact cut tight to the proud backside jutting negligently at the angle of the weight-bearing hip, and close to the long legs. (*BD*, 134)

In Rosa's view, here, there is a clear sensual appreciation of the physicality of Marisa, of neck, back, legs and backside; at the same time, there is a suggestion that this physical and sexual perfection has a political significance. The 'splashing colour' of Marisa's clothing 'include[s] as overall effect the colour of her skin': the identification is a political one because Marisa's outfit depicts 'ancient ideogrammatic symbols' suggestive of an ethnic African culture properly linked with black African identity. Marisa's physical perfection clearly represents for Rosa (and symbolizes in the novel) the health and potential of African culture. The problem remains, however, of locating when Rosa arrives at a position from which to articulate this private/public conjunction. In fact, Rosa's responses to Marisa do not articulate the connection clearly, even though it is implicitly there. A few pages later Rosa uses the analogy of alcoholic intoxication to account for her feeling of wishing to remain in Marisa's orbit, and this indicates an inability to articulate its significance precisely (*BD*, 144). By the end of the novel Rosa has an implicit understanding of what her response to Marisa means: indeed Marisa is the focus of Rosa's return, and this personification of a political ideal sums up the commitment she has discovered by the end of the novel when Rosa and Marisa are in prison together, finding pleasure and inspiration in each other's company (*BD*, 355).

The development in part three of that which was implicit in Rosa's responses in part one limits the function of part two in her progression, and also affects how the novel's structure is interpreted. It seems that the interlude of Rosa's trip to Europe has both positive and negative connotations: one can argue that the cultivation of her personal, emotional side does release and develop important, incipient traits, but it is also clear that the escape is ultimately condemned as an apolitical and irresponsible escapism. The section ends with a phone call

Rosa receives from 'Baasie' which shocks Rosa out of this state and forces her to return to her responsibilities. 'Baasie', here grown up, is the black boy who is taken into the Burger household and who grows up alongside Rosa as her brother when they are small. Following their unexpected meeting at a gathering in London 'Baasie' phones to condemn Rosa for her complicity in white repression, angered by the way she has been fêted by the assembled company of political refugees, sympathizers and journalists. The implicit objection, in effect, is that Rosa (albeit involuntarily) perpetuates a system which suppresses black identity. This is denoted through the caller's fury at Rosa's use of his former pet name 'Baasie' (little boss), bestowed by the well-meaning Burgers: his real name is Zwelinzima Vulindlela (Zwelinzima means 'suffering land'). This insistence by Zwelinzima on his identity seems to be the crucial aspect of a vitriolic attack which finally pushes Rosa to consolidate the redefinition of her own identity, and to articulate her position in relation to the discourse of Black Consciousness, represented by Zwelinzima's accusation.

The reading of the novel adduced here – which is more positive than some interpretations – is reinforced by the way in which different voices are combined. In her narrative Rosa articulates on several occasions the difficulty of perspective (*BD*, 14, 16, 171), and this thematic preoccupation determines the narrative design of the book. One can characterize the narrative as fully dialogized, a narrative which places in opposition and/or in conflict many different voices and perspectives. There are several third-person narrators in the novel offering contending perspectives, as can be seen from the opening scene which offers three views of Rosa waiting outside the prison (*BD*, 9–12). In each section of the novel Rosa's different addressees also affect the style of the third-person narrative, or even take it up themselves (as Katya does at one point (*BD*, 262)). Rosa's first-person narrative is in contention with the various third-person narrators, and is also itself dialogized, both by the effect of her development (which creates different focalizers, as we have seen), and by the different addressees, who elicit varying analyses.

By problematizing the narrative perspective, Gordimer

fashions a novelistic form which reinforces her investigation of ideology and discourse. Rosa's identity can be constructed in different ways – by her parents, by the security forces, by Zwelinzima, by herself at different stages in her life. This mutability of identity is demonstrated both by the problematic narrative perspective, and by (what now seems the deliberate) obfuscation of the overall dialectical structure. The essential point is that personal identity must be appropriately constructed in a given context and in relation to given discursive practices. The resolution of Rosa's identity – and its appropriate historical location – emerges through a relation to an important new discourse which enters the text explicitly in the third section. This new voice is the voice of Black Consciousness, heralded in the epigraph to the section – *'Peace. Land. Bread'* – which is an ANC slogan (*BD*, 327).[11] This is followed up dramatically by Gordimer's inclusion of the text of a pamphlet issued by Soweto Students' Representative Council in June 1977, a document banned for possession as well as publication (*BD*, 346–7).[12] This is the context of Rosa's new commitment and the insertion of this new voice of political opposition into Rosa's narrative indicates its importance in her new emerging consciousness, a point reinforced by the fact that this organization was banned on 19 October 1977, the date on which Rosa herself is detained.[13] The new phase for Rosa is also a new phase for South African history:[14] Black Consciousness, advocating the need for blacks to take responsibility for their own political advancement, is tacitly approved in Rosa's decision to take a subservient role in her political recommitment.

JULY'S PEOPLE

July's People, like *Burger's Daughter*, is an examination of the construction of identities, but the two novels have quite different dynamics. *Burger's Daughter* progressively establishes the fact of ideological interpellation and, in the process, moves to a prescription for an appropriate construction; *July's People*, on the other hand, systematically reveals the deleterious effect of a particular construction: it is a brief and powerful condemnation of consumer capitalism and the identities it creates and sustains.

The novel takes as its epigraph a famous epigraph from Gramsci's *Prison Notebooks*: 'The old is dying and the new cannot be born; in this interregnum there arises a great diversity of morbid symptoms.' It is the project of this novel to examine some of the 'morbid symptoms' of this interregnum through a concentration on a (previously concealed) crisis of identities, exposed in the revolutionary moment.

Gordimer's priorities are underscored by the fact that the novel eschews entirely the depiction of revolution, focusing solely on the issue of identity. In an article on *July's People*, Michael Neill considers the charge that the novel fails to describe the murderous and chaotic effects of the revolutionary process. Neill points out that a novel that *did* focus on such effects may well be counter-productive as it might have a cathartic effect, offering vicarious terror-fantasies which might purge the guilt of whites.[15] The effect of *July's People* is the precise opposite of this: it is a short and intense novel, one of Gordimer's most powerful works, which traces the dissolution of a materially dispossessed white bourgeois family, and which, in the process, systematically exposes the absence of any sustaining or sustainable values in their lives. Gordimer shows, particularly, how the white couple Maureen and Bamford Smales have no meaningful sense of their own identity, and this crisis of selfhood also affects the novel's analysis of its black characters, whose lives have been artificially disrupted and restructured by the effects of apartheid. The novel thus offers a pessimistic prognosis for the moment of revolutionary transition, even though there are some hints of a worthwhile future in the occasional actions and responses of the children in the novel, hints of how a reconstructed post-apartheid identity might emerge.

The problem of identity is announced at the beginning of the novel as Maureen Smales wakes up in the hut given over to herself and her family by her servant July, after their flight from the revolutionary violence of the town to July's village:

Stalks of light poked through ... A thick lip of light round the doorway; a bald fowl entered with chicks cheeping, the faintest sound in the world. Its gentleness, ordinariness produced sudden, total disbelief. Maureen and Bam Smales. Bamford Smales, Smales, Caprano & Partners, Architects. Maureen Hetherington from Western Areas Gold Mines. Under 10s Silver Cup for Classical and Mime at the Johannesburg Eisteddfod. She closed her eyes again and the lurching motion of the vehicle swung in her head as the swell of the sea makes the land heave underfoot when the passenger steps ashore after a voyage. She fell asleep as, first sensorily dislocated by the assault of the vehicle's motion, then broken in and contained by its a-rhythm, she had slept from time to time in the three days and nights hidden on the floor of the vehicle.

People in delirium rise and sink, rise and sink, in and out of lucidity. The swaying, shuddering, thudding, flinging stops, and the furniture of life falls into place. The vehicle was the fever. (*JP*, 2–3, original gap maintained)

The 'culture shock' registered here is a profound one. Maureen, waking to the sights and sounds of a rural peasant existence, responds (for the passage, presented from her perspective, is also infused with her voice) by contesting the empirical evidence with a consciousness of her sense of self as something which does not belong here. Clearly the means she has of reminding herself of her identity, and that of her husband, is exposed as insubstantial: the 'titles' of a bourgeois society – bestowed through marriage, through business partnership, and through children's 'high cultural' competition – these titles are evidently meaningless in the face of a revolutionary dissolution of the institutions which validate them. Even so, the irony is not straightforward. The point is not just that the Smales can be reduced to a series of vacuous titles and roles (though ultimately they can), but that these roles are various, *already* creating a dissipation of individual identities, and these identities *do* have a power and validity within the bourgeois construct: the Smales have drawn sustaining power from their bourgeois identities (even though they prove to be nontransferable) and could have continued to do so. Consequently, Maureen's assertion of her identity involves an implicit appeal to a power that is, in the final analysis, no longer effectual, but which the Smales will continue to try and assert for a while. The personal dissolution will only be fully manifested through the course of the novel, and this initial period of transition is registered in the 'delirium' which Maureen experiences, provoked by the motions of their escape vehicle, the 'bakkie', their safari truck which is a symbol of bourgeois status in normal use (*JP*, 5), the 'a-rhythm' of its new rougher use paralleling and provoking the delirium of Maureen's transition.

The situation of the Smales' new dependence on their former servant creates a simple reversal of the power relationship, but it also produces a complex analysis of the network of forces that has created these individuals and the matrix in which they interact. The Smales' material dispossession robs them also of the terms of their intimacy, and, as the novel progresses, they know each other less and less, finally appearing together in the manner of divorced people trying to give the appearance of normal family life (*JP*, 140). This estrangement is essentially negative since even it is lived in the terms of the bourgeois existence that has gone: the opportunity of a personal redefinition has not been taken up. In one of her reflections Maureen makes the crucial connection between wealth and personal response, understanding that there is a balance between duty and desire which is affected by economic factors, factors which determine how a relationship is lived and experienced (*JP*, 65). July and his wife Martha have for years had a 'marriage' determined by economic forces: July lives in the city with his white family, and his town 'wife', returning to his village only once every two years. For Martha this means conceiving a child every two years, and, in the meantime, living a traditional, but incomplete existence:

Across the seasons was laid the diuturnal one of being without a man; it overlaid sowing and harvesting, rainy summers and dry winters, and at different times, although at roughly the same intervals for all, changed for each for the short season when her man came home. For that season, although she worked and lived among the others as usual, the woman was not within the same stage of the cycle maintained for all by imperatives that outdid the authority of nature. The sun rises, the moon sets; the money must come, the man must go. (*JP*, 83)

The economic restructuring of the community's 'cycles' involves 'imperatives' which have become mystified: the necessity and consequent inevitability of the man's departure has created a pattern which has become accepted by the community as comparable to, and ultimately more significant than, the daily cycle of nature, which is 'outdone'. Martha is out of step with this consensus when the man is there, and out of tune – in her loneliness – with the agricultural routine when he is away. In short, she lives two alienated roles just as July does. The underpinning irony is that the apparently 'traditional' existence which has been disrupted is already a sinister artificiality: the poor quality of the land – this rural region designated for Africans – makes self-sufficiency impossible, and enforces the pursuit of work in the towns. The notionally traditional existence of July's community is an aspect of the regime's discriminatory fantasy, already doomed to a failure which will perpetuate economic dependency, and inequality. The existence to which July's extended family has settled itself indicates a worrying alienation, an implicit acceptance of the racist fantasy, significantly challenged by Martha's non-alignment – a different (less complete) alienation.

For July the experience is a schizophrenic one, as he is forced to live and work as a servant away from his home. It is only towards the end of the novel that the Smales discover that July's real name is 'Mwawate' (*JP*, 120), his two names calling attention to the split-personality enforced upon him: he has a role to play populating his designated rural village (signified by his African name), yet this also necessitates his absence working in service, for which he requires another name that whites can use (*JP*, 120). Both names are, in effect, required by the regime (since it enforces two identities), and the contradiction of naming points merely to the contradictions inherent in the policies it pursues. Identity itself is shown to be determined through the control of spatio-temporal practices.

This issue of control is extended through the question of

marriage: the marriage of July and Martha is contrasted with
that of the Smales. In each case the effects of the political and
economic situation are shown to determine the nature of the
contact allowed and the type of bond that is constructed.
Evidently, the Smales are in large measure complicit with the
system which restricts them, but the positive implications of
revolution are important for both couples: the political revolution must also be a sexual one, since the terms of personal
interaction will be changed. Maureen has occasion to reflect on
this connection too: 'an explosion of roles, that's what the
blowing up of the Union Buildings and the burning of master
bedrooms is.' (*JP*, 117) Maureen, here, clearly associates the
destruction of the political hegemony and its manifestations
with a metonymical destruction of the site of bourgeois
sexuality.

An important scene, in which connections are established
between power, sexuality and bourgeois identity, is Bam's
successful hunt and its aftermath. Bam shoots two wart-hog
piglets, and in doing so reveals to himself an essential fact about
himself. One of the piglets is shot in the body, and, as it lies
kicking in pain, he advances to put it out of its misery:

Bam ... shot it through the head. Its young bones were so light that
the snout smashed. It was horrible, the bloodied pig-face weeping
blood and trailing blood-snot; the clean death from the chromed
barrels that smelled aseptically of gun-oil. Game-birds (his usual
prey) had no faces, really; thin aesthete's bony structure with its
bloodless beak and no flesh, a scrap of horny skin, wrinkled paper
eyelids – a guinea-fowl head doesn't look much different, dead, from
alive. The shattered pig-face hung to the ground, dripping a trail all
the way back to the huts, where his function as a provider of meat
settled upon him as a status. (*JP*, 77)

This passage, presented from Bam's perspective, brings into his
consciousness facts about himself that had hitherto been concealed or mystified. The power of the gun bestows power and
status upon its owner, and evidently this is particularly crucial
where killing is for survival rather than for sport; this is not to
suggest that Bam is here slipping into a new, more purposive
communal role, since he remains the white man with the gun,

his power and status conferred upon him by virtue of the fact that he has a gun for sport killing. He is horrified by the smashed pig's skull, principally through an anthropomorphic identification with the disfigured mammal, an identification he doesn't make with the dead game-birds. This identification suggests a symbolic connotation for the smashed pig's skull, a violent identity beneath the visage previously seen. Again, this implies an underlying reality rather than a new identity: when, on the following page, we read of Bam's new understanding that he is a killer, we perceive a new realization on his part of the latent violence which underpins bourgeois power (*JP*, 78).

After consuming the meat the Smales family becomes intoxicated, and a holiday-campfire atmosphere develops. Afterwards, Bam and Maureen make love for the first time since they have left home, in their hut surrounded by their sleeping children. In the morning Bam has 'a moment of hallucinatory horror when he saw the blood of the pig on his penis – then understood it was hers' (*JP*, 80). Like Maureen's 'delirium', this 'hallucinatory' moment is one of self-revelation, and it completes the episode of demystification: the killing of the pig is now associated with Bam's sexuality as well as with his status in the hegemony. The connection is revealing and suggests a latent violence in the bourgeois channelling of male sexuality, an aspect of appropriation and ownership which is merely one aspect of the male's socially encoded power.

Another scene in which this kind of connection is made is the one in which Maureen tells Bam that she has drowned a litter of kittens:

– Did you find someone to take the kittens? – They were no longer in the hut . . .
– I drowned them in a bucket of water. –
She used sometimes to answer him outlandishly, out of sarcasm, when he suggested she might do something it was beyond question – by nature and intelligence – for her to have done. *Now don't let slip to Parkinson I don't intend to go to the meeting because I've no intention of voting, mmh. – Oh I've already had a good chat with Sandra about it, just to be sure he'll get to hear.*
This kind of repartee belonged to the deviousness natural to suburban life. In the master bedroom, sometimes it ended in brief

coldness and irritation, sometimes in teasing, kisses, and love-making
. . . That she had said 'in a bucket': he understood that as it was
meant, a piece of concrete evidence of an action duly performed.
   – Oh my god. – His lips turned out in disgust, distaste, on her
behalf . . .
   She pulled [her] shirt over her head and shook it . . . – What're you
making a fuss about. – The baring of breasts was not an intimacy but
a castration of his sexuality and hers. (*JP*, 89–90)

At its most immediate level this episode registers a changing
attitude appropriate to more elemental circumstances:
Maureen's act, brutal by bourgeois standards, indicates an
acceptance of necessity in a community directly concerned
with matters of subsistence. The scene also involves the issue of
language and communication, and exposes a convention of
marital banter as quite vacuous: the sarcasm that Bam is
expecting is merely a way of *denying* purposive action, though it
ostensibly indicates assurance and control. It is, therefore, a
contradictory discourse, with a rebounding, self-defeating
irony, and the contradictory nature of the discourse is suggested by its unpredictable effects: it can produce both dispute
and intimacy in the master bedroom. This suggests that the
terms of communication between Maureen and Bam were
already ineffectual, so that Bam's shock at the 'brutality' forced
upon Maureen is, once more, part of a process of more profound demystification: it is not that a genuine mode of communication has been lost, together with an intimacy sometimes
associated with it, but rather the discourse itself is exposed as
vacuous, thereby calling into question those responses associated with it. Consequently the 'castration', remarked upon
here by the narratorial voice, is implicitly redemptive, destroying the terms of a false intimacy, even though, for Bam, the
sense of shock and loss is predominant.
   As several critics of the novel have remarked, the theme of
language and communication is central to *July's People*. Jennifer Gordon, for example, feels that the book demonstrates the
need for a common language as a prerequisite for social integration and advancement in South Africa: language, consequently, may be the instrument of social change.[16] This is a

perceptive overview of the novel which accurately locates the centrality accorded to language and communication in the hegemony, and, as a result, the central role they must occupy in any consideration of revolutionary change. However, no blueprint for a common language emerges from the events of the book – indeed, the focus is consistently on the failure of language; but the importance of the need for change does, at least, emerge from an analysis of the failure.

The inability of the Smales to communicate properly with their hosts is illustrated repeatedly, though for Maureen the issue is complicated by a strong element of self-deception. She is initially confident in her ability to communicate with July feeling that they understand each other well (*JP*, 13); she is disabused of this confidence as the real terms of this 'understanding' manifest themselves. The essential point here is that the hegemonic mistress-servant relationship, conducted in broken English, is structured to serve the interests of Maureen and to deny a genuine voice to July; July knows only scraps of English – orders and responses – acquired from subservient working situations: this is not a language with which he can express ideas or feeling. (*JP*, 96). July's English serves only a utilitarian function for his employers; it is merely a tool to extract useful work from him. For July, therefore, the English he speaks with his employers is a one-way channel only: however considerate the liberal Smales may feel themselves to have been, the imprisoning language they have imposed on their servant – their 'boy' as July insists on calling himself – confirms and reinforces the hegemony. Gradually Maureen comes to a consciousness of this:

How was she to have known, until she came here, that the special consideration she had shown for his dignity as a man, while he was by definition a servant, would become his humiliation itself, the one thing there was to say between them that had any meaning.
Fifteen years
　　　　　your boy
　　　　　　　you satisfy (*JP*, 98)

That which is deemed considerate by bourgeois standards – a token acknowledgement of a dignity which is simultaneously denied – is a contradiction which produces the most oppressive effect of July's existence: the recognition of his sense of self and the concomitant denial of an outlet for it produces a specific frustration and humiliation, which is the insidious result of his 'liberal' treatment. Maureen's consciousness of how July has been manipulated in this way is articulated in her reaction in a crucial late scene in which July begins a tirade at her in his own language:

– You – He spread his knees and put an open hand on each. Suddenly he began to talk at her in his own language, his face flickering powerfully. The heavy cadences surrounded her; the earth was fading and a thin, far radiance from the moon was faintly pinkening parachute-silk hazes stretched over the sky. She understood although she knew no word. Understood everything: what he had had to be, how she had covered up to herself for him, in order for him to be her idea of him. But for himself – to be intelligent, honest, dignified for *her* was nothing; his measure as a man was taken elsewhere and by others. (*JP*, 152)

Michael Neill has commented perceptively on the tone in this passage, which is potentially misleading, indicating how, in a sparely written novel, it has a strained rhetorical effect, apparently projecting an optimism for the future not sustained by the novel. Neill points out that the optimism is undercut by the negative nature of Maureen's 'understanding', but it is the tension between optimism and pessimism – the ambiguity itself – which, I think, is crucial.[17] The tension locates the *need* of a more purposive communication, the lack of which is underscored by Maureen's negative realization.

The problem of communication is shown to have its roots in the economic relationships which interfere with the creation of a common language. The same interference obtains over the related questions of power and ownership, and the control of space: the Smales' preoccupation with commodities, which has also tainted July's village, prevents any genuine cross-racial co-operation and conditions the geopolitical map.

Bam's gun and the bakkie provide the foci for the struggle for possession, and the loss of both causes great anguish for the Smales: without these two things their status and identity in

July's community will be transformed, since both items (in the
short term, at least, while ammunition and fuel last) have a
great utilitarian value. The losses of both gun and vehicle
symbolize, quite straightforwardly, the transition of power
from white to black, but it is the dependence on the easy power
these artefacts supply that is the real issue. For Bam and
Maureen possession of the keys to the bakkie outweighs all
question of their debt to July for saving their lives (*JP*, 58),
since the loss of control of the vehicle, together with the gun,
renders them totally dependent: without their power they will
have a quite different role in the community, one requiring an
alternative identity, an inner resource of adaptability which
they clearly do not have. Concerning the dead carcases of the
wart-hog piglets, Maureen whispers to her husband to give the
larger piglet to July and to keep the smaller one for themselves
(to be eaten by the Smales in their separate family unit),
ostensibly for reasons of protocol, but also because she knows
that the smaller one will be the more tender (*JP*, 78):
Maureen's machinations indicate clearly how a preoccupation
with commodities, driven by self-interest, obstructs the Smales'
participation in communal activities.

The false consciousness induced by the power struggles
which the commodities produce also affects July, and this is a
crucial aspect of the book: this is not merely an analysis of a
white bourgeois family symbolically failing at a time of revolutionary transition; equally important is the fact that a
dependence on the terms of a commodity culture is common to
whites and blacks in the novel. Gordimer's point is that a
simple post-revolutionary 'rebirth' cannot be provided by a
return to the values of ethnic African communities, because
these communities are already tainted by the ideas and effects
of the capitalist system, which has artificially called them into
being for its own exploitative ends. The principal example of
the shared commodity fetishism is July's pride in his possession
of the bakkie, and his apparent fear, sensed by Maureen, of
Bam 'stealing' it back from him (*JP*, 94, 101). Maureen's final
accusation against July on this issue is that he sees the bakkie as
a means of establishing himself as a local gangster, just while he

can find petrol (*JP*, 153): the bakkie, initially established in the novel as a symbol of white bourgeois power (*JP*, 5), is now presented, by extension of its symbolic role, as an instrument of corruption, destructive of community action.

The bakkie also emphasizes the importance of the control of space. A crucial index of the nature of the revolutionary transition is the loss of geographical control, and this is marked for the Smales by their forced retreat to July's village, a place Maureen had previously imagined visiting one day, of her own volition, on a combined shooting, camping and educational jaunt in the bakkie (*JP*, 37–8). But the issue of the control of space is not explored simply as a matter of loss, but rather as a transition naturally resulting from the exposure of false credentials. Bam, as the representative white bourgeois unable to adapt to a new social space, is ironically exposed when we discover that he had once presented a paper on 'Needs and Means in Rural African Architecture' (*JP*, 108); Bam, though able to theorize about the pragmatic use of African social space, is himself quite unable to operate in that environment. There is an important geopolitical point here about a prescriptive paternalism establishing a blueprint for spatial organization which does not originate organically from within a community and a lived understanding of its needs.

The treatment of the issue of space reaches a culmination in the following passage, in which many of the novel's themes are conjoined:

He lingered about in the small space of the hut behind her, she could hear him hitting his fist into his palm as he did back there when he was talking about some building project he was hoping to be commissioned to design. Impossible to imagine what was happening in those suburban malls now, where white families ate ice-cream together . . . bought T-shirts stamped with their names ('Victor' 'Gina' 'Royce'), and looked, learning about foreign parts, at photographic exhibitions whose favoured subject was black township life. (*JP*, 125)

As Bam lingers in the 'small space' of the village hut, Maureen reflects on those diametrically opposed spaces – shopping malls – he had been involved in producing, as an architect; spaces in which stable bourgeois identities are possible and can be proclaimed on T-shirts, and in which the issue of racial and economic equality is reduced to the optional photographic exhibitions – aesthetic representations, apparently incidental to the capitalist routine which such malls epitomize. Of course, this is a concealment of the real causal relation: the creation of these urban shopping spaces is, in important ways, dependent upon the spaces of social deprivation. The suppression of this causal relationship is exposed alongside another reversal: the obvious irony of Bam's transposition – from the designer of capitalist urban space to a lingerer in someone else's mud hut.

Although the general tenor of the novel is negative, however, there are some hints of the possibility of a post-revolutionary rebirth. These hints are carried principally by the Smales children, the daughter Gina in particular, who establishes a 'best friend' bond with one of the small village girls. The most important aspect of Gina's settling in is that it enables her to learn July's language, something which remains beyond Maureen and Bam. The son Victor also shows himself able to adapt, as when he performs a gesture of obeisance, as appears to be customary for the village children when receiving food (*JP*, 42–3; 157). These hints are tenuous, however, and do not amount to a serious projection of future reintegration, since the community to which the children begin to adapt themselves is, itself, tainted by the dying order which had initially constructed it. The 'hope' that the novel can offer is based, rather, on a total exposure and acceptance of the vacuity and bankruptcy of the values epitomized by the Smales. When Maureen runs to the sound of the helicopter at the end of the novel, just such an acceptance is implied: it is not clear whether the helicopter heralds the arrival of revolutionary forces, or of government forces re-establishing the old order. This is an apocalyptic moment for the bankrupt white identity: the white woman finally accepts that she has no inner resource and no residual power or control to deal with her situation. She runs to accept the inevitability that her fate lies in the hands of others.

Gordimer's preoccupation with the construction of identity in *Burger's Daughter* and *July's People* results in novels turning on questions of literary structure, ideology and language; these concerns bespeak the increasing sophistication of Gordimer's writing, a trend which progresses to a phase of self-reflexive self-consciousness in her next two novels.

CHAPTER 5

Self-reflexive reassessments
'A Sport of Nature' and 'My Son's Story'

The most recent phase in Gordimer's novel sequence is characterized by a metafictional quality: this is not an entirely new development since there are deliberations about the function of technique and form in her previous novels. In *A Sport of Nature* (1987) and *My Son's Story* (1990), however, this tendency is both more pronounced and more overtly self-reflexive, focusing – often ironically – on her previous treatment of issues now taken up again. This principle of self-reflexive intertextuality in both novels makes their full signification dependent upon a knowledge of Gordimer's earlier work.

A SPORT OF NATURE

In some ways *A Sport of Nature* is Gordimer's most ambitious novel to date: it offers, as its organizing principle, an exaggerated re-evaluation of the issues and forms of her previous novels. This lends the book a ludic, metafictional quality which sets it apart from her earlier works. This novel is written at one remove: it is a book *about* her previous books, and this is what anchors a work that investigates the variety of interpretation to which personal and historical action can be subjected. The result is a novel which, viewed as a conventional work of realism, appears to be radically uncertain in its narrative stance, in its view of purposive political action, and in its conclusions about historical change. The implicit point is to create a fiction, ultimately free from facile teleological prescriptions, which presents questions of historical and political debate *through its form*. The problem for critics, rather than finding the novel gives no lead for the would-be interpreter, has been that different and conflicting interpretations appear to be endorsed at different times. This is an integral part of the project; the question of its success or failure is one to consider when the formal project has been evaluated in appropriate terms.

A brief summary of *A Sport of Nature* emphasizes its meta-fictional nature: the schematization of its structure and its concerns reveals an intensified reconsideration of ideas pre-viously addressed in the novels. The central character is Hillela, the 'sport of nature' announced in the title. Gordimer draws attention to the *OED* definition of her title by including it as an epigraph. As a 'sport of nature' Hillela represents, following the dictionary definition, 'a departure from the parent stock or type' established in the earlier novels: she is 'a spontaneous mutation' or 'new variety' of protagonist, and takes her meaning from a comparison with previous protagon-ists in Gordimer's work, which have been variations on the notion of typicality. Hillela – a white Jewish girl initially recognizable as a Gordimerian type – is raised by two aunts. She is effectively ejected from both households – that of the bourgeois Olga as well as that of liberal (but ultimately restric-ted) Pauline – after transgressing sexual taboos: she is passed on to Pauline after being seen with a 'coloured' boy (an episode resurrected from *The Lying Days*), and in Pauline's house she is discovered in bed with her cousin Sasha. Her career, in fact, is determined by her sexuality: she either becomes attached to, or is the focus of desire for, a series of men in various situations, initially in South Africa, but subsequently abroad. Her mar-riage to Whaila Kgomani, a black revolutionary, represents a stage of temporary stability: she has a daughter by him, the first of her projected 'rainbow family', but this naive phase is brought to a brutal end with the assassination of Whaila. After an interlude with an American fiancé, Brad, her next sig-nificant relationship is with Reuel, a revolutionary general. Hillela's sexuality is now channelled – in an uncomfortable association – in the service of military ambition. Reuel becomes the Prime Minister of the African nation he has liberated into

socialism, and the novel ends with a fantastical Utopian scene
in which Hillela and Reuel (now her husband) attend the
independence ceremonies in the new African state that was
South Africa.

The novel contains the familiar dialectic between the personal and the political/historical. References to actual figures
such as Mandela, Tambo and Sisulu emphasize a link with
history. But the reverse process of the dialectic – the influence
of fiction upon history – is also implied in similar references to
Gordimer's own fiction: Lionel Burger, for example, is mentioned alongside Bram Fischer, while Rosa Burger actually
appears briefly in this novel. Consequently, the distinction
between actual historical figures and literary characters is
deliberately blurred. Metafictional references to the previous
novels are also discernible where *A Sport of Nature* takes up the
argument of previous novels: for example, Hillela's response to
suffering in the USA leads her into action – doling out soup
powder – which is comparable to the action available to Rosa
at the end of *Burger's Daughter* (see *SN*, 284, 312, 328 for
references to this). This phase is succeeded by Hillela's attachment to Reuel, which offers a progression beyond what now
appears as Rosa's interim stage. The way in which Rosa's story
parallels contemporary South African history is also a point of
reference for the career of Hillela. In a passage detailing some
important political events in the childhood and adolescence of
Hillela and her cousin Carole, we learn of the impact of the
Alexandra bus boycott upon the schoolgirl Carole, and of
Carole's later involvement in protest meetings (*SN*, 64–6). But
this implied direct linkage of historical event and personal
development is a product of Pauline's commitment to the
struggle, something which the novel will clearly expose as
two-dimensional in comparison to Hillela's. We discover that
Hillela had been taken in by Pauline's family in the year before
Sharpeville, and the narrator tells us that this tendency to date
Hillela's history according to public history is a feature of her
existence in Pauline's house (*SN*, 64). The novel resists the kind
of linkage that Pauline favours, and even follows an ironic
cat-and-mouse attempt at it. One section, for example, begins

by speculating on Hillela's whereabouts, at the age of seventeen, on the Day of the Covenant, 16th December 1961, when
several terrorist bombs exploded (*SN*, 121). Undoubtedly such
historical references contribute something important to the
texture of the novel, and the way in which it contextualizes
itself. But the emphasis is on the resistance of Hillela who,
unlike Rosa Burger, pursues her own slippery history which
denies the formulation applied to the previous heroine,
reduced to a flat, walk-on part in this novel. The straightforward association of private and public histories – the ethos
of Pauline's house – is clearly simplistic in the light of the
novel's alternative investigation of how these areas interrelate.
A later moment, which suggests this different interaction,
occurs when Hillela is in Eastern Europe, soon after the killing
of Whaila, left dead for his family to deal with on their kitchen
floor. The character Karel shows Hillela a gruesome war
memento, a canister of the gas used by the Nazis in their gas
chambers, which he discovered on the desk of one of Hitler's
men (after shooting him) in Berlin. Her response to his grim
memorial, keeping the canister just as it was used, like any
other commodity, is visceral:

An urge came upon her crudely as an urge to vomit or void her
bowels. She began to tremble and to flush. Her eyes were huge with
burning liquid she could not hold back. She wept in his arms ... He
knew she was not weeping for the man he had shot dead at his desk,
or even for the innocents for whom death was opened like a can of
beans. The kitchen floor; it was the kitchen floor. (*SN*, 264)

On the face of it Karel appears to have triggered an outburst of
Hillela's grief for her murdered husband, but this grief is
clearly associated with an emerging historical and political
understanding: the violence of the holocaust, symbolically
recontained in the transportable canister, is the violence of
political struggle which, in another context, had found its way,
fatally, into Hillela's marital home. Hillela is here coming to
terms with the actuality of violence and death in her personal
political commitment, something which Whaila had already
tried to convince her of in theory, and which, in contrast, the
liberal Pauline never fully accepts.

Hillela's visceral response to Karel's canister is symptomatic of the kind of vitality which she is shown to offer, and this reaction is itself defined in terms of an intertextual reference to Gordimer's previous concerns. Hillela alights on the canister while looking over the objects Karel has accrued over the years, including framed letters from Georg Lukács and Thomas Mann (*SN*, 263). Hillela shows little interest in these formative influences of Gordimer's, and the novel implicitly consigns them to the past, along with most of Karel's other memorabilia: the coded message here is that Gordimer's new heroine is no figure of Lukácsian typicality, even in a redefined or enlarged sense. She is an intensified version – a near-parody – of the Gordimer hero(ine) for whom sensuality can be the channel of political enlightenment. In Hillela, Gordimer takes to an extreme her consideration of the radical political potential represented by sexuality, for Hillela's personal development, and her influence upon others are both expressed in terms of her sexual relationships, at every stage of the novel. This association of radicalism and sexuality is sometimes unconvincing, but it is never merely uncritical: sexuality has its negative connotations in the novel, as well as directly auspicious ramifications, and this is the result of Gordimer consciously bringing out the various possible implications of the sexual politics in previous novels.

Gordimer's characters frequently dwell on physical difference, and this is an important characteristic of Hillela. With her American fiancé, Brad, she actually caresses his dark birthmark, the blemish that others try to ignore (*SN*, 294), just as with her first husband, Whaila, Hillela refuses merely to accept their different skin pigmentations:

Lying beside him, looking at pale hands, thighs, belly: seeing herself as unfinished, left off, somewhere. She examines his body minutely and without shame, and he wakes to see her at it, and smiles without telling her why: she is the first not to pretend the different colours and textures of their being is not an awesome fascination. (*SN*, 206; original italics)

The Utopian idea that lies behind Hillela's preoccupation with racial difference is clearly indicated here: inter-racial harmony, or 'completion', it is implied, depends upon an initial celebration of racial difference, rather than a denial of it. Such a celebration, which is facilitated by the sensuality of Hillela, may represent a subversion of the racist code which demands separation through difference; the implicit point here would be that it is more appropriate to *address* the very real issue of difference than to gloss over it in a liberal notion of harmony. This strategy of subversion through confrontation has not always been deemed successful, however. Brenda Cooper, for example, considers it to be counter-productive, arguing that the focus on race is accompanied by a playing down, or misrepresentation, of the important issues of class and gender. For Cooper the focus on racial difference may represent an inverse racism which includes its own potential reversal.[1] The other (connected) charge – that issues of class and gender are underplayed in *A Sport of Nature* – has also some validity if the novel is seen strictly as being about South Africa. But an important feature of the novel is how it seeks to place the South African problem in a broader context of the struggle for African liberation, and this, appropriately, places the concerns of this metafiction at a more theoretical level.

An essential feature of the Utopian impulse in the novel concerns a multi-national concept of emerging African brotherhood, as we shall see. More important with regard to the issue of racial difference, however, is the fact that the novel presents no simplistic conclusions in this area, and considers the possibility that Hillela's sensuality may be a naive solution. An indication of this is given in the scene of Hillela's first sexual encounter with her cousin Sasha: as a prelude to the contact, Hillela questions Sasha about her looks, emphasizing her physical difference from Sasha and the rest of the family, and speculating on the possibility that she is half Portuguese (*SN*, 41). There are a number of ways of approaching this scene, which seems, at face value, to offer a plausible account of an 'innocent' seduction, as Hillela finds a way of focusing attention on her looks. Beyond the verisimilitude, Hillela's emphasis on the possibility of difference makes the taboo contact between cousins more acceptable, and this introduces the motif of the exotic. Hillela, effectively, presents herself as an exotic object for Sasha, and their first sexual encounter seems to be based on the eroticism of the pure other, the response criticized as a colonizing impulse in (for example) *A World of Strangers* and *The Conservationist*. Such an encounter may represent the polar opposite of the kind of unification which the book seems elsewhere to celebrate through the conjunction of racial and sexual difference, a pure sensuality which depends upon the *preservation* of difference rather than its effacement. It is through details such as this that Gordimer includes debate about the dangers of emphasizing questions of race.

The idea of Hillela as 'other', in fact, is treated in a complex way throughout the novel. Her sexual encounters, far from presenting an easy route to a unified politics, often produce adverse effects. An important episode in this connection involves Hillela's affair with the French Ambassador, after her progression from Tamarisk Beach into the Embassy. Hillela, working as nanny and tutor for the Ambassador's children, becomes a strange erotic focus for him: one day, making love to Hillela, the Ambassador smells his children on her, and feels the two halves of his life have been brought together in a kind of new erotic wholeness (*SN*, 194). This irony of this 'wholeness', which brings into view a misplaced desire, is echoed later when Brad is aroused by Hillela's small daughter singing in his ear in a way which evokes her mother (*SN*, 297). Hillela, at many points in the novel is shown to embody a powerful and positive force for the breaking of restrictive taboos, but here the reverse side of this force comes into focus. Hillela's sexuality, in short, as an emblem of difference, can elicit predatory male desires which, as in these instances where children are part of the focus, are inimical to the idea of the growing family, an idea which assumes considerable importance in the novel's Utopian theme. Desire, without direction, encourages a predatory psychological underside, a point aptly emphasized in the case of the Johannesburg psychiatrist, reduced, through his infatuation with Hillela, to the condition of one of his patients (*SN*, 127).

The *principal* connotation of Hillela's sexuality, however, appears positive: it is through her sexuality that she is able to break restrictive taboos, and inspire in herself and in others productive committed action. It is through sexuality that the novel establishes its positive links between private and public realms, and this depends on allowing the primacy of personal desire and then channelling it in an appropriate way. Even here, however, the novel is far from straightforward in its presentation, showing sexuality in a strange conjunction with revolutionary (especially military) activity. At the time of Whaila's military ambitions to recapture his country, he has a concentration which is somehow more intense than sensuality, and which Hillela experiences as any woman visited by a general on the eve of a great offensive (*SN*, 234). This association between sexuality and the concentration of military pretensions seems to flow through Hillela herself when she is with Reuel, the General of his troops, before the final successful push on his country:

Her sexuality, evident to every man watching her pass as he sat in the bush oiling his gun, or stood at attention for review before the General, was part of the General's Command. For him it seemed to grow, to be revealed with the success of his push towards the real capital. Her small, generous, urging, inventive body was the deserts of success; some bodies are made only for consolation, their sweetness touches with decay. But he had known from the first time he made love with her that that was only an experience of her possibilities – without realizing exactly what these would turn out to be.

Everyone has some cache of trust, while everything else – family love, love of fellow man – takes on suspect interpretations. In her, it seemed to be sexuality. (*SN*, 330)

There are some arresting associations, here, especially the phallic oiling of guns which accompanies the troops' sexual recognition of Hillela: her sexuality is identified as the source of the General's authority, and, in accordance with this image of ownership, her body is then associated with the actual military capture of terrain, in the ambiguous phrase 'the deserts of success', which suggests the African battlefield as well as the unspecified 'rewards' to which the term ostensibly refers. These are uncomfortable associations; the metaphoric connection between the female body and the male appropriation of land is particularly so, since it reverses the criticism made in *The Conservationist* of the colonizing male psyche. The problem of interpretation is wilfully by-passed by the idea of Hillela's 'cache of trust' – her sexuality – which is invulnerable to 'suspect interpretations'. Gordimer seems here to be announcing the need to withhold judgement in a passage which broaches the uncomfortable subject of the means by which revolutionary success must be achieved. There is an attempt, here, to come to terms with the inevitable brutality of political struggle, and to 'humanize' an acceptance of that brutality. Hillela comes to this acceptance herself through analogous means – through her relationship with Whaila: his indication of the necessity to include soft targets in his campaign, which initially inspired Hillela's concern for ordinary people (*SN*, 241–2), is later implicitly accepted in her concern for both the diplomacy and the practicalities of military means, rather than for older theories of ends (*SN*, 254). The transition is tacitly approved by the novel in that it is one that Pauline is never able to make, but the transition is an uncomfortable one, both for Hillela and for the novel, as indicated by the presence of male predatory desire in Reuel's army, elicited, once more, by Hillela.

The question of interpretation is a central problematic in the novel, and this affects the nature of the narrative stance which becomes fundamentally indeterminate: there are different narrators in the novel with differing perspectives. On occasions a third-person narrator will offer a sardonic reflection on certain characters, as when the presence of protest leaflets in Pauline's house is compared to art dealers' catalogues in Olga's, a comparison which clearly ironizes the nature of Pauline's commitment (*SN*, 75). The narrator who deals with Hillela appears as a biographer, attempting to fill lacunae, and frequently having to admit to uncertainties in the life she or he is attempting to chart. An important question with regard to the treatment of Hillela is whether or not it is ironic, a question which is not easy to answer. Cooper, for example, detects no irony in the treatment, while Peck considers the ironic distance between character and narrator suggests disapproval, and results in a damaging ambivalence.[2] Temple-Thurston may be right that the confusion over Hillela is quite deliberate, something which obliges us to avoid the desire to judge or fix Hillela, thereby aligning ourselves with, for example, the restricted Pauline. Yet Temple-Thurston's reading does locate a kind of certainty in the novel, one which requires the suspension of conventional critical judgement in the pursuit of a new paradigm: the idea, here, is that an acceptance of ambiguity will bring us closer to understanding the dynamic of the book's creative energy, pointing us towards a post-apartheid art.[3] If this appeal to suspend judgement is one aspect of the novel's rhetorical design, a paradoxical *reverse* impetus is also present. As I have already indicated over (especially) the question of sexuality, the novel underscores contradictions which cannot be merely accepted, and these contradictions also affect the narrative stance. As in *A Guest of Honour* the novel seems to imply that value lies in addressing, not glossing over contradictions, and Gordimer here evolves a novelistic form that openly registers these contradictions. I think Judie Newman has come closest to accounting for this form, in arguing that, in effect, the ambivalence is irreducible; it combines fervour and irony, and gives the book a mock-historical tone, leaving the question unresolved as to whether 'mock' or 'historical' is the emphasis.[4]

The deliberate tension which produces the overall interpretive problem can be detected in local details where interpretation is consistently highlighted as being problematic. There are occasions in the novel, for example, where the 'biographical' narrator passes on what is merely gossip about Hillela, and these moments – such as the story of Hillela's involvement with Archie Harper's cross-dressing and champagne sessions with Arab boys – such moments, as with this one visualized by white people's gossip, are in tune with the reactionary perceptions of Hillela's sexuality, typified in Pauline's bitchy observation that Hillela's 'field' is men (*SN*, 188, 325). The interpretation of Hillela is also frequently held up as a problem, both for the characters and for the narrator. A facial expression of Hillela's, for example, stays in Joe's mind as uninterpretable (*SN*, 115); Whaila, we discover, knows only an edited version of Hillela's life, and the narrator, late in the novel, expresses uncertainties about Hillela's racial origins, on the basis of her appearance in a photograph (*SN*, 384). The orientation of this biographical narrator is unclear: irony is sometimes present, but not consistently so, appearing as only one position among several that the narrator takes. The ironic treatment appears as an experiment, the narratorial voice 'trying out' a position in the absence of concrete evidence to validate any one position. The clearest example of this irony occurs in, perhaps, the most withdrawn moment of bio-graphical speculation: 'In the lives of the greatest, there are such lacunae – Christ and Shakespeare disappear from and then reappear in the chronicles that documentation and human memory provide.' (*SN*, 120) Even here, however, the irony is double-edged: the manifest absurdity of the com-parison is predominant, but, given the novel's implicit criti-cism of placing and judging, the huge historical importance conventionally assigned to key figures is also questioned. The tacit point is that perhaps there is no good reason why this young woman should not also acquire great historical importance.

The uncertainty of the biographical narrator in the novel stands in contrast to other voices which do seem to be privi-leged in a quite different way. One of these voices is that of Sasha, coming through his letters to Hillela, even though they never reach their destination. These letters contain the kind of historical overview that other aspects of the novel would seem to endorse, as in this extract from Sasha's last letter:

> *There has been madness since the beginning, in the whites. Our great-grandfather Hillel was in it from the moment he came up from the steerage deck in Cape Town harbour . . . It's in the blood you and I share. Since the beginning. Whites couldn't have done what they've done, otherwise. Madness has appeared among blacks in the final stage of repression. It is, in fact, the* unrecognized last act of repression, transferred to them to enact upon themselves. *It is the horrible end of all whites have done.* (*SN*, 374–5; original italics)

The inevitable culpability of colonizing whites in this historical overview is something which is implied in the novel's condem-

nation of even politically 'enlightened' whites, such as Pauline
and Joe. As Sasha indicates, Hillela is also implicated in this
blood-line, and this is something which may help to explain the
ambivalence surrounding her in the novel. The explanation of
internecine black aggression as a kind of metaphorical in-
fection – the madness involved in, and perpetuated by, repression – leaves open the novel's speculations on the possibility of
a black African Utopia.

The most significant of the 'privileged' voices in the novel is
that of Hillela herself, though her voice is not easy to extract
from that of a different, third-person narrator; these crucially
dialogized passages occur in italicized sections which become
more explicitly Hillela's as the novel, and her personal development, progress. An early passage of this kind describes the
young Hillela at the hairdresser's, and clearly vacillates
between a predominant external focalizer and hints of Hillela's
own perspective (*SN*, 14). These hints begin to surface in these
italicized sections as they come to punctuate Hillela's development. There is a process of transition in the novel, though this
is not neatly defined, in which Hillela's voice becomes an
increasingly dominant presence in the dialogized pieces. One
'transitional' passage occurs midway through the novel in
which third-person and first-person perspectives seem to be
deliberately blurred, the pronouns 'she' and 'I' relating to
Hillela being switched with no consistency (*SN*, 189–90). The
confusion is reduced as Hillela's voice comes to the fore, offering, in a later passage, a speculation on the connection between
sexuality and power (*SN*, 230–1). Towards the end of the novel
a passage of italicized narrative interjection is taken over
entirely by Hillela: this is the section headed 'Liberated Territory', which is a kind of stream of consciousness appearing to
present Hillela's sense of her progression through her relationships, culminating in her new attachment to Reuel (*SN*, 327).

The emergence of Hillela's voice, articulating the nature of
her development does provide some kind of interpretive yardstick to set against the novel's general narrative uncertainty,
making an implicit point about the external rendering of an
individual's history: the character does grow in the novel even

though Gordimer ensures that the external narrative voice is not the voice which authoritatively records this growth. It is when the balance switches to Hillela's internal reflections that some authority is established, though even this is uncertain given the variety of voices in the novel and its governing problematic of interpretation.

The problematizing of interpretation in *A Sport of Nature* has important implications for the conclusion of the novel with its Utopian projection of a liberated Africa. Some critics consider this ending to be naive: Peck, for example, is dismissive of what he sees as a simplistic, and hence unconvincing triumph for the liberation movement in South Africa; Cooper also finds the ending reductive since it is posited on the positive personal attributes of Hillela and her General, and an unambiguously triumphant conclusion.[5] There is, certainly, a Utopian element to the novel's conclusion, though there may be significant ways in which this is qualified. The link between Hillela's sexuality and her General's military power seems one such qualification, and perhaps the most important qualification is also a modification of how Hillela's sexuality is perceived: this concerns Hillela's idea of the rainbow family – containing a spectrum of skin shades – which she comes to reject as an aspect of a naive revolutionary perspective.

When Nomzamo is born Hillela is delighted to have produced a black child, a delight which indicates a clear political orientation: Hillela sees her conception of a black child as a gesture of her solidarity with Whaila's cause (*SN*, 220). When she is expecting their second child, this notion of the political significance of conception is extended: this time she does not ask Whaila what colour he thinks the child will be; she wants their many children to form a 'rainbow' (*SN*, 241). This is Hillela's idea, this rainbow family which will be a literal manifestation of inter-racial harmony. After the killing of Whaila, however, Hillela's idealistic notion of the political potential of her maternal role is dispelled. In another passage of italicized narrative, which appears as Hillela's stream-of-consciousness, she realizes that '*There is no rainbow-coloured family ... that kind of love can't be got away with, it's cornered, it's*

easily done away with in two shots from a 9mm. Parabellum pistol.'
(*SN*, 269) This realization – that domestic harmony may be a
travesty of commitment rather than an expression of it – is
concretized in a later section of Hillela's italicized reflections:

*The real family, how they smell. The real rainbow family. The real rainbow
family stinks. The dried liquid of dysentery streaks the legs of babies and old
men and the women smell of their monthly blood. They smell of lack of water.
They smell of lack of food. They smell of bodies blown up by the expanding
gases of their corpses' innards, lying in the bush in the sun.* (*SN*, 291–2)

The brutal reality of oppression and deprivation, Hillela
understands, destroys the dignity of the African family, the
'real rainbow family', when it doesn't threaten its very existence. The naive idealism of the rainbow family is explicitly
rejected, and, accordingly, Hillela occupies a very different
role as Reuel's wife. Her function here is *not* to perpetuate a
blood-line (*SN*, 359), and her place in Reuel's family, though
central, is no longer that of maternal fount: she occupies a
'non-matrilineal centre' of her own invention (*SN*, 360). The
novel, here, withdraws from its simplistic domestic Utopia,
and, in the configuration of the new marriage, it also eschews
the danger of a facile treatment of African sexual politics, and
of a bourgeois domestic solution: Hillela is not to be the chattel
of her husband, one wife among many, for their marriage is
secure, but not sexually exclusive on either side (*SN*, 386–7).

The Utopian drive of the novel is also clearly ironized: the
bleaker side of Reuel's successful military action – bars and
brothels are looted, for example (*SN*, 334) – is glossed over, and
this treatment embodies an implicit irony which is clearer in
the narrator's account of the new regime, which celebrates its
economic rather than its social successes, and which indicates,
wryly, that human rights are 'rarely' violated (*SN*, 383). *Plus ça
change.* This undercutting extends, also, to the question of
sexuality, as Nomzamo, named after Winnie Mandela, fails to
embody and continue the positive aspect of Hillela's vitality,
and, instead, exploits her fashionable African looks in a
modelling career (*SN*, 227).

Yet the irony is not conclusive; the postive Utopian under-
current remains a powerful presence to the end of the novel.

The idealistic unity, and dignified brotherhood of Africa, with which Whaila had been involved, resurfaces in Reuel's articulation of a new holistic politics, which embraces a politics of the body, and which unifies 'work, love-making, religion, politics, economics. We've taken all the things the world keeps in compartments, boxes, and brought them together. A new combination, that's us.' (*SN*, 310) This is a new political matrix, the essence of a continent rather than a single state; it is also the sudden realization of the Utopian realm which Gordimer's micropolitics in all her novels has gently hinted at. The new matrix is represented in the meeting of new black African leaders, including the new black South African president, as the novel closes (*SN*, 391–6). The idealism, here, is tacitly acknowledged, since political specificity is entirely abandoned in the expression of the ethos of an entire continent, an extravagant Utopian gesture to conclude the novel, which really represents the attitude to Utopia outlined earlier by Sasha, that, although Utopia is unattainable, you have to aim for it, in order to fall some way short (*SN*, 217). The novel, as a whole, embodies a self-conscious recognition of the importance of this strategy: the ambivalence between celebration and irony, which is irreducible, is the result of Gordimer's simultaneous delineation of an idealized African politics and its inevitable points of compromise; and this ambivalence is articulated through the novel's re-evaluation of the previous novels, a re-evaluation which both celebrates the ideological orientation, and ironizes the shortcomings of the earlier work. The reassessment is conducted, principally, through the exaggerated construction of Hillela, a semi-parody of the typical Gordimer protagonist, and this problematizes the question of judgement itself.

MY SON'S STORY

My Son's Story sees Gordimer attempting a new artistic direction, yet again, though, as a self-conscious, metafictional work, it belongs to the same phase as *A Sport of Nature*. The novel turns on familiar concerns – the connections between public and private realms of action; the function of literature – but there is here a new conjunction: the ideologies previously examined by Gordimer are shown to have different ramifications for the family of 'coloured' activists treated in the novel. The origins of Sonny and his family are ambiguous, and Gordimer's own comments on this suggest a desire to create a family of immediate relevance to all South Africans, an attempt to 'cover all colours and no colour' by eschewing racial categorization.[6] This seems to be an implicit recognition that the promotion of racial difference is no longer an appropriate strategy, and in this respect the novel confirms the rejection of Hillela's progression beyond the naive phase in which difference was to be marvelled at. But if the presentation of family in *My Son's Story* seems notionally Utopian – the projection of a new typicality for a post-apartheid South Africa – the novel also undercuts this gesture by delineating the struggles of people whose lives have been (and remain) dominated by racial prejudice. Commitment for these characters involves a catastrophic interference between public and private identities; and, through the authorial persona of Will – the 'son' whose story this is – the novel offers a bleak indictment of a traditional ideology of the 'improving' function of literature, an indictment which also raises crucial questions about the possibility of intervention through artistic production. The treatment of these issues represents a reconsideration of their implications.

As does *A Sport of Nature*, *My Son's Story* offers a reconsideration of how private relationships fit public requirements, and the relationship between Sonny and his white mistress Hannah is the fulcrum of this concern. Their relationship, in its origins, seems to represent an ideal fusion of public and private, a union of people committed to the same cause, who can turn from caresses to political discussion because, in them, it is 'all one' (*MSS*, 84). This unity, or oneness, is announced several times in the narrative, most explicitly when we read that, between them, there is a unity of sexual happiness and political commitment (*MSS*, 125). But this symbiotic relationship is unstable, something which is hinted at in the later reformulation of this idea, that cause and lover are transposable (*MSS*, 223). The cause, and his lover, are both capable of causing Sonny distress as well as a sense of happiness and purpose; beyond this, the point is that both 'objects' of his commitment cannot always contain or satisfy his personal desire. This suggests that the two can become misaligned, that the cause can negate the requirements of the personal relationship, as does occur in the novel. There is also the suggestion that the cause is like a lover, capable of rejecting as well as embracing, of embittering as well as satisfying.

An important aspect of Sonny's initial fascination with Hannah is his delight at her ability to quote – from both literary and political texts – especially as a way of communicating clandestinely while visiting him in prison. The ideology of 'improvement' through literature, a powerful formative force on Sonny's consciousness, also determines his idea of Hannah. Her use of the phrase (from *As You Like It*) 'sermons in stones' (*MSS*, 49) causes particular delight for Sonny, and it becomes elevated in his mind to something of a private love-tag. Later in the novel, Hannah gives the phrase to a colleague to use as a password, to ensure Sonny will offer him shelter, an instance which lays bare the disjunction between the private and the public through Sonny's wounded reaction (*MSS*, 164). The contradiction within Sonny is apparent here, the phrase, 'sermons in stones, and good in everything', initially used by Hannah for political expediency, is appropriately re-used by her in the same way, despite Sonny's appropriation of it as an instance of personal/literary communion. The recurring phrase 'needing Hannah' emphasizes Sonny's dependence on her, and his later desire to create a parallel dependence in her – 'needing Sonny' (*MSS*, 216) – implies an inner lack which the relationship cannot resolve: the self-serving need to create a need is a vicious circle of private emotion.

Notionally, the 'anti-bourgeois' idea of Sonny's affair is an appropriate revolutionary challenge to the family unit; yet it is his relationship with Hannah that, ultimately, channels the aspects of bourgeois life which reside in his consciousness, while his family all progress in an opposite direction, quite opposed to the inward-looking archetypal family cell. A scene which crystallizes Sonny's inner confusion is that of the cleansing of the graves, a demonstration and memorial for nine youngsters shot by the police (*MSS*, 99).[7] The event results in more shooting, and a crisis moment for Sonny in which, instead of staying to help with the wounded, he runs with Hannah from the guns. This act is later articulated – through Sonny's perspective – as the saving of himself through the preservation of Hannah (*MSS*, 126). In the chaotic scene a young man is shot and falls before Hannah and Sonny who continue to flee the shots, despite an initial impulse to stay and help. The man has been shot in the head, as is clear when a distraught woman attempts to revive him: blood runs from his hair, obscuring the slogan on his T-shirt, '*An Injury To One Is An Injury To All*' (*MSS*, 117). The solidarity of the slogan is evidently undermined by the fleeing lovers.

Sonny's confusion becomes a crisis of identity, a crisis examined in this important passage:

> The construction he had skilfully made of his life was uninhabitable, his categories were useless, nothing fitted his need. *Needing Hannah*. His attraction to Hannah belonged to the distorted place and time in which they – all of them – he, Aila, Hannah, lived. With Hannah there was the sexuality of commitment; for commitment implies danger, and the blind primal instinct is to ensure the species survives in circumstances of danger, even when the individual animal dies or the plant has had its season. In this freak displacement, the biological drive of his life, which belonged with his wife and the children he'd begotten, was diverted to his lover. He and Hannah begot no child; the revolutionary movement was to be their survivor. The excitement of their mating was for that.
>
> But Aila was the revolutionary, now. (*MSS*, 241–2)

This is a complex passage which occurs after Sonny and Hannah have broken up, and she has gone to work abroad, and after the subversive activities of both Baby and Aila are known. The association between sexual and revolutionary liberation has broken down since Sonny's 'family unit' has proved to be a source of revolutionary commitment, rather than a reactionary building block: there was nothing, here, to react against. It may be that Sonny's affair is never explicitly predicated on this opposition, but the switching of terminology in this passage suggests that such an opposition is to be questioned: Sonny's 'biological drive' has been channelled in a direction of sterility, while Aila is able to keep, at least, some semblance of family progression in her life *through* her commitment, as is indicated by her exile with Baby and her granddaughter. This is a matter of planning, a family nucleus which dovetails with political commitment, rather than the expression of the biological drive it resembles. Or, more precisely, this new family nucleus represents a consciously socialized version of the familial biological drive, the synthesis which Sonny fails to achieve. The forces operating on Sonny have caused the 'freak displacement' in which his energies have been dissipated in an ephemeral affair, while the female members of his family have managed to salvage an ongoing communal sense of themselves. It may be that Will's apparently obsessive and oedipal reflections on the attraction that blonde white women have for black men is significant, here: the stereotypical notion of this attraction, which Will likens to a disease, may be the kind of transgression that years of apartheid rule have made subliminally compelling (at least symbolically so, in terms of Sonny's reactions in the novel). Here Gordimer returns to a theme dealt with in *Occasion for Loving* – in the consideration of Gideon's attraction to Ann – and makes her critique more explicit. Sonny's compulsive attraction can be seen to be the 'freak' product of a repressive ideology, much as another restrictive ideology – Sonny's idea of literature – also colours his feelings for Hannah, blinding him to the cultural hegemony embodied in this aspect of her appeal.

Although there are hints of a new, productive 'family' existence for Aila and Baby in exile, there remains the issue of the dissolution of the original family unit. Of particular significance here is the gender divide: the failure of the men, Sonny and Will, left behind amid the smouldering ruins of their burnt-out house in a hostile white suburb. The decision to move to the white suburb – a sponsored political challenge, which is eventually confronted with violence – is an initial undermining of the family's standing: Sonny's family is required to function as a gestural challenge, divorced from the possibility of genuine community. It is this dislocation – in which the geographical aspect is merely one part of a broader psychological dislocation – which results in the rupture of this family; and Sonny's decision to relocate is clearly not the cause of the problem, but rather the symptom of – in forming an appropriate reaction to – a broader cause: that of a repressive state structure.

Considerations of social space recur in the novel and they are intimately related to the presentations of the identity of Sonny and those of his family. In the new house in the white suburb the family dynamic appears to change, as it is now possible to co-exist in the larger house with the luxury of privacy. From Will's perspective this is a way in which his parents (especially his mother) conceal from themselves their marital estrangement:

If she's busy in another room he's sometimes home for half an hour or so before she knows he's there. In her innocence she takes this as one of the benefits we've won for ourselves, for the cause, for freedom: this house has privacy, it's not like the old one in the ghetto where we were together all the time. It's a space he deserves. *It's something we have to be grateful to him for.* He's been to prison for principles like this. (*MSS*, 44; original italics)

Will's early perspective may include an element of impercipience regarding his mother's knowledge of Sonny's affair, but, reading against Will's heavy irony, this passage fittingly associates the estrangement with the new, sterile social space that facilitates isolation. An important point emerges from this: the old 'ghetto' house embodied social possibility, by enforcing a sense of community, whereas this new bourgeois space embodies and creates social separation. Will misunderstands the nature of the 'freedom' and the 'space' which is being fought for: the idea of a radical social restructuring is not to repopulate existing social space, but to effect its break-up and rearrangement. The infiltration of the white suburb is an interim phase, a means rather than an end in itself, and the larger objective is actually fulfilled by the eventual destruction of the house.

The connections between space, power and community are made in this resonant passage which occurs during the cleansing of the graves episode, in which white activists join with blacks in the political demonstration:

The blacks were accustomed to closeness. In queues for transport, for work permits, for housing allocation, for all the stamped paper that authorized their lives; loaded into overcrowded trains and buses to take them back and forth across the veld, fitting a family into one room, they cannot keep the outline of space – another, invisible skin – whites project around themselves, distanced from each other in everything but sexual and parental intimacy. But now in the graveyard the people from the combis were dispersed from one another and the spatial aura they instinctively kept, and pressed into a single, vast, stirring being with the people of the township. The nun was close against the breast of a man. A black child with his little naked penis waggling under a shirt clung to the leg of a professor. A woman's French perfume and the sweat of a drunk merged as if one breath came from them. And yet it was not alarming for the whites; in fact, an old fear of closeness, of the odours and heat of other flesh, was gone. One ultimate body of bodies was inhaling and exhaling in the single diastole and systole, and above was the freedom of the great open afternoon sky. (*MSS*, 110)

Gordimer here returns to the notion of a black heterotopia, first broached in *The Lying Days*. In this passage spatial repression is shown, paradoxically, to have created the possibility of a community, an integrated body politic: it is a community of proximity, a vitality which is alien to the privileged whites who are, nevertheless, soon infected by its sense of possibility. A heterotopia is a space which is connected to all other social sites, in a contradictory relationship. The sites of black urbanization in South Africa – symbolically represented here – clearly fulfil this function since they are connected to the other sites defined in the nation's economic hegemony, sites which they also challenge or contradict. Yet if uncontrollable black urbanization represents a challenge to the racist social organization of South Africa, it does so, perhaps, through the formation of sites which could be termed *homo*topias as much as Foucauldian heterotopias: the challenge is a unification of a repressed, collective identity. The image of unity in this body

politic – 'the single diastole and systole' – is made to adumbrate
the nation's possibility, in the image of 'the freedom of the
great open afternoon sky', an unlimited space above this land,
and above these people, presumably heralding the change they
will bring to it; and if a homotopian impulse generates the'
communal possibility, it opens out into something non-
sectarian: significantly, whites feel themselves to be *contained
within* this heterotopia/homotopia, for the first time in Gordimer's work. However, the fleeting vision of an alternative
future is dissipated by the chaotic break-up of the protest, in
which the self-absorption of Sonny and Hannah effaces their
communal impulse.

If there is a clear hint of political change in *My Son's Story*,
however, the novel still maintains a steady gaze on the interim
phase, on the personal dissolution of Sonny and Will, examples
of the human sacrifice that the period of resistance must entail.
Other instances of the control of social space indicate the
exclusion of Sonny from the new dawn, as when the idyll of
Hannah's rented cottage garden oppresses Sonny with its arti-
ficial beauty and greenery which screens 'the smashed symmetry of shot bodies' (*MSS*, 143): there is a violence embodied in
the symmetry of the garden, the domain of the rich white man,
a violence which produces the parallel asymmetry in order that
the domain may be preserved. A description of the spatial
discrimination which has governed the lives of Sonny and his
family ends with an account of Sonny's exclusion from the
library:

The lover of Shakespeare never had the right to enter the municipal
library and so did not so much as think about it while white people
came out before him with books under their arms; he did not
recognize what the building represented for him, with its municipal
coat of arms and motto above the pillared entrance: CARPE DIEM.
(*MSS*, 12)

This is the edifice of cultural exclusion, which equates power
with opportunism, available for whosoever can enter these
portals and 'seize the day'. It is the importance of this ideology
which Sonny comes to recognize, rightly understanding that
advancement is facilitated through the acquisition of certain

cultural knowledge. Sonny's problem is that he is never able to separate his idea of 'improvement' from a complicity with the cultural hegemony – the opportunism – which the incipient black community spirit implicitly challenges. This, again, may be another instance of the interim phase, a necessary working within the modes of production, which Sonny also encourages in Will by transposing onto him his idea of improvement and the importance of literature. When, at the end of the novel, Will effectively announces himself as the 'author' of the novel, we realize – as the title has indicated all along – that he has accepted his father's legacy, despite the resentment he has continually felt towards his father's cultural elitism. This may imply that Will accepts the mantle of scribe as a compromise, as a necessary act of complicity in finding a voice that will challenge the hegemonic system in a language it can recognize. But there may be something beyond this, an advancement beyond Sonny's confusion about the relationship between culture and power; a more explicit understanding on Will's part, perhaps, of the nature and implications of the compromise that is being made. In one sense this has to be the case, since Will is identified as the 'author' of the novel which can be made to reveal just such an understanding. There are also instances in the novel which indicate the process of this advancement, as in Will's account of his father's reaction to the wreck of their burnt-out house, when, after his apparent sense of loss,

the old rhetoric took up the opportunity. We can't be burned out, he said, we're that bird, you know, it's called the phoenix, that always rises again from the ashes. Prison won't keep us out. Petrol bombs won't get rid of us. This street – this whole country is ours to live in. Fire won't stop me. And it won't stop you.

Flocks of papery cinders were drifting, floating about us – beds, clothing – his books?

The smell of smoke, that was the smell of her.

The smell of destruction, of what has been consumed, that he first brought into that house. (*MSS*, 274)

Sonny's own distaste for rhetoric, even for the articulation of ideas with which he is in agreement (*MSS*, 192), casts an ironic doubt over this stubborn outburst, which is merely automatic, gestural. The infiltration of the white suburb has here met its anticipated confrontation, and the interim phase is passed, just as the memory of Hannah, the smoker, appears to be simultaneously exorcised in this destruction. Most importantly, perhaps, the books have also been destroyed, implying an accompanying exorcism of Sonny's 'idea' of literature, the appeal with which Hannah is associated. Sonny, it appears, is restricted in this conclusion, a victim of the interregnum, unable to progress beyond a gestural language of confrontation.

Here there is the first part of an extended allusion to the ending of Gordimer's first novel, *The Lying Days*, where Helen Shaw's 'phoenix illusion' of accepting disillusionment as a potential new beginning is associated with her intention of returning one day to face her country's problems; the association establishes an ironic distance between character and (more mature) character-narrator (*LD*, 367). Sonny's 'phoenix speech' is illusory in that it fails to register the element of salutary exorcism in the destruction before him; but his illusion concerns strategies and attitudes of practical resistance, casting an ironic shadow on the free choice of Helen in *The Lying Days* as to whether she will commit at all.

For Will, at the end of the novel, there is a partial advancement, but a compromise and restriction, too. Will's situation is indicated in the novel's final passage: 'What he did – my father – made me a writer. Do I have to thank him for that? Why couldn't I have been something else? I am a writer and this is my first book – that I can never publish.' (*MSS*, 277) The overt metafictional conclusion to the novel raises important questions about the function of literature, questions specific to the South African context. The passage quoted represents a complex conjunction. Will's reluctance at his 'enforced' vocation stems from the appropriation of his personal life for public need: as for Sonny, the interregnum demands this sacrifice from him. The final line presents an important ambiguity: the avowed impossibility of publication suggests a paradoxical reluctance to make the sacrifice, which has in fact already been made. It also suggests, quite apart from the spectre of censorship, an impossibility imposed by political expediency, the need to protect the sensitive details of the activism Will has described in his translation of his family's 'reality' into fiction. Here there is a tacit acknowledgement on Gordimer's part of the effects of racial discrimination on literary production: the freedom she has to create a fictional representation of the forces operating on a family of committed activists, is a freedom and a luxury which could not have been enjoyed by the family she has created.

Here Gordimer alludes again to her first novel, *The Lying Days*, recreating the effect used at the end of that novel when the (semi-autobiographical) narrator, Helen Shaw, also announces herself as the 'author'. The end of *My Son's Story* forms an ironic contrast with that luxurious moment of self-definition which had implied an emerging bridge between world and text for the young white writer finding a voice. The metafictional moment here emphasizes the impossibility of such a bridge for Will, the kind of South African 'author' who has had to be invented by a privileged white. There is a fitting sense of closure in Gordimer's inclusion of such a self-reflexive moment in *My Son's Story*, the last of her novels to be written in the apartheid era: her novel articulates its point about South African literary identity and literary production by re-evaluating the metafictional ending of her first novel, written in the early days of Nationalist rule.

CHAPTER 6

The short stories

Gordimer's reputation as a short story writer is difficult to pin down. Especially since Robert Haugh's study privileged the 'poetic intensity' of the short stories above the novels, which he regarded as relative failures, the stories have often been seen as examples of a kind of technical perfection, or aesthetic completeness, which some critics deem to be a feature of fully realized short stories.[1] My view of the Gordimer stories is that they work *ironically* with this notion of 'aesthetic completeness' in the tradition of key modernist innovators such as Joyce and Mansfield. The importance of Gordimer's contribution to the short story genre is not in doubt, even if the nature of this contribution (and, consequently, the nature of short story poetics) is a matter for debate. The major problem with the Gordimer stories, however, is manifested through the inevitable comparison with the novels.

Establishing an overview of a writer's short story oeuvre is always a difficult venture, particularly if clear stages of development are sought, and this is especially the case with a writer like Gordimer who has produced a series of major novels: the short stories may appear as a more occasional means of expression. This does make it difficult to trace lines of development, and, if such lines are found, one has to consider carefully how much significance should be attached to them. In contrast to Haugh's study, subsequent books on Gordimer have tended to concentrate on the novels while ignoring the stories: Clingman considers the stories to be of far less significance, for example, while Newman omits them for evident reasons of space, but also because of their quite specific narrative qualities which

indicate that they require a separate study.[2] Barbara Eckstein
may be right when she argues that the short stories do not
represent the same kind of immediate response to the political
context embodied in the novels. Eckstein feels that, whereas
the novels move away from the personal towards a more
complete social vision, the short stories, from the 1950s
onwards, have presented problematic ambiguities in the interaction of self and other.[3] The short stories may evince a relative
lack of contextualization, but the element of ambiguity can be
seen as more purposive in Gordimer's stories than this criticism
suggests: ambiguity, a fundamental property of the short story
genre, is a property that Gordimer pointedly exploits. Another
critic, Michael King, stands opposed to Eckstein on the question of development, and considers Clingman's conception of a
developing consciousness of history in the novels to be applic-
able also to the short stories.[4] Something of this developing
consciousness does emerge from a chronological reading of
Gordimer's story collections, but this should not be over-
emphasized. The development, which is not a purely linear
one through Gordimer's career, can be illustrated with reference to particular points of technical advancement.

Clingman's own comments on the short stories, however,
raise a further question about the properties of the genre,
which is seminal to this discussion. He acknowledges that the
stories *do*, indeed, have a connection with social developments,
but he makes a striking evaluative distinction based on formal
generic properties, and it is this distinction which is important
to address:

To put it simply, the novel is both more intensive and more extensive
historically than the short story could ever be; it is a question of
degree, but one that approaches 'kind'. Gordimer's short stories,
while often rooted in an identifiable social world, turn in general on
human intricacies of a psychological or emotional nature, and this is
the basis of the short story as a form. Also, because the stories are by
definition shorter, and expressions of a more coherent moment of
conception, they are more easily susceptible to what is normally
called aesthetic 'perfection', a feature for which Gordimer's stories
are rightly renowned. For us, however, this is a disability; we need
the significant contradictions, silences and gaps revealed in the longer

work. And the novels, due to the sheer expanse of their exploration in space and time, of necessity investigate their social and historical situation in greater depth and at greater length.[5]

There is a general point of comparison here which is illuminating: the Gordimer novels, without doubt, do offer scope for a more involved treatment of social and historical issues than do the stories; but the formal properties to which this distinction is attributed, as I have indicated, are problematic. Clingman reproduces an aesthetic of the short story – based on notions of its unity, or 'aesthetic perfection' – commonly found in traditional short story criticism. I have taken issue with this at length elsewhere, arguing that the disunifying and disruptive potential of the short story was significantly developed during the modernist period; and this is important since Gordimer's stories, in their turn, are influenced by, and develop, modernist innovations.[6] This means that the 'significant contradictions, silences and gaps' which Clingman celebrates in the novels, are to be found in the stories as well. It may be that the effect of these disruptive elements is less marked in shorter fiction than it is in the novels, but the aesthetic seems to me to be similar in both cases. Also problematic is Clingman's assertion that short stories 'turn in general on human intricacies of a psychological or emotional nature'. This is an astute observation, but it suggests a link between Gordimer's novels and her stories, rather than the distinction Clingman seeks to make: both investigate the public through the private, the political ramifications of personal actions, even though the novels may develop the embryonic kind of investigations the stories can offer. The (justified) privileging of the novels over the stories seems a matter of degree *rather than* one of kind.

Gordimer's literary influences – and intertextual references – are various, and can supply a basis for the evaluation of the short stories. Critics have sometimes discerned a manifest intertextuality in her writing, and this applies to the stories as well as the novels. Viktor Link, for example, considers 'The African Magician' (1965) to be a commentary on – and a partial retelling of – Conrad's *Heart of Darkness*.[7] One can also discern an implicit reference to the Conrad novella in 'Inkalamu's

Place' (1971). Other, more overtly innovative modernist writers have exerted their influence over Gordimer: the author has herself acknowledged D. H. Lawrence as an important early influence, for example.[8] The affinity between Gordimer and Mansfield – as well as Gordimer's admiration for her modernist precursor – is recorded in the anonymous 'Foreword' to Gordimer's first book, the short story collection *Face to Face* (*FF*, 5). In interview, however, Gordimer has cast doubt upon the importance of Mansfield as an influence on her work, claiming, in 1978, that she finds her almost unreadable as a consequence of her femininity and breathlessness.[9] This seems to be a way of taking issue with belittling comparisons based on a conception of Mansfield as a delicate female stylist: Haugh, for example, had written in his survey (1974) of Gordimer as 'a stylist, a gem-polisher', comparable to Mansfield in the ability to create a 'shimmering immediacy of image'.[10] Mansfield, however, should be seen as a modernist innovator who (with Joyce) is a crucial formative influence on the modern short story, using it as a site for disruptive and dissonant modernist expression quite consciously opposed to the notion of aesthetic perfection in the genre. Gordimer acknowledges the influence of Mansfield on her as a young writer;[11] but affinities are discernible beyond her earliest stories, indicating that she has continued and appropriated Mansfield's important generic innovations, even if there is not a continuing and direct influence.

One example of these affinities is 'The Gentle Art' (1960), an account of a Johannesburg couple, the McEwens, taken as guests on a crocodile hunt. When the forehead of a young crocodile is blown apart by a hunter's gun, from point-blank range, Vivien McEwen, the young wife, finds herself intoxicated by the display of power. This recalls the children's reactions to the duck-decapitation scene in Mansfield's 'Prelude', as well as the confused responses of the title character in Mansfield's 'Millie'. Millie finds herself delighted at the sight of a young fugitive she had been harbouring being chased by a 'posse', including her husband, armed with guns; and this instance of the maternal being effaced by female excitement at male violence is replicated in the response of Vivien in 'The Gentle Art', who, significantly, cannot comprehend the long suffering mood of Mrs Baird, the wife of the successful hunter. Another striking parallel is that between 'A Company of Laughing Faces' (1965) and Mansfield's 'The Garden Party', for both stories involve an episode of significant adolescent development, occasioned by the experience of death, in which a daughter begins to grow beyond the restrictive social parameters of her mother.[12]

Gordimer's importance as a short-story writer stems from her ability to utilize certain formal properties of the genre. One such property is ambiguity, a quality which Gordimer continually exploits in her short stories, extending the challenge to the 'single effect' or simple revelation short story; a challenge associated with (especially) Joyce and Mansfield. Gordimer's stories display a consciousness that a particular strength of the short story – far from making a single point – is how it is able to yoke together different possibilities in a challenging, yet rewarding conjunction. This quality of *productive ambiguity* is apparent in Gordimer's earliest stories: 'Is There Nowhere Else Where We Can Meet' (1949), for example, generates its effects through a resonant ambiguity. This brief story describes an encounter between a black man and a white woman walking on a road: after a tussle, the man robs the woman of her bag and her parcel. The ambiguity is suggested by the ironic title, which suggests the desire for a more intimate contact that a situation of material disparity prevents, and this title does jar with the narrative perspective of the story, focalized through the woman, which replicates her fear of, and repulsion from, the black man. In this sense the story is restricted by its own narrative perspective, unable to begin to formulate the desired 'somewhere else'. The earlier stories are restricted by this kind of limited narrative perspective, but there is still scope for Gordimer to create resonantly ambiguous scenarios.

This quality of productive ambiguity is often most evident in the resonant ending of a short story, as is the case with 'The Catch' (1952); the story is presented from the perspective of a young white couple on holiday in a coastal resort who befriend (tentatively) an Indian – on his two weeks' annual leave from work at a nearby sugar refinery – who spends each day fishing. This delicate, inter-racial contact is boosted when the Indian catches an enormous salmon which the husband and wife insist on photographing for posterity. Later in the day three friends visit the couple unexpectedly, and they fall back into the habits of their own racial 'enclave'. On their way to Durban for a night out, the five whites drive past the Indian, unable to carry home his great fish. The husband and wife are obliged to offer their new friend a lift, despite the tacit resentment of their companions, and only the wife attempts to converse with him. Her crucial remark, which the new passenger repeats, as its metaphorical connotation accrues, indicates that the big catch is proving to be more trouble than it's worth (*SS*, 41). The story ends when the whites are rid of the Indian, and the wife attempts to re-establish 'normality' with their scandalized friends:

'The things we get ourselves into!' she said, spreading her skirt on the seat. She shook her head and laughed a high laugh. 'Shame! The poor thing! What on earth can he do with the great smelly fish now?'

And as if her words had touched some chord of hysteria in them all, they began to laugh, and she laughed with them, laughed till she cried, gasping all the while, 'But what have I said? Why are you laughing at me? What have I said?' (*SS*, 42)

The significance of this resonant ending is indicated in the story's title which, as Kevin Magerey suggests, operates as a pun on several levels; particularly important, here, is the implication that, for the whites, their new Indian friend comes with a 'catch': he is more trouble than he's worth to them, just as his own catch is to him. As Magerey suggests, the laughter indicates a subconscious recognition of the parallel.[13]

Another aspect of the 'catch', of course, is that this Indian man's new white friends prove to be more trouble to him than they are worth, in their insulting discomfort in the friendship. The title pun indicates the different elements embraced by the story, and drawn together in the resonant ending in which the racist, contradictory behaviour of the whites gives rise to an hysterical outburst which exposes the personal schism. In the final scene the wife is both annoyed at the rudeness of her white companions, and irritated at having to talk to the Indian in this situation. The social force of peer group pressure enforces the contradiction: the couple must repress a full and open acknowledgement of an acquaintance which transgresses the dictates of social division, and find themselves pulled in both directions without fully understanding why. The clearest aspect of the story's resonant ending is the slightly crazy expression of the mutually exclusive responses. A sense of personal duality is expressed through the formal structure, in a moment in which conflicting forces are revealed operating simultaneously.

In 'The Catch' the contradictory behaviour of the ruling class is represented in the story's form – in its resonant ending. Of course, one might expect contradictions to emerge in the Gordimer stories concerning the reactions of white South Africans. The same principle can be applied, however, to the stories dealing with political activism. A good example here is the story 'Some Monday for Sure' (1965), in which Gordimer deals with the ambition and ultimate sense of dispossession of a cell of black activists, forced into exile, after their holdup of a truck carrying explosives for the mining industry. The piece is marked by a duality of tone, a duality also reflected in its form. A tension between optimism and disillusionment pervades the story by virtue of a narrative stance containing different accents: it both engages with the narrator, Willie's, enthusiasm, and yet exposes his naivety through an implied authorial distantiation and critique. Willie's thought that 'on Monday, or another Monday, the truck will stop down there and all the stuff will be taken away and . . . we'll win forever' represents an optimism which is captured in the cadence of his narrative (*SS*, 268); yet also significant here are the lack of specificity, and the imagined perfect stability of the future society. These are aspects of a dream evidently divorced from the process of political change: the process of achieving victory after an explosives robbery involves the key stage which Willie eschews, that of a sustained bombing campaign. His uncertainty in this area reveals a key contradiction, that of using violence in the short term to establish long-term political stability. Yet, there is also a satisfaction in this strategy which, as the story tacitly acknowledges, is the only one available.

The overall organization of the story encapsulates its ambivalence which is clearly apparent at the ending where Willie's dream of an amenable future persists, as he imagines his exile in Dar es Salaam is no more than a stopover on the road to victory:

> One day I suppose I'll remember it and tell my wife I stayed three years there, once. I walk and walk, along the bay, past the shops and hotels and the German church and the big bank, and through the mud streets between old shacks and stalls. It's dark there and full of other walking shapes as I wander past light coming from the cracks in the walls, where the people are in their homes. (*SS*, 274)

The final image – one of (relative) domestic comfort from which the narrator is excluded – emphasizes the illusion. The narrative has reached a point, in terms of events, where the possibilities for future prosperity seem to have diminished, for Willie, so the progression of the story – in epical terms – runs counter to the lyricism of Willie's dream. The tension between these elements, lyrical and epical, accounts for the resonance of this poignant ending in which aspirations are shown to endure, though badly tarnished.[14]

'An Intruder' (1971), offers another example of Gordimer's use of a pointed ambiguity. This is a story of male sexual repression, of how a condescending paternalistic male perspective is allied to a demanding and misogynistic sexual appetite. An objective correlative for the effects of this repression is offered when the couple in the story – the womanizing James, and his new wife-victim Marie, whom he treats like a pet – return home after a late Saturday-night drinking session. The following morning Marie finds the house ransacked, indicating an intruder. Nothing has been stolen, but everything has been disordered or defaced, including her discarded underwear which has been rearranged as part of an 'obscene collage' (*SS*, 327). There are no signs of a break-in, and the story ends with the indication that Marie – now pregnant – is shocked into an awareness of her situation: she is described as suddenly having grown-up (*SS*, 328). Karen Lazar argues that the intruder is James, the external manifestation of sexual violence being merely an exaggerated representation of legitimized male intrusions on the safety and the peace of mind of women.[15] Lazar also cites the alternative reading of Dorothy Driver, in which it is Marie's 'maddened self' which, possibly, emerges. Actually, Driver considers that this positive feminist possibility is ultimately negated by an ending which asserts joint responsibility: Driver argues that the couple are presented as a unit, both implicated in the latent violence of their relationship.[16] It seems to me that the readings of Lazar and Driver are both invited by the resonant ending of this story which focuses the nature of James's repression, and also highlights the need for its overthrow. The element of withdrawal which Driver detects, from the unequivocal feminist message, is in tune with this effect of productive ambiguity, and it also ensures a wider significance: the fact that husband and wife are both implicated in a system of repression indicates how white female passivity colludes with a system of racial oppression.

In the stories discussed so far there is something static: the resonant (and pointed) ambiguities expose contradictions through disruptive formal gestures, but the omniscient narrative voice is constrained by a predictable stability. In other stories, however, Gordimer utilizes an additional short story property: an unreliable or incomplete narrative perspective which extends her possibilities in the genre.

Gordimer's interest in this capacity of the short story is evident throughout her writing career, though this is a feature that can be seen operating most effectively in more recent works. An early story which is interesting in this regard, and also for its intertextual features, is 'Another Part of the Sky' (1952). The story has as its focalizer a reformatory principal, working in a 'reforming' system based on an ideology of Christian-liberalism. Alan Paton's famous novel of this era, *Cry, the Beloved Country* (1948), appears to offer the selfsame ideology as a way forward for South Africa, and Gordimer appears to be alluding to Paton's work: Paton was, himself, a reformatory principal (before retiring to work as a writer full time), and a main focus of *Cry, the Beloved Country* is reconsidered in Gordimer's story. Paton's novel concerns the search of the rural black clergyman, The Reverend Kumalo, for (in particular) his son, in Johannesburg. The son, who has turned to a life of crime, kills a white man, having been released from a reformatory. Paton's novel consciously constructs a plot worthy of a classic nineteenth-century novel, yet the high-Biblical diction of the work is explicitly anti-realistic, creating a powerful dissonance. The novel's affinities with parable – the implication that a positive lesson can be learned from the novel's events; the uniform quasi-Biblical diction which implies faith in an order temporarily concealed – these affinities locate the novel as an organic statement of Christian-liberalism. The principal literary effect of *Cry, the Beloved Country*, however, derives from its subtext: the brutality of the political reality which is not properly addressed in the novel's diction, or its implied grounds for hope. One is led to conclude (especially reading with hindsight) that this is not a language that can properly deal with its subject, hence the unsettling resonance of the work, arising from a dissonance between the importance of the diagnosed subject, and the naivety of the proffered way forward.

In 'Another Part of the Sky' Gordimer does not have the advantage of analyzing the liberal ideology with hindsight, yet is able to subject it to a critical analysis. As with the early novels, this story indicates Gordimer's initial attempts to think beyond the inadequacies of the liberal position in South Africa. Her focalizer in the story anguishes over an escaped inmate, suspected of robbing and assaulting an old woman. His preoccupation with how the system may have failed in this instance means that when he is woken by his distraught black assistant Ngubane, whose brother has been killed travelling on the outside of a bus, this white reformer, anticipating news of his runaway, cannot immediately deal with the new crisis. The story ends with a moment of realization for the reformer:

If there is room for the boy, there is no room for Ngubane. This conscience like a hunger that made him want to answer for all the faces, all the imploring of the dispossessed – what could he do with it?

What had he done with it? The man who pulled down prison walls and grew geraniums . . .

He did not know how he would live through this moment of knowledge, and he closed his lids against the bitter juice that they seemed to crush out, burning, from his eyes. (*SVS*, 154–5)

This is a personification of classic liberal humanism in crisis: the burden of a particular kind of reverence for the individual is too great, since there are too many individuals with problems (a whole nation dispossessed, is the implication) for personal, paternalistic attentions. The protagonist here (also a prison reformer, like Paton himself) ends having to face the bankruptcy of the ideology of liberal-paternalism. The story, in effect, explicitly invites an interpretation which corresponds to my re-reading with hindsight of *Cry, the Beloved Country*.

One of the most significant uses of narrative voice in Gordimer is that which represents the consciousness of the reactionary white landowner. This line of development, which culminates in the character Mehring in *The Conservationist*, can be traced back to some early stories. The story 'No Luck To-night' (1949), from the first collection, is about the 'Civic Guard' trying to catch the narrator's black servants brewing illicit beer. The narrator, who, with his wife, colludes with the concealment of the illicit brew, makes a partial advancement beyond an initially utilitarian position: that of desiring to protect servants from prosecution to obviate the inconvenience of training new ones. In conversation with one of the Civic Guard, the narrator, on being apprised of the money to be made in illicit brewing, acknowledges to himself the attractiveness of the proposition to a servant, on the basis of how little a servant (his own, presumably) is paid. This Sergeant-Major is also prepared to reveal significant contradictions in the policy he is enforcing: having given the government line that drinking produces violence and crime, he then admits that the government actually gathers significant monies from the fines imposed. This explains why no measures are taken to prevent the brewing in the first place – by restricting sales of yeast, for example (*FF*, 138, 142). The story is notable for encapsulating a system of social repression reinforced by economics into a very few pages. The story's narrator is confronted with the fact of this system, but chooses to reinforce it, rather than attempt to reform it, at the story's end: realizing that his wife has helped conceal the tin of beer in her sewing work-basket, he reflects that his servant, Letty, (who had been pretending to do some mending work, to help deceive the Civic Guard) should probably do the mending work in future. Tacitly, the narrator expects a pay-off from Letty for the collusion, thus extending, and unequivocally aligning himself with, the system of economic and social repression. This explicit alignment – between the repressive system and the story's narrative perspective – makes 'No Luck To-night' a deceptively brutal story: there is no ideological obfuscation for the narrator, but a full and open acceptance of oppressive power.

A more equivocal piece in this line of development is 'Six Feet of the Country' (1956), one of Gordimer's best stories. This story anticipates not only the narrative stance of *The Conservationist*, but also the idea central to the novel: the resonant significance of the death of a black stranger on a white man's property. The narrator of the story, like Mehring, is a city businessman whose farming activities represent a back-to-the-land dilettantism; the episode he recounts is that of the death of his servant Petrus' brother – an illegal immigrant – who has walked to the farm from Rhodesia in pursuit of work. The authorities dispose of the body, assumed to be unknown in the area, and the narrator then, after some difficulty, manages to retrieve the corpse for the grieving Petrus, who has had to collect from his community a substantial fee for this purpose. The dead boy's old father travels for the funeral, and the story's crisis point occurs in the almost farcical funeral scene: the narrator, annoyed with his wife, is outside with his eight iron, practising approach shots, when the funeral procession arrives at the old burial ground outside the farm boundary. There is a commotion when the coffin is removed from the donkey cart which has brought it from the city, and is being lifted towards its grave: the narrator approaches to intervene, and discovers that the old man is complaining that the coffin is too heavy for the slight stature of his son. The coffin is duly

opened to reveal the corpse of a heavily-built stranger. The end
of the narrative details the vain attempts of the narrator and
his wife to obtain the correct body or to retrieve Petrus's
substantial sum of money. A crucial aspect of this ending is the
clearly implied distinction between the narrator and his wife:
her interest in the matter suggests a compassion which is at one
with her apparent affinity with Petrus, whereas the narrator's
dogged engagement with the authorities is no more than a
matter of principle (*SS*, 68). The isolation of the narrator's
perspective parallels the physical isolation indicated by his
sexual estrangement from his wife. The association between
the wife, Lerice, and Petrus suggests they are both victims of
white male oppression, as previous critics have noticed.[17] This
process of isolating the narrative point of view also represents
an economical way of requiring a reading against the grain of
the narrative line.

   A significant development of point of view in some of Gordimer's stories in the 1980s and 1990s is a more consistent
attempt to create convincing black narrators. In *Jump and
Other Stories*, for example, the story 'Amnesty' (1991) presents
the suffering domestic voice of a young mother awaiting the
return of the political prisoner who is her partner. He,
however, will remain away from 'home' even when released
from a five-year prison sentence: the life of an activist in the
'Movement' removes all domestic certainties and financial
securities. The story's poignancy lies clearly in the simple needs
and wishes of the mother – needing to accept, in part, a
repressive situation – which needs are thwarted by a political
context which breaks up her family. One reviewer found this
kind of perspective in the collection inappropriate, arguing
that the stories 'written from inside an African character ...
are the least convincing. There is something *faux-naif* about the
perception and diction; it feels patronising – which must be far
from the author's intention. It seems odd that Gordimer even
tries to feel black.'[18] This complaint raises some important
issues. Clearly in trying to give a voice to African characters
Gordimer runs the risk of being perceived as patronising; but
that kind of perception itself – of a necessary divide between

white and black Africans – is precisely that which Gordimer's
work seeks to problematize. From this perspective there is no
good reason why white writers should not create black narrators, even if they are not fully realized: an exploration of this
problematic area seems vital for a writer with Gordimer's
interests and, indeed, such an exploration has formed a central
part of her recent work, especially in *My Son's Story*. As the
opening chapter indicated, Gordimer is sensitive to the limitations on inter-racial experience (and consequently on narrative
possibilities) imposed on the writer in South Africa; but narrative can be used as a way of resisting these imposed restrictions,
and this transgressive gesture is a crucial element, for Gordimer, in the forging of a new national literature for South
Africa, even if there is an inherent risk of artistic failure in such
transgressions.

The problems, then, in the use of black narrators, can be
seen as necessary teething problems, and, in any case, Gordimer has evolved strategies for dealing with the inevitable
difficulties. The most effective instances of this exploration in
the short stories are fictions which juxtapose white and black
narrators: here the question of difference receives an appropriately dialogic presentation. In 'What Were You Dreaming?'
(1991), two whites (an Englishman and the mature woman
who is showing him the country) stop their car to pick up a
black hitchhiker. The story begins with the black man's monologue, revealing how his conversation with whites in cars is
necessarily pragmatic and scheming: he must create the
impression of himself he imagines his interlocutors hope for, in
order to reach his destination. On this occasion he begins to
cotton on to the fact that the white woman is using him as an
illustration of oppression for her companion, and he readily
supplies information (not all true) about enforced relocation,
effective slave labour, disease, and so on. The crucial point is
that the fact of oppression must be reproduced as a kind of
circus act in repayment for the patronage of these 'concerned'
whites. This effect is reinforced by the contrast between the
monologue, and the sensationalist, sometimes prurient conversation the whites indulge in about the black situation, while

their passenger sleeps in the back of the car: there is an integrity about the hitcher's monologue – even in acknowledging the lies he is telling – and this comes partly from the cohesion of a single mind reasoning with itself; this contrasts with the jokey superficiality of the whites in both form and substance. An aspect of this superficiality is represented in the title image: the passenger is woken up, and the Englishman, 'with the voice . . . of one who is hoping to hear something that will explain everything', asks '"What were you dreaming?"' (*J*, 224). This bespeaks a liberal preoccupation with the single identity which the splintered political actuality renders ineffectual: the hitcher does not produce dream images which encapsulate his situation, and so has no answer, but the whites sense that 'if pressed, he will produce for them a dream he didn't dream, a dream put together from bloated images on billboards, discarded calendars picked up, scraps of newspapers blown about' (*J*, 224). Again, the felt need to jump through hoops crystallizes the situation: the hitcher, now, seems prepared to imitate the Englishman's notion of the psyche from the scraps of white culture that may clutter his life. But this notionally coherent identity is a fiction. The irony is that the forms of the story represent the dispossessed hitcher as having a more coherent view of the situation than do the confused whites, who blend voyeurism with concern seamlessly in their behaviour. As the hitcher is dropped off the woman hands him a two-rand note, payment for the display, and turns to her companion, knowing she is 'accountable' for the events of the story, and, by implication, for the situation beyond them (*J*, 225).

A story which blends narrative modes in a similar way is 'A City of the Dead, A City of the Living' (1984) in which a third-person narrative is interspersed with italicized sections of first-person narrative; this narrator is Nanike Moreke, a township woman who finally betrays a fugitive her husband, Samson, has brought to their crowded home. Her reporting of the fugitive to the security police represents a protection of the domestic environment, and an associated fearful rejection of the incipient sexual attraction Nanike feels for this man. A

treatment of the theme of social space – a theme contained in
the suggestive title-image – is introduced into the story by the
fugitive himself as he spends one night describing his travels to
the Morekes: he tells them about the oldest city on the African
continent, which has a city of the dead – a city of tombs – as
well as a city of the living (*SOT*, 18). The living/dead dichotomy supplies an obvious parallel to the 'two cities' formed
by a township and an adjacent city, though there is an ambiva-
lance about which should be seen as 'living', and which 'dead'.
J. U. Jacobs points out how Nanike's interior monologue –
esteemed to be a 'living' narrative voice – alternates with the
'dead' sections of omniscient narration, resulting in an ambivalent narrative structure which progresses beyond the restrictions of a purely omniscient stance.[19] The danger implicit in a
white writer's representation of black township life is avoided
by the juxtaposition of narrative voices which enables Gordimer to acknowledge the danger of a reductive or stereotypical
presentation, and to *separate this out* from the creation of the
black character herself. This involves, of course, a carefully
constructed pattern of narrative, the artificiality of which
strengthens the link between narrative and living space. The
limitations of the narrative, in Jacobs' reading, relate not
simply to the inability of the third-person narrator to *know* that
which lies beyond typification, but also to the problem of
inauthenticity in Gordimer's creation of Nanike's narrative.[20]
Yet these inauthenticities, in replicating the artificialty (in a
political sense) of township life, also replicate the context
which produces the contradictory behaviour of Nanike: the
dual-narrative represents the incoherences and restrictions of a
repressed urban existence in which individual need clashes
with external interpellation.

As in the novels, the issue of social space and its control forms
a constant theme in the short stories, and adds an important
extra dimension to the effects of the more complex stories.
Architectural motifs form an important part of the exploration
of spatial issues. 'Monday is Better Than Sunday' (1949), ends
with a dystopian, imprisoning chinese-box city motif which
encapsulates the situation of the servant Elizabeth, whose life

of drudgery is compounded by the Sunday-depression of the whites for whom she works. In the story 'Inkalamu's Place' (1971) the empty house, formerly owned by the eponymous Kurtz-type character, is a succinct image of colonial disso-lution, while, in the same collection, the narrator of 'Africa Emergent' (1971) is himself an architect; having once spent time designing sets for an inter-racial theatre group, the nar-rator's embourgeoisement, his gradual withdrawal from an engagement with black rights and black intellectuals, is suc-cinctly represented by his new professional commitments, which anticipate those of Bam Smales in *July's People*: he has been too busy building shopping malls, and a cultural centre, to carry on his work for the theatre group (*LC*, 247). The story condemns the attitudes of sympathetic whites, including the narrator, who have to see a black man imprisoned before they cease suspecting him of acting as a police agent; the lack of faith in the individual is mirrored in the failure to commit to the hit-and-miss theatre group. Faith is placed, instead, in capital finance and the opportunities for building it creates.

Gordimer's preoccupation with social space has continued in her short stories into the 1990s. 'Teraloyna' (1991), for example, is an allegory of racism and ecological mis-management in a fictional island, in which brutal environ-mental controls are explicitly linked with violent racial repress-ion. In the same collection is 'The Ultimate Safari', narrated from a child's point of view, which concerns the 'safari' of a group of refugees from the war in Mozambique, through the Kruger park. Not all survive, and the blind optimism of the child at the story's end (now in a refugee camp) emphasizes the bleakness of the future. The story's epigraph – a travel adver-tisement for the 'ultimate' safari in Africa – makes quite explicit the point about how power and the control and repre-sentation of space are inextricably linked.

Gordimer's single most impressive short fiction, which best illustrates the technical features in her shorter work, is 'Some-thing Out There' (1984); this is a complex novella written in an ambivalent, seriocomic tone. The parallel plots – of a baboon terrorizing white suburbs, and that concerning an

activist cell targetting a power station – raise a host of familiar
Gordimerian concerns: social space and its control; sexuality;
racial politics; cultural expression. These issues are profoundly
interrelated in what is one of Gordimer's finest works.

In examining these issues, the novella also utilizes each of the
major features of the short story form identified in this chapter:
the pointed ambiguity of its effects, incorporating a resonant
ending; the succinct and powerful use of intertextual reference
to imply much which cannot be dealt with explicitly; a careful
juxtaposition of narrative perspectives, often allied to the
development of important themes, such as social space.

The two plots are overtly interrelated: the baboon's terrorizing of white suburbia in Johannesburg is an ironic metaphor
for the activities of the terrorists, planning their attack on a
power station. The act of sabotage is described immediately
after an account of the baboon's most vicious attack – on a Mrs
Lily Scholtz, whose home, protected by elaborate anti-burglar
arrangements and by a half-breed Rottweiler, proves no
defence against attack from the 'something out there'. This is
no surprise since the threat is, simultaneously, an internal fear
produced by a racist psyche, and the actual, inevitable threat
of historical revolution which this psyche brings in its wake.
The careful interweaving of scenes in the story makes clear this
link between the internal fear and its external realization,
though this is a complex process of accretion, to which only a
full reading of the novella can do full justice. In one scene, a
couple take their clandestine affair to an untenanted cottage,
where the baboon spies on them in their passion, as they realize
after the event. At the end of this episode the woman tells her
male partner that she does not mind having been watched, and
here the voyeurism of the baboon is implicitly associated with
the forbidden pleasures of the affair: the baboon becomes
associated with that which is forbidden and, since the creature
is repeatedly mistaken for a black man, this suggests that a
denial of desire, a psychological repression, is a root cause of
racism – an idea that Gordimer pursues in much of her fiction.
In another episode, further apparent sightings of the baboon
produce the rumour of a 'spook', explicitly internalizing the

irrationality of the fear of the something out there, and, in the following scene, one of the terrorists reads out a newspaper transcript of a Prime Ministerial speech exploiting such fears of '*those who lurk, outside law and order, ready to strike in the dark*'. The government '*will not see the food snatched from your children's mouths by those who seek the economic destruction of our country through boycotts in the so-called United Nations and violence at home*' (*SOT*, 148, 149; original italics). Here the convenient alignment between the fear of the other and government policy is clear, and is extended by a particular obfuscation in the implication that only a recalcitrant attitude to international relations can protect the domestic necessities. The later episode involving the police interrogator Sergeant Chapman extends some of these links when his wife discovers a piece of venison has been snatched from inside their house, presumably by the baboon. Government policy is confirmed: the something out there will snatch food, though the implicit irony of a *luxury* cut having been taken is obvious.

This kind of explicit linking and development supplies the narrative momentum of the piece as a whole, and indicates a clear view on the novella's serious issues. These are: a consideration of the acceptability of violence as a means of furthering political ends; and the crucial issue of topographical history and continuity. On the first issue the nature of the target – a power station to be sabotaged – indicates a campaign designed to minimize injuries to people; but the nature of the weaponry the saboteurs surround themselves with reveals the potential need for a less selective extension of the campaign. The following passage follows a sketch of saboteur Vusi's past, a catalogue of repression and an urge for self-improvement, leading, apparently inevitably, to political confrontation and commitment, and an associated destruction of a domestic existence:

He [Vusi] had left a girl and baby without hope of being able to show himself to them again. You could not eat the AKM assault rifles that Charles had brought in golf-bags, you could not dig a road or turn a lathe with the limpet mines, could not shoe and clothe feet and body with the offensive and defensive hand-grenades, could not use the AKM bayonets to compete with the white man's education, or to thrust a way out of solitary confinement in maximum security, and the wooden boxes that held hundreds of rounds of ammunition would not make even a squatter's shack for the girl and child. But all these hungers found their shape, distorted, forged as no one could conceive they ever should have to be, in the objects packed around him. These were made not for life; for death. He and Eddie lay there protected by it as they had never been by life. (*SOT*, 146)

In this passage the narrative perspective is fused with that of Vusi, and this gives it a validity, especially in comparison with the flippant irony that characterizes the descriptions of white suburbia, and which is absent here. The contrast in tone is matched in substance: the privileged domesticity of white Johannesburg is mirrored by the deprivation of Vusi's life at each crucial stage. These 'hungers' of deprivation provide implicit comment on the contrived fear of hunger perpetuated by the white regime. The combination of privileged narrative perspective and pointed contrast provides a clear framework for interpreting the social distortion described here: terroristic violence, so the logic of the passage indicates, is produced by a social system of inequality and repression, as an inevitable response.

The novella ends with a resonant description of the mine-working where Eddie and Vusi hide, with their arsenal of weapons, prior to the attack on the power station:

The mine-working where Eddie and Vusi hid, that Charles identified as belonging to the turn of the 19th century, is in fact far, far older. It goes back further than anything in conventional or alternative history, or even oral tradition, back to the human presences who people anthropology and archaeology, to the hands that shaped the objects or fired the charcoal which may be subjected to carbon tests. No one knows that with the brief occupation of Vusi and Eddie, and the terrible tools that were all they had to work with, a circle was closed; because before the gold-rush prospectors of the 1890s, centuries before time was measured, here, in such units, there was an ancient mine-working out there, and metals precious to men were discovered, dug and smelted, for themselves, by black men. (*SOT*, 203)

The genuine 'something out there', as this passage makes clear, is the actual history of the country, the archaeological evidence that disproves the fundamental tenet of racial superiority and pioneering ownership which underpins the mythology of Afrikaner history. The resonance of this ending – a discourse of asserted historical validity – is set to jar with other discourses in the novella, in particular the comic portrayal of the whites and their fears. In this way the novella condenses – through its ambivalent narrative voices – a view of the geopolitical situation. Here, however, an omniscient accent summarizes the stage, claiming a superior knowledge of that which 'no one knows': this privileged accent has a pointed function at this point, underscoring an appalling fact of historical ignorance. From this perspective comes also the moral approval of terroristic means: we are told that Eddie and Vusi have nothing else to work with but their 'terrible tools'. The productive work potential (and consequent self-definition) of black men, we infer, is repressed and inevitably subverted into an alternative violent assertion.

In summary, Gordimer's shorter fiction betrays an increasing sophistication which parallels the development discernible in the novel sequence, though the curve of this progression is by no means so clear. An important feature of the shorter fiction is a cultivated use of ambiguity in the tradition of the modernists, indicating a skilled use by Gordimer of dissonant fictional form for her particular purposes. Although a constant ideological perspective is present, an increasingly destabilized narrative texture is also evident, and this has an importance for the incorporation of a black perspective and for the pointed ironizing of authoritative discourses, a process which the potentially disruptive frame of the short story intensifies. These are developments which replicate, in miniature, the progression of the novels towards more urgent formal innovation and an increasingly explicit literariness.

CHAPTER 7

Conclusion
Gordimer: postmodernist?

The interpretations of Gordimer's work I have offered indicate strong connections with contemporary intellectual trends. I have characterized her fiction as containing a working-through of her own micropolitics, and an associated articulation of geopolitical concerns. The novel sequence betrays a development and refinement of central themes, and the early work is very significant in this development: even in the first three novels Gordimer conducts a critical examination of European literary forms, evincing a concern to fashion a cultural identity and expression appropriate to the goal of political change in South Africa. A phase then ensues in which the politics of textuality assumes central significance: the novels up to *The Conservationist* express with an increasing urgency a conviction about the importance of discursive practices as the *sites* of power, and here the concern with micropolitics and geopolitics is closely allied with the construction of narrative form. This becomes more explicit in *Burger's Daughter* where Gordimer fashions a novelistic form which, through its problematized narrative perspective, reinforces her implications about the ideological function of discourse. There is, then, an increasing literary self-consciousness in Gordimer's work which reaches a peak in the self-reflexiveness of *My Son's Story*, and (especially) *A Sport of Nature*.

This characterization of Gordimer's career – in which the logic of the early novels produces an increasingly explicit literariness in the later ones – is an account which suggests affinities between Gordimer's work and important post-modernist trends, where one finds a stress on textual construction as one of several areas of crossover with poststructuralist thought. If certain affinities are immediately apparent, however, the extent to which Gordimer can be seen as a postmodernist writer is more problematic than it might at first appear. Postmodernism, for example, is often taken to be concerned with problematizing ideas about the centred self, a concern which strikes a chord with the Gordimer novels.[1] From her first semi-autobiographical novel – which challenges conventions of the *Bildungsroman* – Gordimer has been concerned with de-centring the self, and re-siting individual identity in a reciprocal and interactive relationship with larger social structures. However, this, in itself, does not a postmodernist make, and is an aspect of Gordimer's work which is treated ambivalently: single, major protagonists dominate her novels indicating a formal centring of self which one does not find in overtly experimental postmodernist writing, even if notions of unified selfhood are continually questioned.

Further connections are suggested in Linda Hutcheon's presentation of postmodernism as a mode which combines realist reference and modernist self-reflexiveness, and makes simultaneous use and abuse of these features, in both photography and narrative.[2] Gordimer has shown an ambivalent interest in photography: she has collaborated with photographer David Goldblatt to produce two works combining her text with Goldblatt's black-and-white photography. In *Lifetimes: Under Apartheid*, for example, powerful images of black dispossession are interspersed with extracts from the novels which describe similar scenes. This book does not display the kind of problematizing of representation that one associates with postmodernist photography: the collaborative work with Goldblatt has its own polemical intention, and is constructed to suggest a straightforward illustrative function for the extracts from the novels. The novels, of course, do not function in this way, and often contain critical references to photography: for example, Liz Van Den Sandt's hankering for a family photo-album in *The Late Bourgeois World* belongs to the bourgeois world she must grow beyond; in *July's People* there is even an ironic reference to the kind of work that Gordimer and

Goldblatt have produced when we learn that photographs of
township life had often been displayed for the aesthetic enjoy-
ment of shoppers in malls designed by Bam Smales (*JP*, 125).
As with the question of the centred self, a glance at Gordimer's
interest in photography suggests only a partial manifestation of
postmodernist tendencies.[3]

Gordimer seems, then, to occupy a 'border' position, moving
towards a mode of postmodernist expression, but having been
heavily influenced by the realists and the modernists at vital
stages in her career. Brian McHale's account of the distinction
between modernism and postmodernism (in his first book on
postmodernism) helps to articulate Gordimer's 'border' position in relation to these movements. McHale's formulation of a
changing dominant – from the epistemological dominant of
modernist poetics to the ontological dominant of postmodernist
fiction – makes sense of the postmodernist anxiety over states of
being: the modernist concern over ways of knowing, expressed
in fragmented and uncertain narrative forms and perspectives,
is, effectively, intensified into an anxiety about the nature of
our existence in the world – or rather worlds – we inhabit.
Ontology, in McHale's account of postmodernism, may
involve the description of different universes, including the
fictional universe, or 'heterocosm' of fiction.[4] Gordimer's
fiction, however, incorporates continual references to a specific
'world', which distinguishes it from the ontological questioning
of the plurality of worlds in much postmodernist fiction. Yet
these specific references may, if presented in a certain way,
embody postmodernist ontological concerns. Gordimer's comments on *Burger's Daughter*, for example, indicate a certain
alignment with these concerns: she indicates that the book's
focus is the nature of commitment, but not 'commitment'
defined in just a narrow political sense: the concept is part of a
broader 'ontological problem'.[5] Gordimer's fiction refers continually to actual people, places, and ideas – key political
figures and ideologies – references which might be said to
anchor the text in the specific historical and ideological
struggle. For McHale, references to actual people/places/ideas
mean that these are incorporated rather than reflected in

fiction: they comprise areas of ontological difference within a fictional heterocosm that is otherwise homogeneous.[6] In postmodernist fiction an overtly disruptive principle highlights this ontological difference, the mingling of different worlds, whereas Gordimer's novels generally appear to try to efface this difference, and reinforce, through such references, their connection with the 'real'. However, the overlap between the fictional world and the real inevitably raises the spectre of ontological difference, even if such a difference is not usually signalled overtly in Gordimer. There is an order in Gordimer's world-projections which contrasts with the 'anarchism' McHale detects in the postmodernist tendency to sustain a plurality of possible ontological levels. Such an anarchic presentation of plural worlds is clearly absent, but something of this postmodern anxiety filters into her fiction on occasions. The ambiguity with which *July's People* ends is, in part, a conflict of ontological possibilities, with Maureen Smales giving herself up to a contradictory moment in which an unresolved choice between different political orders – between different states of being – resonates.

One of the most damaging and powerful criticisms of postmodernist fiction stems from the ontological anarchism that Gordimer eschews. There is an apparently uncritical openness to the conditions of postmodernity in postmodernist fiction which, for McHale, involves a paradoxical return to mimesis: the form of postmodernist fiction imitates the splintered ontological experience of life in developed industrial cultures. McHale employs Foucault's concept of heterotopia to account for the arena of this pluralism, the fictional space – also called 'the zone' by some practitioners – in which worlds that are mutually exclusive can be accommodated. McHale goes on to define the fictional heterotopia in terms of a key difference from realist and modernist modes: in realism and modernism, the spatial construct is organized around a perceiving subject – either character or narrator; the space of postmodernist writing is differently ordered (or disordered) – deconstructed at the same time as it is constructed.[7]

According to this distinction Gordimer would seem to have a

greater affinity for modernist modes. Her novels, as do many modernist novels, problematize the nature of perception, especially that of a selected individual. But this is normally a learning process, governed by an epistemological dominant, often buttressed by a disembodied narrator who provides ontological stability: there is a certitude about the world which Gordimer's protagonists must learn to know better. As the novel sequence progresses, however, the voice of a disembodied narrator is heard less often, and that yardstick of ontological stability is less accessible. This may involve an increasing reliance on the kind of unity which even the most heterotopian fiction can rely on: the paradoxical creation of a homotopia, which, in this context, is used to designate the space projected and concretized by readers in the reading process.[8]

In the postmodernist texts analyzed by McHale the possibility of this homotopia is disrupted by the deliberate incorporation of elements drawn from other ontological levels, such as the device of *retour de personnages*, pushed to its limit. The device of *retour de personnages* – in which the same characters crop up in different novels by the same writer – has the effect of reinforcing realism by appearing to give characters an existence beyond the text in which they first appear.[9] There is one memorable instance of this in Gordimer: the fleeting reappearance of Rosa Burger in *A Sport of Nature*, and this has quite the opposite effect as it is combined with Gordimer's usual reference to actual people: the customary connection between world and text is exaggerated by the self-parodying reference which deliberately confuses fiction and history. The cultivation of such confusion may conform to an important postmodernist tendency identified by McHale, discussing a revisionist creation of historical reference in postmodernist fiction where, as fiction and history exchange places, the straightforward location of the 'real world' is made problematic.[10] This question, which lies beneath the surface of the earlier novels, becomes explicit in *A Sport of Nature* and (to some extent) *My Son's Story*.

This may suggest a break in Gordimer's writing signalled, in particular, by the self-reflexiveness of *A Sport of Nature*, with its ironic revision of certain structures in *Burger's Daughter*. There may also be a principle of mock-allegory about Hillela's story, another mode characteristic of postmodernist fiction according to McHale:[11] Hillela becomes representative of the Gordimerian revolutionary principle pushed to its limits; in this sense she is a disembodied essence whose power, in a further irony, is predicated upon bodily attributes. There is already, perhaps, a hint of mock-allegory in *Burger's Daughter* in which a single life is shown so scrupulously to be representative of the experiences – and moral obligations – of a community; but despite the self-consciousness of its structure, other elements of the narrative signal a particular seriousness; the full realization of the principle of representativeness which Gordimer had been working up to in previous novels. Only after its full realization could this principle of representativeness – typicality *in extremis* – be subjected to the overt self-parody of *A Sport of Nature*.

The most convincing aspect of McHale's case for the positive potential of postmodernist fiction concerns its treatment of discourse, based on Bakhtinian principles. McHale follows Bakhtin's insights concerning the novel as a medium primarily concerned with the dialogue between different discourses, and allies this to the concept of heterotopia: there is a non-hierarchical mingling of both incommensurable spaces and different discursive orders in the postmodernist novel, and this produces a genuine polyphony since there is no privileging of any one discourse or voice. For McHale, this is a way of foregrounding the ontological aspect of different discourses in conflict, thus creating 'a polyphony of *worlds*'. In the modernist novel, however, the plurality of voices – the heteroglossia – is suppressed by the unifying effect of a monological perspective, integrating the various worlds of discourse within one ontological plane, or at least striving so to do. This means that polyphony, a positive feature of postmodernism, can only be inadvertent in modernist texts.[12] This seems to me to be, in part, a useful initial technical distinction between many modernist and postmodernist texts, and a distinction, moreover, which helps locate the ambivalence of Gordimer's techniques: it seems clear that there is a unifying perspective in Gordimer's novels, though one which diminishes in importance through the sequence, implying a transition from modernist to post-modernist according to McHale's distinction.

One way of indicating this transition is through the self-consciousness of some of Gordimer's narrators. Some post-modernist narrators deliberately destroy the illusory frame of their narrative, drawing attention to its artificiality and con-structedness. Such frame-breaking, which ostensibly supplies 'an absolute level of reality', actually has a destabilizing effect on ontology, because the gesture, instead of installing a higher plane of 'reality' (the author's) only places the author within the fiction, and its ontological structure.[13] In this connection one might compare the ending of Gordimer's first novel, *The Lying Days*, with that of her most recent, *My Son's Story*: in both cases the narrator breaks the frame by announcing her- or himself as the 'author' of the fiction. In *The Lying Days* the gesture signals a crucial stage in Helen Shaw's development, an advancement in her understanding of her place in a crystal-lizing social world. The emphasis is on how an individual subject can know or reconstruct her social role. This suggests an 'epistemological dominant' which is harder to detect at the end of *My Son's Story* where Will announces himself as the 'author' of the novel realized before us, which he also claims he can never publish. This contradiction suggests an ontological discrepancy in McHale's terms: the fictional world in which Will can create is separated from the evocation of the real society in which he would be silenced. Of course, this is not an anarchic representation of plural worlds, but it is a pointed use of a particular ontological contradiction: that between a Utopian realm of free expression – effectively created in the space of the novel – and the given of South African reality.

A Sport of Nature is clearly the novel which most explicitly betrays Gordimer's slowly growing affinity with the attributes of postmodernist fiction. One significant area of commonality between the novel and postmodernist fiction is the element of carnival. Carnivalized literature, typically, involves a picares-que adventure, in which the protagonist seeks answers to essential questions, through episodes that see him or her violating social norms, and experimenting with extreme mental and physical states. These features of carnivalized literature accurately locate key stages in Hillela's career, and this is significant if such features are also characteristic of postmodernist fiction.[14] Of course, parodies of official ceremonies and rituals are essential features of popular carnival; and if *A Sport of Nature* as a whole is taken as carnival (it is an extended carnivalization of Gordimerian concerns) then we can see such a parody included in the too-easy transition to South African independence celebrated in the ceremony at the end of the novel. The most significant connection at this point, however, may be with the revolutionary impulse: 'At the point where representations of carnival converge with carnivalized literature's Utopian themes we find the postmodernist topos of revolution. This is not political or social revolution, however, so much as it is ludic and sexual revolution, revolution as carnival; its real-world models are the May Events in Paris and the Prague Spring.'[15] If *A Sport of Nature* can be seen to incorporate a genuine revolutionary moment, it is in precisely this ludic postmodernist sense, where the celebratory moment is double-edged, involving self-parody as an integral part of the Utopian theme. This account of the novel would also locate it as postmodernist according to Hutcheon's notion of postmodernism's ambivalence, involving a critique in which a work reveals its own complicity with power.[16]

The value of postmodernism is often said to reside in its ability to analyze and explicate processes of representation, revealing how our ideas of self are constructed. The self-consciousness that often goes hand-in-hand with such investigations has also a positive – self-critical – dimension.[17] If the analysis of representation has always been an aspect of Gordimer's fictions, it is only in *A Sport of Nature* that it becomes overtly and self-reflexively parodic.

One could, however, make a case for earlier novels showing affinities here on the basis of a preoccupation with representation combined with parody: the parodic rejection of Forsterian representation in the early novels, for example, betrays a critical examination of fictional constructions of selfhood. Yet

Hutcheon's notion, that by making representation into an issue postmodernism challenges mimetic assumptions, is one which does not distinguish postmodernism from modernism as clearly as McHale's formulations do. Hutcheon acknowledges that modernism had already challenged the realist notion of mimesis that presumes a direct link between sign and referent, word and world. The difference, for Hutcheon, is that modernist art, in making the same challenge, emphasized the self-contained nature of the signifying system, thus creating a gulf between world and text. Postmodernism can then be seen to bridge the gulf by 'de-naturalizing' both the transparency of realism and the reflexive response of modernism; this double de-mystification would seem to recoup experimentalism for purposive comment, though this is a formulation which presents modernist art as inevitably divorced from life in a way that is questionable: it seems to me that the self-conscious ambivalence Hutcheon assigns to postmodernism – a challenge to the ideology which still recontains it – is an implicit aspect of the modernist project. A more convincing aspect of Hutcheon's account is her claim that postmodern representation challenges totalization and mastery, replacing the search for totality with an interrogation of limits. This postmodern questioning of representation is particularly evident in the pointed critiques of those working in post-colonialism and feminism. For Gordimer, a post-colonial, (arguably) feminist writer, whose project has affinities with a poststructuralist micropolitics, there are many resonances in this account of postmodern representation.[18]

A Sport of Nature is a postmodernist parody in that it foregrounds the *politics* of representation: Gordimer, at one level, allows the negative implications of her previous representations of sexuality to be expressed at their logical extreme, alongside similarly extreme versions of her positive, Utopian representations. According to Hutcheon this is typical of postmodernist irony which rejects the urge of modernism towards resolution, closure or distance. If there is no 'resolving urge' in *A Sport of Nature*, there may still be a principle of critique at the level of representation – rather than an unresolved, apolitical ambiguity. All of Gordimer's novels, of course, focus on the political dimension of the personal, but this novel uses a self-consciously ambivalent presentation of sexuality and desire, and can be seen, therefore, as one of those feminist works which, for Hutcheon, have occasioned the postmodernist analysis of the female body and its desires, and how these are socially constructed through modes of representation. If *A Sport of Nature* courts the danger of a phallocentric version of female sexuality, this is precisely the grounds of its postmodernism, since the parodic use (even the abuse) of male representations of women is characteristically postmodernist in that it contains a paradoxical self-critique. If the extreme manner in which the personal and the political are linked in the novel is a self-parody – Hillela's sexuality as a wellspring of revolutionary violence is the clearest instance – it is also a strategy for presenting the idea in an arresting form, something which would conform to the iconoclasm Hutcheon seems to detect in the feminist-postmodernist challenge to a traditional separation of public and private history.[19]

The problem that remains to be addressed is how postmodernism can establish a position from which a genuinely politicized critique can be made: the element of complicity which even defenders of postmodernism like McHale and Hutcheon discuss evidently compromises the comment on offer. It may be that this is an inevitable feature of any art, yet the postmodernist tendency to remain open to a plurality of discourses does represent a denial of 'judgement' in any traditional sense. Here, however, we must return to the issue of totality and the grand narrative: postmodernism's rejection of conventional forms of monologic critique is an implicitly political rejection of the dominating effects of master codes of narration; as such, this is a potentially liberating impulse.

For Ernesto Laclau the postmodern challenge to 'meta-narratives' and master codes is defined in terms of its reaction to 'the central categories of the discourses of modernity', or rather to the ontological status of these categories. Laclau's analysis reinforces the credibility of the change to an onto-logical dominant that McHale detects in the transition from modernist to postmodernist fiction: ontological questioning is a way of eschewing the restrictions of totalizing thought, thereby facilitating an extension of the values of modernity, both in terms of content and operability.[20] For Laclau (as for Gordimer) modernity's key contribution is to be found in the discourses of Marxism, which can be recouped from their totalizing ontological certitude when seen as historically specific, and 'not as the ground of History but as pragmatic and limited syntheses of a historical reality that subverts and surpasses them'.[21] Once the totalizing tendency has been relinquished, analytical discourses can be appropriated and reapplied to shifting situations. For Laclau this does not produce nihilism, because the resulting proliferation of discourses is representative of social existence, rather than of any illusory 'extradiscursive reality'. Argument and discourse themselves constitute the social, and so their open-endedness can produce a greater activism, with humankind no longer perceived as imprisoned by necessary Historical laws, but liberated to see itself as the *constructor* of its history.[22] The objection that can be levelled at this kind of formulation is that it enforces a situation of radical undecidability in which judgement, and consequently political mobilization, is impossible; but the challenge to the ontological status of universal structures does not preclude the formation of judgement: it merely requires an acknowledgement of the mutability and contingency of all discursive judgements.

Previous chapters have shown how Gordimer's micropolitics (a challenge to metanarrative) is combined in her novels with a (consequently) modified presentation of Marxist revolutionary themes. In *The Late Bourgeois World*, for example, the dominant intertextual presence of Ernst Fischer's *The Necessity of Art* – a work in Marxist aesthetics – is utilized and challenged in the presentation of Elizabeth Van Den Sandt's struggle to define her personal sense of historical commitment; another good example is *A Guest of Honour* in which Fanon's *The Wretched of the Earth* supplies the post-colonial revolutionary context for another formal problematic, centring on characterization in the novel, and the private route to public commitment. If the challenge to grand narrative does not preclude a position of judgement – an ideological orientation – it may be that Gordimer's work combines a postmodernist decentring with a necessary ideological recentring. Just as Hillela, in *A Sport of Nature*, occupies a 'non-matrilinear centre' of her own invention, Gordimer's work may well occupy a newly recentred space that establishes the necessary principles of a post-apartheid literature (*SN*, 360).

Yet if Gordimer's writing shows an increasing connection with the technical properties of a composite definition of postmodernist fiction, different constructions of postmodernism suggest her work is less easy to place: her roots in realism and modernism, and her appropriation of techniques drawn from realist and modernist writers, are postmodernist credentials, in Hutcheon's conception. Gordimer might also, at times, be formulating a 'double-coded' fictional form – combining modernist with earlier codes – in the kind of combination which Charles Jencks sees as characteristically postmodernist.[23] McHale's 'ontological dominant', however, might be something that gradually assumes importance, most notably in *A Sport of Nature*, and this gradualism might locate her as a borderline figure. There is, however, an insistent preoccupation with micropolitics from Gordimer's earliest work, and this indicates an implicit challenge to the grand theories of macropolitics; the same challenge is encoded in the gathering significance of her metafictional interrogations of representation and power.

Ultimately, it may be the South African situation which lends the appearance of a borderline position to Gordimer's fiction: there is a laudable certitude in her radical criticisms of her nation, which are forced to resemble analyses of a universal given. Yet, as Gordimer knows, the twentieth century's most infamous and sustained situation of oppression is mutable: it was only the racist conception of apartheid which was founded on a misplaced notion of the ontological fixity of a racially divided world. New social forms, inevitably, will elicit new fictional forms. Only Gordimer's subsequent novels will reveal whether or not her recent self-conscious phase is a fleeting, or sustained engagement with postmodernist tendencies, and whether or not a new creative phase will characterize her work in the post-apartheid era.

Notes

1 John Cooke, in particular, has seen this phase of Gordimer's youth as crucially formative: he has shown how a pervasive theme in Gordimer's fiction – that of breaking free from the influence of the maternal house – has its roots in this episode. See Cooke, *The Novels of Nadine Gordimer: Private Lives/Public Landscapes* (London and Baton Rouge: Louisiana State University Press, 1985).

2 Gordimer's Jewish identity may be another significant factor, though this has not been a consistent or primary concern. Michael Wade offers a preliminary discussion of Jewish identity as a repressed theme in Gordimer's work in '*A Sport of Nature*: Identity and Repression of the Jewish Subject', *The Later Fiction of Nadine Gordimer*, edited by Bruce King (London: Macmillan, 1993), pp.155–72. This subject is also considered in Andrew Vogel Ettin's *Betrayals of the Body Politic: The Literary Commitments of Nadine Gordimer* (Charlottesville: University Press of Virginia, 1993), which was published after this work was originally drafted.

3 Robert Green, 'From *The Lying Days* to *July's People*: The Novels of Nadine Gordimer', *Journal of Modern Literature*, 14 (1987–8), 543–63 (563).

4 Gordimer has not always been clear about the distinction between literature and history. See Stephen Clingman, *The Novels of Nadine Gordimer: History From the Inside* (1986; second edition, London: Bloomsbury, 1993), chapter one, on this. Clingman's book as a whole is an extended attempt to articulate how Gordimer's fictional presentation of the effects of South African history – her 'history from the inside' – evolves. Clingman clearly shows how such an inside history is properly seen as a matter of evolution in which the novelist's developing historical consciousness is subject to change, and also to various stages of complicity with historically located ideologies.

5 C. Servan-Schreiber, 'Learning to Live With Unjustice', *World Press Review*, 27 (January 1980), 30.

6 See Robert Boyers, et al., 'A Conversation With Nadine Gordimer', *Salmagundi*, 62 (Winter, 1984), 3–31 (13–14).

7 'A Wilder Fowl', *London Magazine*, 15 (June, 1975), 90–2 (92).

8 'South Africa: Towards a Desk-Drawer Literature', *Classic*, 2 (1968), 4, 64–74 (70–1).

9 *The Black Interpreters* (Johannesburg: Ravan Press, 1973), p.5.

10 Abiola Irele, 'The African Imagination', *Research in African Literatures*, 21 (1990), 1, 49–67 (60, 63).

11 Cooke, *The Novels of Nadine Gordimer*, pp.34–7.

12 On 'white consciousness' see her essay 'What Being a South African Means to Me', *South African Outlook*, 107 (1977), 87–9, 92; Gordimer expresses disapproval of the separatist philosophy in an interview with Anthony Sampson: 'Love Among the Madness', *The Observer*, 29 March 1987, p.21.

13 See 'Introduction' to *Selected Stories*, p.11.

14 'English-Language Literature and Politics in South Africa', *Journal of Southern African Studies*, 2 (1975), 131–50 (149).

15 Ibid., p.139.

16 See, for example, Mongane Serote's *To Every Birth Its Blood*, Sipho Sepamla's *A Ride on the Whirlwind* and *The Children of Soweto* by Mbulelo Vizikhungo Mzamane.

17 *Apartheid* (Paris: UNESCO, second edition, 1972), p.189.

18 'South African Writers Talking: Nadine Gordimer, Es'kia Mphahlele, André Brink', *English in Africa*, 6 (September, 1979), 1–23.

19 Edmund Morris, 'A Visit with Nadine Gordimer', *New York Times Book Review*, 7 June, 1981, 26–7 (27).

20 'An Interview' in *Momentum: On Recent South African Writing*, edited by M. J. Daymond, J. U. Jacobs and Margaret Lenta (University of Natal Press, Pietermaritzburg, 1984), pp. 32–4 (p.33).

21 'Turning the Page', in *Soho Square V*, edited by Steve Kromberg and James Ogude (London: Bloomsbury, 1992), pp.270–8 (p.274).

22 'What Being a South African Means to Me', 89.

23 Such a transitional position can, however, be seen as typically postmodern. See the concluding chapter on this.

24 *The Black Interpreters*, pp.31–2.

25 See *The Meaning of Contemporary Realism*, translated by John and Necke Mander (London: Merlin, 1979). In an early interview Gordimer argues that it is 'a betrayal' to put writing at the service

of a cause: Arthur Ravenscroft, 'A Writer in South Africa: Nadine Gordimer', *London Magazine*, 5 (May, 1965), 20–8 (22).

26 *Studies in European Realism*, translated by Edith Bone (London: Merlin Press, 1989), p.10.

27 *The Essential Gesture* (London: Cape, 1988), pp.106–7.

28 Irving Howe, *Politics and the Novel* (Morningside Edition, New York: Columbia University Press, 1992), pp.23, 256.

29 See Clingman and Cooke on this, as well as Elisabeth Gerver, 'Women Revolutionaries in the Novels of Nadine Gordimer and Doris Lessing', *World Literature Written in English*, 17 (1978), 38–50, and Kelly Hewson, 'Making the Revolutionary Gesture: Nadine Gordimer, J. M. Coetzee and Some Variations on the Writer's Responsibility', *Ariel*, 19 (1988), 4, 55–72.

30 Clingman, p.10.

31 Fredric Jameson, *Marxism and Form* (Princeton University Press, 1974), p.196.

32 Lukács, *Writer and Critic*, translated by Arthur Kahn (London: Merlin, 1978), pp.116, 130, 146.

33 Ibid., p.143.

34 Eugene Lunn, *Marxism and Modernism* (London: Verso, 1985), p.79.

35 Cooke, *The Novels of Nadine Gordimer*, p.37.

36 Robert, Boyers, et al., 'A Conversation With Nadine Gordimer', *Salmagundi*, 62 (Winter, 1984), 3–31 (27–8).

37 'The Idea of Gardening', *New York Review of Books*, January 2, 1984, 3–6 (6).

38 In an early interview Gordimer numbers, among her influences: Lawrence, James, Hemingway, Forster, Yeats, Auden, Rilke, Donne, Woolf, George Eliot, Gide, Joyce, Proust, Welty, Conrad and Camus. Arthur Ravenscroft, 'A Writer in South Africa: Nadine Gordimer', 24–5.

39 Robert Boyers, et al., 'A Conversation With Nadine Gordimer', 19–20.

40 Ibid., 20–1.

41 Karen Lazar, 'Feminism as "Piffling"? Ambiguities in Some of Nadine Gordimer's Short Stories', *Current Writing*, 2 (1990), 1 (Oct), 101–16 (103).

42 Dorothy Driver, 'Nadine Gordimer: The Politicisation of Women', *English in Africa*, 10 (1983), 2, 29–54 (46). On this issue see also Martin Trump, 'The Short Fiction of Nadine Gordimer', *Research in African Literatures*, 17 (1986), 3, 341–69.

43 Robin Visel, 'A Half-Colonization: The Problem of the White Colonial Woman Writer', *Kunapipi*, 10 (1988), 3, 39–45 (39).

44 Robin Visel, 'Othering the Self: Nadine Gordimer's Colonial Heroines', *Ariel*, 19 (1988), 4, 33–42 (34–5).

45 Ibid., 39.

46 'Writers and Politics' (conversation with Susan Sontag), in *Voices: Writers and Politics*, edited by Bill Bourne, Udi Eichler and David Herman (Nottingham: Spokesman, 1987), pp. 25–39 (pp.34–5).

47 Jana Sawicki's summary of the significance of Foucault's thinking in these areas is very helpful. See *Disciplining Foucault* (London: Routledge), 1991, pp.21–2.

48 See David Harvey, *The Condition of Postmodernity* (Oxford: Blackwell, 1990), p.205.

49 Ibid., p.226.

50 Cooke, *The Novels of Nadine Gordimer*, pp.11, 29.

51 Robert Boyers, et al., 'A Conversation With Nadine Gordimer', 6.

52 Edward Soja, *Postmodern Geographies* (London: Verso, 1990), p.50.

53 On this see *The Apartheid City and Beyond: Urbanization and Social Change in South Africa*, edited by David M. Smith (London: Routledge, 1992), editorial gloss to part one, p.11.

54 Foucault, 'Of Other Spaces', *Diacritics*, 16 (1986), 22–7 (24).

55 Soja, *Postmodern Geographies*, pp.17–18.

56 David M. Smith, 'Introduction' to *The Apartheid City and Beyond: Urbanization and Social Change in South Africa*, p.1.

57 Such a contradiction is not an unusual factor in the control of power-space practices. (See, for example, Harvey on this: *The Condition of Postmodernity* , p.226.)

58 See David M. Smith, 'Introduction' to *The Apartheid City and Beyond*, for a useful summary of these developments.

59 For an exhaustive treatment of the relationship between Gordimer's work and the political history of South Africa see Clingman, *The Novels of Nadine Gordimer*.

2 THE EARLY NOVELS

1 As Stephen Clingman has pointed out there is a close correspondence between the descriptions of Atherton and the description of Springs in the essay 'A South African Childhood', where Gordimer grew up. Clingman, *The Novels of Nadine Gordimer*, p.27.

2 Kolawole Ogungbesan feels that the narrator is not the focus of the novel's autobiographical element: he points out that Gordimer seems to have projected onto Joel Aaron the ambiguities of her own situation as a Jew in South Africa, creating a heroine with a Scottish background instead. See 'The Way Out of South

Africa: Nadine Gordimer's *The Lying Days*', *Ba Shiru*, 9 (1978), 1–2, 48–62 (60–1). John Cooke argues that the novel, as auto-biography, displays a significant omission in Gordimer's failure to confront fully the question of her relationship with her own mother. See *The Novels of Nadine Gordimer*, p.49.

3 Michael Wade, *Nadine Gordimer* (London: Evans Brothers, 1978), p.13.

4 John Cooke, for example, believes this to be 'Gordimer's only novel in which private and public responsibilities are avoided and nothing learned'. See *The Novels of Nadine Gordimer*, p.48.

5 See, for example, Clingman p.41.

6 The process of rescinding 'coloured' voting rights involved various constitutional manipulations and was only finally 'legal-ized' in 1956 (three years after the publication of *The Lying Days*). See Leonard Thompson, *A History of South Africa* (New Haven: Yale University Press, 1990), pp.190–1.

7 Clingman, p.45.

8 Robert Green, 'Nadine Gordimer's *A World of Strangers*: Strains in South African Liberalism', *English Studies in Africa*, 22 (1979), 1, 45–54 (45).

9 Clingman, p.45. The Congress Alliance was an association between the ANC and other political organizations. See Clingman p.46 on this, and the whole chapter on *A World of Strangers* (pp.45–71) for the argument I summarize here.

10 Newman, p.24.

11 Clingman, p.60.

12 Clingman, p.56.

13 Green, 'Nadine Gordimer's *A World of Strangers*: Strains in South African Liberalism', 50.

14 John Barkham, 'South Africa: Perplexities, Brutalities, Absurdi-ties', *Saturday Review*, 12 January, 1963, 63.

15 Tom Lodge's figures are 69 dead, 180 wounded: *Black Politics in South Africa since 1945* (London: Longman, 1983), p.210.

16 See Clingman, *The Novels of Nadine Gordimer*; Mike Nicol, *A Good-Looking Corpse* (London: Secker and Warburg, 1991).

17 See Thompson, *A History of South Africa*, p.197.

18 Clingman, following a lead given by Gordimer in her essay 'The Novel and the Nation in South Africa', claims that the affair, in Gordimer's treatment is 'normalized', in contrast to the customary over-explicit preoccupation with cross-racial relation-ships in South African fiction. See *The Novels of Nadine Gordimer*, p.80.

19 See Newman, *Nadine Gordimer*, pp.30–1.

20 Clingman, p.82

21 This is how Clingman reads the novel. See *The Novels of Nadine Gordimer*, pp.88–9.

22 Cooke, *The Novels of Nadine Gordimer*, p.65.

23 Thompson, p.87. Gordimer recalled in an interview that, in the 1970s, black writers had a 'need for myths which fed fervour' and consequently they expressed much interest in black heroes such as Chaka. (Anthony Sampson, 'Love Among the Madness', *The Observer*, 29 March 1987, 21.)

24 See, for example, 'English-Language Literature and Politics in South Africa'. (Mofolo's novel is actually itself critical of Chaka's reign.)

25 See Thompson, *A History of South Africa*, pp.80–7.

26 Abdul R. JanMohamed, *Manichean Aesthetics: The Politics of Literature in Colonial Africa* (Amherst: University of Massachusetts Press, 1988), p.88.

3 DEVELOPING NARRATIVE MUSCLE

1 J. Riis, 'Nadine Gordimer', *Kunapipi*, 2 (1980), 20–6 (20).

2 Jannika Hurwitt, 'The Art of Fiction 77: Nadine Gordimer', *Paris Review*, 88 (Summer, 1983), 83–127 (100).

3 'South Africa: Towards a Desk-Drawer Literature', 71. See also 'English-Language Literature and Politics', 142.

4 For summaries of the role of the African Resistance Movement see Leonard Thompson, *A History of South Africa*, p.211; Tom Lodge, *Black Politics in South Africa since 1945*, pp.240–1; and Clingman, *The Novels of Nadine Gordimer*, pp.92–8.

5 Newman, p.35.

6 Fischer, *The Necessity of Art*, pp.8, 9, 223, 214–15.

7 Ibid., pp.193–4. References in the preceding paragraph to pp.129–30, 152.

8 Ibid., p.130.

9 See chapter 6 for some reflections on this influence.

10 Fischer, p.217.

11 See Gordimer, 'The Flash of Fireflies', in *Short Story Theories*, edited by Charles May (Ohio University Press, 1976). Originally appeared as 'South Africa' in an 'International Short Story Symposium', *Kenyon Review*, 30 (1968).

12 For the passage quoted in the novel see Frantz Fanon, *The Wretched of the Earth* (Harmondsworth: Penguin, 1990), p.116.

13 For further references in this paragraph see Fanon, *The Wretched of the Earth*, pp.132, 125, 140, 29, 118, 142, 115, 36–7.

14 E. G. Burrows, 'An Interview with Nadine Gordimer', *Michigan Quarterly Review*, 9 (1970), 4, 231–4 (233–4).

15 Clingman, pp.113–15.

16 The acceptance of the necessity of violence in the pursuit of political aims, is summarized in references to *Satyagraha* – which means 'truth-force' (Gandhi's philosophy of non-violent opposition) and which occupies the reverse pole of the position arrived at by Bray through the course of the novel. The inadequacy of passivity in the face of capitalist violence is clearly indicated by Bray's experiences, and the assumption of an identifiable 'truth' is clearly invalidated by the novel's analysis of complexity and contradiction as being the condition of political reality. A condemnatory reference to the Gandhi Hall, and the political philosophy it commemorates, is made during the rioting (*GH*, 416), when the Hall is burned down. Among the things salvaged from it, Bray sees a chest labelled 'THE MAHATMA GANDHI NON-VIOLENCE STUDY KIT' (*GH*, 454), and this manifest irony compounds the judgement offered earlier on the adequacy of *Satyagraha*.

17 Elaine Fido reads the scene as illustrating a connection between masculinity and power in '*A Guest of Honour*: A Feminine View of Masculinity', *World Literature Written in English*, 17 (1978), 30–7 (32); Newman, on the other hand, considers that the emphasis on desire together with silence indicates an attempt to resist the control and repression of sexuality through language (48).

18 Fido, 32, 36.

19 For an important discussion of this narrative shift see Mary Donaghy, 'Double Exposure: Narrative Perspective in Gordimer's *A Guest of Honour*', *Ariel*, 19 (1988), 4, 19–32.

20 Henry Callaway, *The Religious System of the Amazulu* (facsimile reprint, Cape Town: Struik, 1970). The quoted passages appear on the following pages: *The Conservationist*, p.35, Callaway, p.182; *The Conservationist*, p.55, Callaway, p.182; *The Conservationist*, p.77, Callaway, p.194; *The Conservationist*, p.87, Callaway, p.194 (modified slightly in *The Conservationist*); *The Conservationist*, p.107, Callaway, p.194; *The Conservationist*, p.155, Callaway, pp.12–13; *The Conservationist*, p.183, Callaway, pp.134, 136; *The Conservationist*, p.201, Callaway, pp.77, 78–9; *The Conservationist*, p.217, Callaway, pp.391, 392 (modified slightly in *The Conservationist*); *The Conservationist*, p.233, Callaway, pp.15–16 (modified slightly in *The Conservationist*).

21 Michael Thorpe, 'The Motif of the Ancestor in *The Conservationist*', *Research in African Literatures*, 14 (1983), 184–92.

22 There is something problematic in viewing the quotes from Calla-

way as an authentic account of Zulu culture: some of the quotes given in *The Conservationist* are taken from informants who are either converts to Christianity or have been exposed to missionary teachings (see, Callaway pp.10, 185). One of the quotes is actually Callaway's own gloss rather than the words of an informant (*C*, 155, Callaway, pp.12–13). For one critic the Zulu myths are 'already contaminated' with the religious ideology of Callaway as recorder, something which Gordimer is able to make use of. (Brian Macaskill, 'Interrupting the Hegemonic: Textual Critique and Mythological Recuperation From the White Margins of South African Writing', *Novel*, 23 (1990–1), 2, 156–81 (161).) Indeed, any lack of 'purity' serves the purpose: this is a buried culture struggling to re-emerge.

23 See Stephen Gray, 'An Interview With Nadine Gordimer', *Contemporary Literature*, 22 (1981), 263–71 (268).

24 'Golden Reclining Nudes of the Desert', *Encounter*, 43 (July, 1974), 3–6.

25 Irene Gorak, 'Libertine Pastoral: Nadine Gordimer's *The Conservationist*', *Novel*, 24 (1990–1), 241–56 (242, 250).

26 Thorpe, 190.

4 THE CONSTRUCTION OF IDENTITY

1 For speculation on some of the possible models for Lionel Burger see Rina Leeuwenburg, 'Nadine Gordimer's *Burger's Daughter*: Why Does Rosa Go Back?', *New Literature Review*, 14 (1985), 23–31 (29).

2 Gordimer's admiration for Fischer is recorded in two essays: 'The Fischer Case', *London Magazine*, 5 (March, 1966), 21–30; 'Why Did Bram Fischer Choose Jail?', *New York Times Magazine*, 14 August 1966, 30–1, 80–1, 84 (reprinted in *The Essential Gesture*). For more detail on the correspondences between Fischer and Lionel Burger see Clingman pp.171–3.

3 In her account of the novel Gordimer has indicated that in the 1920s and 1930s in South Africa only the Communist Party (legal at that time) offered a political framework which articulated blacks' entitlement to participate as equals in government (*What Happened to 'Burger's Daughter'*, p.18).

4 Naomi Mitchison comments on this in *A Life for Africa: The Story of Bram Fischer* (London: Merlin Press, 1973), p.120.

5 See, for example: Richard Peck, 'One Foot Before the Other into an Unknown Future: The Dialectic in Nadine Gordimer's *Burger's Daughter*', *World Literature Written in English*, 29 (1989),

26–43 (26); M. J. Daymond, '*Burger's Daughter*: A Novel's Reliance on History', in *Momentum: On Recent South African Writing*, edited by M. J. Daymond, J. U. Jacobs and Margaret Lenta (University of Natal Press, Pietermaritzburg, 1984), pp.159–70 (p.166); Leeuwenburg, 'Nadine Gordimer's *Burger's Daughter*: Why Does Rosa Go Back?', 30; Rowland Smith, 'Living For the Future: Nadine Gordimer's *Burger's Daughter*', *World Literature Written in English*, 19 (1980), 163–73 (166, 172).

6 Richard Peck, 'One Foot Before the Other into an Unknown Future'.

7 The episode of the dead man in the park, as most critics of the novel point out, is an important one in the delineation of Rosa's career: it contributes significantly to Rosa's acquisition of a wider social apprehension which she claims to have 'seen' for the first time, as a consequence of this early episode, and to have retained from this point onwards (*BD*, 77–80).

8 Liscio considers the possibility that the stepmother's house recalls the writer Colette, and approximates both her residence in Southern France and the sensual appetite for which she was renowned. The most significant aspect of Liscio's claim is that there is a similarity between the third-person narrator in part two and Colette's style. See Lorraine Liscio, '*Burger's Daughter*: Lighting a Torch in the Heart of Darkness', *Modern Fiction Studies*, 33 (1987), 245–61 (254).

9 Liscio, '*Burger's Daughter*: Lighting a Torch in the Heart of Darkness', 257.

10 Leeuwenburg, 'Nadine Gordimer's *Burger's Daughter*: Why Does Rosa Go Back?', 27, 28.

11 There was a significant Africanist element in the creation of the Black Consciousness movement which is, perhaps, glossed over by Gordimer here. Even so, there were important differences between the movement and its Africanist precursors; commentators also disagree as to the extent of the ANC's involvement in the movement, and the extent to which Black Consciousness directly inspired the Soweto uprising. For an overview of these debates see Tom Lodge's *Black Politics in South Africa since 1945*, chapter 13.

12 See *What Happened to 'Burger's Daughter'*, p.11.

13 The inclusion of an actual historical document does not, it should be stressed, collapse the distinction between literature and history; rather it serves to enrich the process of interaction. As Richard Martin points out, the novel is representational – it is to be understood in terms of actual historical events – and yet it resists the illusion of direct access to the 'real' by emphasizing the

mediatory role of language and ideology, factors which are themselves historically determined, as is the text itself. See Richard G. Martin, 'Narrative, History, Ideology: A Study of *Waiting For the Barbarians* and *Burger's Daughter*', *Ariel*, 17 (1986), 3, 3–21 (11).

14 Daymond has commented on this new, post-Soweto phase, and its significance for Gordimer: see '*Burger's Daughter*: A Novel's Reliance on History', 161.

15 Michael Neill, 'Translating the Present: Language, Knowledge, and Identity in Nadine Gordimer's *July's People*', *Journal of Commonwealth Literature*, 25 (1990), 1, 71–97 (72).

16 Jennifer Gordon, 'Dreams of a Common Language: Nadine Gordimer's *July's People*', *African Literature Today*, 15 (1987), 102–8 (102, 108); see also Neill, 'Translating the Present: Language, Knowledge, and Identity in Nadine Gordimer's *July's People*'.

17 Neill, 'Translating the Present: Language, Knowledge, and Identity in Nadine Gordimer's *July's People*', 82.

5 SELF-REFLEXIVE REASSESSMENTS

1 Brenda Cooper, 'New Criteria for an "Abnormal Mutation"? An Evaluation of Gordimer's *A Sport of Nature*', in *Rendering Things Visible: Essays on South African Literary Culture*, edited by Martin Trump (Athens: Ohio University Press, 1990), pp.68–93 (p.72).

2 Brenda Cooper, 'New Criteria for an "Abnormal Mutation"? An Evaluation of Gordimer's *A Sport of Nature*', 83; Richard Peck, 'What's a Poor White to Do? White South African Options in *A Sport of Nature*', 86–9.

3 Barbara Temple-Thurston, 'Nadine Gordimer: The Artist as *A Sport of Nature*', *Studies in Twentieth Century Literature*, 15 (1991), 1, 175–84 (178).

4 Judie Newman, *Nadine Gordimer*, p.96.

5 Richard Peck, 'What's a Poor White to Do? White South African Options in *A Sport of Nature*', 90; Brenda Cooper, 'New Criteria for an "Abnormal Mutation"? An Evaluation of Gordimer's *A Sport of Nature*', 83.

6 See Mike Nicol, 'A Thorn in the Side of Apartheid', *The Guardian*, Friday 4 October 1991, 34: Nicol records Gordimer remarking that the origins of the family are ambiguous, and that this is intentional. For Gordimer, the family appears to be a 'mixture of "coloureds" with a dash of Malay and Indian'.

7 The episode has its source in Gordimer's own experience. See

Anthony Sampson, 'Love Among the Madness', and also Clingman, *The Novels of Nadine Gordimer*, p.xxiv.

6 THE SHORT STORIES

1 Robert F. Haugh, *Nadine Gordimer* (New York: Twayne Publishers, 1974), p.161.
2 Clingman, *The Novels of Nadine Gordimer*, p.19; Newman, *Nadine Gordimer*, p.13.
3 Barbara Eckstein, 'Pleasure and Joy: Political Activism in Nadine Gordimer's Short Stories', *World Literature Today*, 59 (1985), 3, 343–6 (343).
4 Michael King, 'Race and History in the Stories of Nadine Gordimer', *Africa Insight*, 13 (1983), 3, 222–6 (222).
5 Clingman, *The Novels of Nadine Gordimer*, p.19.
6 See Dominic Head, *The Modernist Short Story: A Study in Theory and Practice* (Cambridge University Press, 1992).
7 Link, Viktor, 'The African Magician and His Western Audience: Norms in Nadine Gordimer's "The African Magician"', *Commonwealth Essays and Studies*, 11 (1989), 2, 104–9 (104). The dates given for individual stories in this chapter are for first publication in story collections.
8 See, for example, Gordimer, 'Notes of an Expropriator', *TLS*, 4 June, 1964, 484; Pat Schwartz, 'Interview – Nadine Gordimer', in *New South African Writing* (Hillbrow: Lorton, 1977), pp.74–81.
9 Pat Schwartz, 'Interview – Nadine Gordimer', p.78.
10 Haugh, *Nadine Gordimer*, p.13.
11 Schwartz, 'Interview – Nadine Gordimer', p.78.
12 In Gordimer's first novel, *The Lying Days*, Helen Shaw – like Laura Sheridan in Mansfield's 'The Garden Party' – sees garden parties as representative of the bourgeois world she must outgrow.
13 Kevin Magerey, 'Cutting the Jewel: Facets of Art in Nadine Gordimer's Short Stories', *Southern Review* (Adelaide), 7 (1974), 3–28 (8).
14 In her essay, 'The Lyric Short Story: The Sketch of a History', Eileen Baldeshwiler uses the terms 'epical' and 'lyrical' to distinguish between different story types. The terms can also be usefully employed to account for opposing tendencies within individual stories. (See *Short Story Theories*, edited by Charles E. May (Ohio University Press, 1976), pp.202–13.
15 Karen Lazar, 'Feminism as "Piffling"? Ambiguities in Some of Nadine Gordimer's Short Stories', *Current Writing*, 2 (1990), 1 (Oct), 101–16 (113).

16 Dorothy Driver, 'Nadine Gordimer: the Politicisation of Women', *English in Africa*, 10 (1983), 2, 29–54 (44).

17 See Martin Trump, 'The Short Fiction of Nadine Gordimer', *Research in African Literatures*, 17 (1986), 341–69; Dorothy Driver, 'Nadine Gordimer: the Politicisation of Women'; Karen Lazar, 'Feminism as "Piffling"? Ambiguities in some of Nadine Gordimer's Short Stories'.

18 Gabrielle Annan, 'A Prize Out of Africa', *The Sunday Times*, 13 October 1991, section 7, p.3.

19 J. U. Jacobs, 'Living Space and Narrative Space in Nadine Gordimer's *Something Out There*', *English in Africa*, 14 (1987), 2, 31–43 (37).

20 Ibid., 37–8.

7 CONCLUSION GORDIMER: POSTMODERNIST?

1 See Linda Hutcheon, *The Politics of Postmodernism* (London: Routledge, 1989), p.40.

2 Ibid., p.141.

3 For a fuller account of the relationship between photography and Gordimer's fiction see Cooke, *The Novels of Nadine Gordimer*. Especially interesting is Cooke's argument that Gordimer moves away from a principle of 'verbal' photography in the early novels to a more complex mode incorporating a painterly imagination.

4 Brian McHale, *Postmodernist Fiction* (1987; rep. London: Routledge, 1991), p.27. My use of McHale's book is merely instrumental in constructing a preliminary account of Gordimer's postmodernism. McHale's later book, *Constructing Postmodernism* (London: Routledge, 1992) is different in orientation, and examines various critical constructions of postmodernism.

5 Jannika Hurwitt, 'The Art of Fiction 77: Nadine Gordimer', 100.

6 Brian McHale, *Postmodernist Fiction*, p.28.

7 Ibid., pp.38, 44, 45.

8 Ibid., p.56.

9 Ibid., pp.56, 57–8.

10 Ibid., p.96.

11 Ibid., p.145.

12 Ibid., pp.163, 166, 167.

13 Ibid., p.197.

14 Ibid., pp.172, 173. The link is further emphasized in André Brink's account of *A Sport of Nature* as picaresque: 'Mutants of the Picaresque: *Moll Flanders* and *A Sport of Nature*', *Journal of Literary Studies/Tydskrif Vir Literaturwetenskap*, 6 (1990), 4, 261–74.

15 McHale, *Postmodernist Fiction*, pp.174, 175.

16 Hutcheon, *The Politics of Postmodernism*, p.4.

17 Ibid., p.7.

18 Ibid., pp.32, 34, 37.

19 Ibid., pp.94, 99, 143, 150, 160.

20 Ernesto Laclau, 'Politics and the Limits of Modernity', printed in *Postmodernism: A Reader*, edited by Thomas Docherty (London: Harvester, 1993), pp.329–43 (p.332).

21 Ibid., p.340.

22 Ibid., p.341.

23 See, for example, Charles Jencks, *The Language of Post-modern Architecture* (sixth edition; London: Academy Editions, 1991).

Select bibliography

WORKS BY GORDIMER

NOVELS

The Lying Days (London: Gollancz; New York: Simon & Schuster; 1953)

A World of Strangers (London: Gollancz; New York: Simon & Schuster; 1958; rep. London: Cape, 1976)

Occasion for Loving (London: Gollancz; New York: Viking; 1963)

The Late Bourgeois World (London: Cape; New York: Viking; 1966)

A Guest of Honour (New York: Viking, 1970; London: Cape, 1971)

The Conservationist (London: Cape, 1974; New York: Viking; 1975)

Burger's Daughter (London: Cape; New York: Viking; 1979)

July's People (London: Cape; New York: Viking; 1981)

A Sport of Nature (London: Cape; New York: Knopf; 1987)

My Son's Story (London: Bloomsbury; New York: Farrar, Straus and Giroux; 1990)

SHORT STORY COLLECTIONS

Face to Face (Johannesburg: Silver Leaf Books, 1949)

The Soft Voice of the Serpent (New York: Simon & Schuster, 1952; London: Gollancz, 1953)

Six Feet of the Country (London: Gollancz; New York: Simon & Schuster; 1956)

Friday's Footprint (London: Gollancz; New York: Viking; 1960)

Not for Publication (London: Gollancz; New York: Viking; 1965)

Livingstone's Companions (New York: Viking, 1971; London: Cape, 1972)

Selected Stories (London: Cape, 1975; New York: Viking; 1976)

Some Monday for Sure (London: Heinemann, 1976) (contains previously collected stories)

A Soldier's Embrace (London: Cape; New York: Viking; 1980)

Six Feet of the Country (Harmondsworth: Penguin, 1982) (A collection of previously collected stories, different to the 1956 collection with the same title)

Something Out There (London: Cape; New York: Viking; 1984)

'*Jump and Other Stories* (London: Bloomsbury; New York: Farrar, Straus and Giroux; 1991)

Why Haven't You Written: Selected Stories 1950–1970 (Harmondsworth: Penguin, 1992) (contains previously collected stories)

OTHER BOOKS

South African Writing Today (joint editor, with Lionel Abrahams) (Harmondsworth: Penguin, 1967)

The Black Interpreters: Notes on African Writing (Johannesburg: Spro-Cas/Ravan, 1973)

On the Mines (with David Goldblatt) (Cape Town: Struik, 1973)

What Happened to 'Burger's Daughter'; or How South African Censorship Works (with others) (Johannesburg: Taurus, 1980)

Lifetimes: Under Apartheid (with David Goldblatt) (London: Cape, 1986)

The Essential Gesture: Writing, Politics and Places, edited by Stephen Clingman (London: Cape; New York: Knopf; 1988) (a collection of important essays)

Conversations with Nadine Gordimer, edited by Nancy Topping Bazin and Marilyn Dallman Seymour (Jackson and London: University of Mississippi Press, 1990) (a collection of all significant interviews and conversations up to 1989)

ESSAYS AND REVIEWS

'A Bolter and the Invincible Summer', *London Magazine*, 3 (May, 1963), 2, 58–65. Reprinted in *The Essential Gesture*

'Alberto Moravia's Africa' (Review of *Which Tribe Do You Belong To?*), *London Magazine*, 14 (October/November, 1974), 53–6

'Apartheid', *Holiday*, 25 (April 1959), 94–5

'Apartheid and the Primary Homeland', *Index on Censorship*, 1 (1972), 25–9

'Apprentices of Freedom', *New Society*, December 24/31, 1981, ii–v. Printed in a different version as 'Relevance and Commitment', in *The Essential Gesture*

'Censored, Banned, Gagged', *Encounter*, 20 (June 1963), 59–63. Reprinted in *The Essential Gesture*

'Censors and Unconfessed History', in *The Essential Gesture*. First published as 'New Forms of Strategy – No Change of Heart', *Critical Arts*, 1 (June, 1980), 2, 27–33

'Chief Luthuli', *Atlantic Monthly*, 203 (April, 1959), 4, 34–9. Reprinted in *The Essential Gesture*

'The Congo River', *Holiday*, 29 (May, 1961), 5, 74–103. Reprinted in *The Essential Gesture*

'At the Crossroads of Culture' (Review of Chinua Achebe, *Morning Yet on Creation Day*), *TLS*, 17 October, 1975, 1227

'Egypt Revisited', *National and English Review*, 152 (January 1952), 47–53. Reprinted in *The Essential Gesture*

'English-Language Literature and Politics in South Africa', *Journal of Southern African Studies*, 2 (1975), 131–50

'The Essential Gesture', in *The Tanner Lectures on Human Values*, edited by Sterling M. McMurrin (Cambridge University Press, 1985). Reprinted in *The Essential Gesture*

'The Fischer Case', *London Magazine*, 5 (March, 1966), 21–30

'The Flash of Fireflies', in *Short Story Theories*, edited by Charles May (Ohio University Press, 1976), pp.178–81. Originally appeared as 'The International Symposium on the Short Story: South Africa', *Kenyon Review*, 30 (1968)

'Great Problems in the Street', in *I Will Still Be Moved*, edited by Marion Friedmann (London: Arthur Barker, 1963), pp. 117–22. Reprinted in *The Essential Gesture*

'The Idea of Gardening' (Review of J. M. Coetzee, *Life and Times of Michael K*, *New York Review of Books*, 2 January, 1984, 3–6

'The Interpreters: Some Themes and Directions in African Literature', *Kenyon Review*, 32 (1970), 9–26

'Johannesburg', *Holiday*, 18 (August 1955), 46–57

'Leaving School II', London Magazine, 3 (1963), 2, 59–65

'Letter from Johannesburg, 1976', in *The Essential Gesture*. First published as 'Letter from South Africa', *New York Review of Books*, 23:20, (9 December, 1976), 3–4, 6, 8, 10

'Living in the Interregnum', *New York Review of Books*, 29:21–2, 20 January 1983, 21–9. Reprinted (in a slightly different form) in *The Essential Gesture*

'Merci Dieu, It Changes', in *The Essential Gesture*. First published as 'The Life of Accra, the Flowers of Abidjan: A West African Diary', *Atlantic*, 228 (November, 1971), 5, 85–9

'98 Kinds of Censorship', *American Pen*, 5 (1973), 16–21. Reprinted in *Hekima* (Nairobi), 1 (December, 1980), 115–19

'Notes of an Expropriator', *TLS*, 4 June, 1964, 484

'The Novel and the Nation in South Africa', in *African Writers on African Writing*, edited by G. D. Killam (London: Heinemann, 1973), pp. 33–52

'One Man Living it Through', *The Classic*, 2 (1966), 1, 11–16. Reprinted in *The Essential Gesture*

'Politics: A Dirtier Word Than Sex!', *Solidarity*, 3 (1968), 69–71

'The Prison-House of Colonialism', *TLS* 15 August 1980. Reprinted in *Olive Schreiner*, edited by Cherry Clayton (Johannesburg: McGraw-Hill, 1983), pp.95–8

(Reply to) 'The Politics of Commitment', by N. Z., *African Communist*, 80 (1980), 109

'Pula', in *The Essential Gesture*. Published in a different version in *London Magazine*, 12 (February/March, 1973), 6, 90–103

'Selecting My Stories', introduction to *Selected Stories*. Reprinted in *The Essential Gesture*

'South Africa: Towards a Desk-Drawer Literature', *Classic*, 2 (1968), 4, 64–74

'The South African Censor: No Change', *Index on Censorship*, 10 (1981), 4–9

'A South African Childhood: Allusions in a Landscape', *New Yorker*, 16 October, 1954, 121–43

'Taking into Account' (Review of Simone de Beauvoir, *Force of Circumstance*), *London Magazine*, 5 (January, 1966), 73–7

'Themes and Attitudes in Modern African Writing', *Michigan Quarterly Review*, 9 (Autumn, 1970), 221–31

'Turning the Page', in *Soho Square V*, edited by Steve Kromberg and James Ogude (London: Bloomsbury, 1992), pp.270–8

'The Unkillable Word', in *The Essential Gesture*. First published as 'Censorship and the Word', *Bloody Horse*, 1 (September/October, 1980), 20–4

'A Vision of Two Blood-Red Suns', in *The Essential Gesture*. First published as 'Transkei: A Vision of Two Blood-Red Suns', *Geo*, 4 (April, 1978), 8–42

'What Being a South African Means to Me', *South African Outlook*, 107 (1977), 87–9, 92

'Why Did Bram Fischer Choose Jail?', *New York Times Magazine*, 14 August 1966, 30–1, 80–1, 84. Reprinted in *The Essential Gesture*

'A Wilder Fowl', (Review of William Plomer, *Turbott Wolfe*), *London Magazine*, 15 (June, 1975), 90–2

'The Witwatersrand: A Time and Tailings', *Optima*, 18 (January, 1968), 22–6 (Also in *On the Mines*)

'A Writer in South Africa', *London Magazine*, 5 (1965), 2, 21–8

'A Writer's Freedom', *English in Africa*, 2 (1975), 2, 45–9. Reprinted in *The Essential Gesture*

'Writers in South Africa: The New Black Poets', *Dalhousie Review*, 53
     (1973–4), 645–66

INTERVIEWS AND CONVERSATIONS

'An Interview' in *Momentum: On Recent South African Writing*, edited by
     M. J. Daymond, J. U. Jacobs and Margaret Lenta (University
     of Natal Press, Pietermaritzburg, 1984), pp.32–4
Barkham, John, 'South Africa: Perplexities, Brutalities, Absurdities',
     Saturday Review, 12 January, 1963, 63
Beresford, David, 'Caught in the Chains of Idealism', *The Guardian*,
     Thursday 18 June, 1992, 25
Boyers, Robert, et al., 'A Conversation With Nadine Gordimer',
     Salmagundi, 62 (Winter, 1984), 3–31
Bragg, Melvyn, 'The Solitude of a White Writer', *The Listener*, 21
     October, 1976, 514
Burrows, E. G., 'An Interview with Nadine Gordimer', *Michigan
     Quarterly Review*, 9 (1970), 4, 231–4
Gardner, Susan, '"A Story for This Place and Time": An Interview
     With Nadine Gordimer About *Burger's Daughter*', *Kunapipi*, 3
     (1981), 2, 99–112
Gray, Stephen, 'An Interview With Nadine Gordimer', *Contemporary
     Literature*, 22 (1981), 263–71
Hurwitt, Jannika, 'The Art of Fiction 77: Nadine Gordimer', *Paris
     Review*, 88 (Summer, 1983), 83–127
Kakutani, Michiko, 'Nadine Gordimer: South African Witness',
     New York Times, 28 December 1981, Sec.C, 11
Morris, Edmund, 'A Visit with Nadine Gordimer', *New York Times
     Book Review*, 7 June, 1981, 26–7
Ravenscroft, Arthur, 'A Writer in South Africa: Nadine Gordimer',
     London Magazine, 5 (May, 1965), 20–8
Riis, J., 'Nadine Gordimer', *Kunapipi*, 2 (1980), 20–6
Salkey, Andrew, 'Nadine Gordimer Talks to Andrew Salkey', *The
     Listener*, 82, 7 August 1969, 184–5
Sampson, Anthony, 'Love Among the Madness', *The Observer*, 29
     March, 1987, 21
Schwartz, Pat, 'Interview – Nadine Gordimer', in *New South African
     Writing* (Hillbrow: Lorton, 1977), pp.74–81
Servan-Schreiber, C., 'Learning to Live With Unjustice', *World Press
     Review*, 27 (January 1980), 30
'South African Writers Talking: Nadine Gordimer, Es'kia Mphah-
     lele, André Brink', *English in Africa*, 6 (September, 1979), 1–23
Uhlig, Mark, 'Shocked by Her Own Heroine', *New York Times Book
     Review*, 3 May, 1987, 1, 20, 22

Wachtel, Eleanor, 'Nadine Gordimer', *Queen's Quarterly*, 98 (1991), 4, 899–910

'Writers and Politics' (conversation with Susan Sontag), in *Voices: Writers and Politics*, edited by Bill Bourne, Udi Eichler and David Herman (Nottingham: Spokesman, 1987), pp. 25–39

WORKS ABOUT GORDIMER

BOOKS AND JOURNAL SPECIAL ISSUES

Ariel: A Review of International English Literature, 19 (1988), 4

Clingman, Stephen, *The Novels of Nadine Gordimer: History From the Inside* (1986; second edition, London: Bloomsbury, 1993)

Cooke, John, *The Novels of Nadine Gordimer: Private Lives/Public Landscapes* (London and Baton Rouge: Louisiana State University Press, 1985)

Ettin, Andrew Vogel, *Betrayals of the Body Politic: The Literary Commitments of Nadine Gordimer* (Charlottesville: University Press of Virginia, 1993)

Haugh, Robert F., *Nadine Gordimer* (New York: Twayne Publishers, 1974)

JanMohamed, Abdul R., *Manichean Aesthetics: The Politics of Literature in Colonial Africa* (1983; rep. Amherst: University of Massachusetts Press, 1988)

Journal of the Short Story in English, 15 (Autumn 1990): 'A Special Nadine Gordimer Issue'

King, Bruce, (ed.), *The Later Fiction of Nadine Gordimer* (London: Macmillan, 1993)

Newman, Judie, *Nadine Gordimer* (London and New York: Routledge, 1988)

Salmagundi, 62 (Winter, 1984): 'Nadine Gordimer: Politics and the Order of Art'

Smith, Rowland, (ed.), *Critical Essays on Nadine Gordimer* (Boston: G. K. Hall & Co, 1990)

Trump, Martin, (ed.), *Rendering Things Visible: Essays on South African Literary Culture* (Athens: Ohio University Press, 1990)

Wade, Michael, *Nadine Gordimer* (London: Evans Brothers, 1978)
White on Black in South Africa (London: Macmillan, 1993)

ESSAYS AND ARTICLES

Alexander, Peter F., 'Political Attitudes in Nadine Gordimer's Fiction', *Journal of the Australasian Universities' Language and Literature Association*, 70 (1988), 220–38

Bailey, Nancy, 'Living Without the Future: Nadine Gordimer's *July's People*', *World Literature Written in English*, 24 (1984), 215–24

Boyers, Robert, 'Public and Private: On *Burger's Daughter*', *Salmagundi*, 62 (Winter, 1984), 62–92

Brink, André, 'Mutants of the Picaresque: *Moll Flanders* and *A Sport of Nature*', *Journal of Literary Studies/Tydskrif Vir Literaturwetenskap*, 6 (1990), 4, 261–74

Burton, Robert S., 'The Composition of Identity in Nadine Gordimer's *Burger's Daughter*', *Notes on Contemporary Literature*, 17 (1987), part 5, 6–7

Clingman, Stephen, 'History from the Inside: The Novels of Nadine Gordimer', *Journal of Southern African Studies*, 7 (1980–1), 165–93
'Literature and History in South Africa', *Radical History Review* 46–7 (1990), 145–59
'Multi-racialism, or *A World of Strangers*', *Salmagundi*, 62 (Winter, 1984), 32–61
'Writing in a Fractured Society: The Case of Nadine Gordimer', in *Literature and Society in South Africa*, edited by Landeg White and Tim Couzens (Harlow: Longman, 1984), pp.161–74

Cooper, Brenda, 'New Criteria for an "Abnormal Mutation"? An Evaluation of Gordimer's *A Sport of Nature*', in *Rendering Things Visible: Essays on South African Literary Culture*, edited by Martin Trump (Athens: Ohio University Press), pp.68–93

Daymond, M. J., '*Burger's Daughter*: A Novel's Reliance on History', in *Momentum: On Recent South African Writing*, edited by M. J. Daymond, J. U. Jacobs and Margaret Lenta (Pietermaritzburg: University of Natal Press, 1984), pp.159–70

Devoize, Jeanne, 'Elements of Narrative Technique in Nadine Gordimer's "Is There Nowhere Else We Can Meet?"', *Journal of the Short Story in English*, 15 (Autumn 1990), 11–16

Devonshire, Christine and Susan Cordwell, '"You Will Use My Words to Make Your Own Meaning": Listening to Nadine Gordimer's *Burger's Daughter*', in *Reception and Response: Hearer Creativity and the Analysis of Spoken and Written Texts*, edited by Graham McGregor and R. S. White (London: Routledge, 1990), pp.196–215

Donaghy, Mary, 'Double Exposure: Narrative Perspective in Gordimer's *A Guest of Honour*', *Ariel*, 19 (1988), 4, 19–32

Driver, Dorothy, 'Nadine Gordimer: The Politicisation of Women', *English in Africa*, 10 (1983), 2, 29–54

Eckstein, Barbara, 'Pleasure and Joy: Political Activism in Nadine Gordimer's Short Stories', *World Literature Today*, 59 (1985), 3, 343–6

Engel, Lars, 'The Political Uncanny: The Novels of Nadine Gordimer', *Yale Journal of Criticism*, 2 (1988–9), 2, 101–27

Fido, Elaine, '*A Guest of Honour*: A Feminine View of Masculinity', *World Literature Written in English*, 17 (1978), 30–7

Gardner, Susan, 'Still Waiting for the Great Feminist Novel: Nadine Gordimer's *Burger's Daughter*', *Hecate*, 8 (1982), 1, 61–76

Gerver, E., 'Women Revolutionaries in the Novels of Nadine Gordimer and Doris Lessing', *World Literature Written in English*, 17 (1978), 38–50

Githii, Ethel W., 'Nadine Gordimer's *Selected Stories*', *Critique: Studies in Modern Fiction*, 22 (1981), 3, 45–54

Goodheart, Eugene, 'The Claustral World of Nadine Gordimer', *Salmagundi*, 62 (Winter, 1984), 108–17

Gorak, Irene, 'Libertine Pastoral: Nadine Gordimer's *The Conservationist*', *Novel*, 24 (1991), 3, 241–56

Gordon, Jennifer, 'Dreams of a Common Language: Nadine Gordimer's *July's People*', *African Literature Today*, 15 (1987), 102–8

Gowda, H. H. A., 'The Design and Technique in Nadine Gordimer's *The Conservationist*', *Literary Half-Yearly*, 20 (1979), part 2, 3–10

Gray, Rosemary, 'Text and Context: A Reading of Elizabeth Charlotte Webster's *Ceremony of Innocence* and Nadine Gordimer's *The Conservationist*', *Commonwealth Essays and Studies*, 13 (1990), 1, 55–67

Gray, Stephen, 'Gordimer's *A World of Strangers* as Memory', *Ariel*, 19 (1988), 4, 11–16

Green, Robert, 'From *The Lying Days* to *July's People*: The Novels of Nadine Gordimer', *Journal of Modern Literature*, 14 (1987–8), 543–63

'Nadine Gordimer: A Bibliography of Works and Criticism', *Bulletin of Bibliography*, 42 (1985), 1, 5–11

'Nadine Gordimer: The Politics of Race', *World Literature Written in English*, 16 (1977), 256–62

'Nadine Gordimer's *A Guest of Honour*', *World Literature Written in English*, 16 (1977), 55–66

'Nadine Gordimer's *A World of Strangers*: Strains in South African Liberalism', *English Studies in Africa*, 22 (1979), 1, 45–54

Greenstein, Susan M., 'Miranda's Story: Nadine Gordimer and the Literature of Empire', *Novel*, 18 (1984–5), 227–42

Haarhoff, Dorian, 'Two Cheers for Socialism: Nadine Gordimer and E. M. Forster', *English in Africa*, 9 (1982), 1, 55–64

Hanley, Lynne, 'Writing Across the Colour Bar: Apartheid and Desire', *Massachusetts Review: A Quarterly of Literature, the Arts and Public Affairs*, 32 (1991), 4, 495–506

Head, Dominic, 'Positive Isolation and Productive Ambiguity in Nadine Gordimer's Short Stories', *Journal of the Short Story in English*, 15 (Autumn 1990), 17–30

Heinemann, Margot, '*Burger's Daughter*: The Synthesis of Revelation', in *The Uses of Fiction: Essays on the Modern Novel in Honour of Arnold Kettle*, edited by Douglas Jefferson and Graham Martin (Milton Keynes: Open University Press, 1982), pp. 181–97

Hewson, Kelly, 'Making the Revolutionary Gesture: Nadine Gordimer, J. M. Coetzee and Some Variations on the Writer's Responsibility', *Ariel*, 19 (1988), 4, 55–72

Irele, Abiola, 'The African Imagination', *Research in African Literatures*, 21 (1990), 1, 49–67

Jacobs, J. U., 'The Colonial Mind in a State of Fear: The Psychosis of Terror in the Contemporary South African Novel', *North Dakota Quarterly*, 57 (1989), 3, 24–43

'Living Space and Narrative Space in Nadine Gordimer's *Something Out There*', *English in Africa*, 14 (1987), 2, 31–43

King, Michael, 'Race and History in the Stories of Nadine Gordimer', *Africa Insight*, 13 (1983), 3, 222–6

Knipp, Thomas, 'Going all the Way: Eros and Polis in the Novels of Nadine Gordimer', *Research in African Literatures*, 24 (1993), 1, 37–50

Lazar, Karen, 'Feminism as "Piffling"? Ambiguities in Some of Nadine Gordimer's Short Stories', *Current Writing*, 2 (1990), 1 (October), 101–16

Leeuwenburg, Rina, 'Nadine Gordimer's *Burger's Daughter*: Why Does Rosa Go Back?', *New Literature Review*, 14 (1985), 23–31

Link, Viktor, 'The African Magician and His Western Audience: Norms in Nadine Gordimer's "The African Magician"', *Commonwealth Essays and Studies*, 11 (1989), 2, 104–9

'The Unity of *Something Out There*', *Journal of the Short Story in English*, 15 (Autumn 1990), 31–40

Liscio, Lorraine, '*Burger's Daughter*: Lighting a Torch in the Heart of Darkness', *Modern Fiction Studies*, 33 (1987), 245–61

Lomberg, A., 'Withering Into the Truth: The Romantic Realism of Nadine Gordimer', *English in Africa*, 3 (1976), 1, 1–12

Louvel, Liliane, 'Divided Space: A Reading of Nadine Gordimer's Short story "The Termitary"', *Journal of the Short Story in English*, 15 (Autumn 1990), 41–53

Macaskill, Brian, 'Interrupting the Hegemonic: Textual Critique and Mythological Recuperation From the White Margins of South African Writing', *Novel*, 23 (1990), 2, 156–81

Magerey, Kevin, 'Cutting the Jewel: Facets of Art in Nadine

Gordimer's Short Stories', *Southern Review* (Adelaide), 7 (1974), 3–28

'The South African Novel and Race', *Southern Review*, 1 (1963), 1, 27–45

Martin, Richard, G., 'Narrative, History, Ideology: A Study of *Waiting For the Barbarians* and *Burger's Daughter*', *Ariel*, 17 (1986), 3, 3–21

Mazurek, Raymond A., 'Gordimer's *Something Out There* and Ndebele's *Fools and Other Stories*: The Politics of Literary Form', *Studies in Short Fiction*, 26 (1989–90), 71–9

Moss, Rose, 'Hand in Glove: Nadine Gordimer, South African Writer', *Pacific Quarterly* (Moana), 6 (1981), 3–4, 106–22

Neill, Michael, 'Translating the Present: Language, Knowledge, and Identity in Nadine Gordimer's *July's People*', *Journal of Commonwealth Literature*, 25 (1990), 1, 71–97

Newman, Judie, 'Nadine Gordimer and the Naked Southern Ape: *Something Out There*', *Journal of the Short Story in English*, 15 (Autumn 1990), 55–73

N., Z., 'The Politics of Commitment', *African Communist*, 53 (1980), 100–1

Ogungbesan, Kolawole, 'The Liberal Expatriate and African Politics: Nadine Gordimer's *A Guest of Honour*', *Nigerian Journal of the Humanities*, 1 (1977), 1, 29–41

'Nadine Gordimer's *The Conservationist*: A Touch of Death', *International Fiction Review*, 5 (1978), 109–15

'Nadine Gordimer's *The Late Bourgeois World*: Love in Prison', *Ariel*, 9 (1978), 1, 31–49

'Reality in Nadine Gordimer's *A World of Strangers*', *English Studies*, 61 (1980), 142–55

'The Way Out of South Africa: Nadine Gordimer's *The Lying Days*', *Ba Shiru*, 9 (1978), 1–2, 48–62

O'Sheel, P., 'Nadine Gordimer's *The Conservationist*', *World Literature Written in English*, 14 (1975), 514–19

Parker, Kenneth, 'Nadine Gordimer and the Pitfalls of Liberalism', in *The South African Novel in English: Essays in Criticism and Society*, edited by Kenneth Parker (London and Basingstoke: Macmillan, 1978), pp. 114–29

Parrinder, Patrick, 'What His Father Gets Up To', *London Review of Books*, 13 September 1990, 17–18

Peck, Richard, 'One Foot Before the Other into an Unknown Future: The Dialectic in Nadine Gordimer's *Burger's Daughter*', *World Literature Written in English*, 29 (1989), 26–43

'What's a Poor White to Do? White South African Options in *A Sport of Nature*', *Ariel*, 19 (1988), 4, 75–93

Ravenscroft, Arthur, 'African Novels of Affirmation', in *The Uses of Fiction: Essays on the Modern Novel in Honour of Arnold Kettle*, edited by Douglas Jefferson and Graham Martin (Milton Keynes: Open University Press, 1982), pp.171–80

Rich, Paul, 'Apartheid and the Decline of the Civilization Idea: An Essay on Nadine Gordimer's *July's People* and J. M. Coetzee's *Waiting for the Barbarians*', *Research in African Literatures*, 15 (1984), 365–93

'Romance and the Development of the South African Novel', in *Literature and Society in South Africa*, edited by Landeg White and Tim Couzens (Harlow: Longman, 1984), pp.120–37

'Tradition and Revolt in South African Fiction: The Novels of André Brink, Nadine Gordimer and J. M. Coetzee', *Journal of Southern African Studies*, 9 (1982–3), 54–73

Roberts, Sheila, 'Character and Meaning in Four Contemporary South African Novels', *World Literature Written in English*, 19 (1980), 19–36

'Nadine Gordimer's "Family of Women"', *Theoria: A Journal of Studies in the Arts, Humanities and Social Sciences*, 60 (1983), 45–57

'South African Censorship and the Case of *Burger's Daughter*', *World Literature Written in English*, 20 (1981), 41–8

Smith, Rowland, 'Inside and Outside: Nadine Gordimer and the Critics', *Ariel*, 19 (1988), 4, 3–9

'Leisure, Law and Loathing: Matrons, Mistresses, Mothers in the Fiction of Nadine Gordimer and Jillian Becker', *World Literature Written in English*, 28 (1988), 1, 41–51

'Living For the Future: Nadine Gordimer's *Burger's Daughter*', *World Literature Written in English*, 19 (1980), 163–73

'Masters and Servants: Nadine Gordimer's *July's People* and the Themes of Her Fiction', *Salmagundi*, 62 (Winter, 1984), 93–107

'The Seventies and After: The Inner View in White, English-Language Fiction', in *Olive Schreiner and After: Essays on Southern African Literature in Honour of Guy Butler*, edited by Malvern van Wyk Smith and Don Maclennan (Cape Town: David Philip, 1983), pp.196–204

'Truth, Irony and Commitment', in *International Literature in English: Essays on the Major Writers*, edited by Robert L. Ross (New York and London: Garland, 1991), pp.171–80

Smyer, Richard I., 'Risk, Frontier, and Interregnum in the Fiction of Nadine Gordimer', *Journal of Commonwealth Literature*, 20 (1985), 1, 68–80

'*A Sport of Nature*: Gordimer's Work in Progress', *Journal of Commonwealth Literature* 27 (1992), 1, 71–86

Temple-Thurston, Barbara, 'Madam and Boy: A Relationship of

Shame in Gordimer's *July's People*', *World Literature Written in English*, 28 (1988), 51–8

'Nadine Gordimer: The Artist as *A Sport of Nature*', *Studies in Twentieth Century Literature*, 15 (1991), 1, 175–84

Thorpe, Michael, 'The Motif of the Ancestor in *The Conservationist*', *Research in African Literatures*, 14 (1983), 184–92

Trump, Martin, 'The Short Fiction of Nadine Gordimer', *Research in African Literatures*, 17 (1986), 3, 341–69

Van Donge, Jan Kees, 'Nadine Gordimer's *A Guest of Honour*: A Failure to Understand Zambian Society', *Journal of Southern African Studies*, 9 (1982–3), 74–92

Viola, André, 'Communication and Liberal Double Bind in *July's People* by Nadine Gordimer', *Commonwealth Essays and Studies*, 9 (1987), 2, 52–8

'The Irony of Tenses in Nadine Gordimer's *The Conservationist*', *Ariel*, 19 (1988), 4, 45–54

Visel, Robin, 'A Half-Colonization: The Problem of the White Colonial Woman Writer', *Kunapipi*, 10 (1988), 3, 39–45

'Othering the Self: Nadine Gordimer's Colonial Heroines', *Ariel*, 19 (1988), 4, 33–42

Visser, Nicholas, 'Beyond the Interregnum: A Note on the Ending of *July's People*', in *Rendering Things Visible: Essays on South African Literary Culture*, edited by Martin Trump (Athens: Ohio University Press, 1990), pp.61–7

Wade, Michael, 'Nadine Gordimer and Europe-in-Africa', in *The South African Novel in English: Essays in Criticism and Society*, edited by Kenneth Parker (London and Basingstoke: Macmillan, 1978), pp.131–63

Weinhouse, Linda, 'The Deconstruction of Victory: Gordimer's *A Sport of Nature*', *Research in African Literatures*, 21 (1990), 2, 91–100

Wettenhall, Irene, 'Liberalism and Radicalism in South Africa since 1948: Nadine Gordimer's Fiction', *New Literature Review*, 8 (1980), 36–44

Wheeler, Katherine, 'Irony and the Politics of Style', *Journal of the Short Story in English*, 15 (Autumn 1990), 75–91

Yelin, Louise, 'Exiled In and Exiled From: The Politics and Poetics of *Burger's Daughter*', in *Women's Writing in Exile*, edited by Mary Lynn Broe and Angela Ingram (Chapel Hill: University of North Carolina Press, 1989), pp. 396–411

Index